PRAISE FOR IAN MOORE

Don't miss a single word... Moore is a cultured comic.
LONDON EVENING STANDARD

Relaxed, laconic, hilarious.
THE STAGE

A brilliant storyteller.
THE BOSTON PHOENIX

PRAISE FOR *VIVE LE CHAOS*

*I hate mods, I hate France and I hate reading
but I still loved this book.*
LEE MACK, COMEDIAN AND ACTOR

*[This book] is everything its author is: immaculately turned
out, sharp and consistently hilarious.*
MARK BILLINGHAM, BEST-SELLING AUTHOR AND ACTOR

Charming, witty, a brilliant read.
SARAH MILLICAN, COMEDIAN AND AUTHOR

C'est mod-nifique.
MARCUS BRIGSTOCKE, COMEDIAN AND ACTOR

T0349933

I've seen Ian Moore on the stage and I'm happy to report that he's just as good on the page. A light-hearted and wry look at life for the Moore family in the Loire Valley, with a passing and amusing nod to Durrell's My Family and Other Animals.

NICK HEWER, BROADCASTER

Plunges you straight in to Ian Moore's strange, endearingly funny world. Zips along with nippy energy, although there are pages you have to read twice, they make you laugh so much.

ANNIE CAULFIELD, WRITER AND BROADCASTER

A warm and witty journey into a foreign land. Like much of the produce in the French village where the Moore family shops, the humour is organic.

MARTIN KELNER, JOURNALIST

If you are looking for a stylish laugh, you need look no further than [this book].

MARK BAXTER, CO-AUTHOR OF *THE A–Z OF MOD*

VIVE LE CHAOS

An Hachette UK Company
www.hachette.co.uk

Summersdale Publishers
Part of Octopus Publishing Group Limited
Carmelite House
50 Victoria Embankment
LONDON
EC4Y 0DZ
UK

This FSC® label means that materials used for the product have been responsibly sourced

MIX
Paper | Supporting responsible forestry
FSC® C104740

www.summersdale.com

The authorized representative in the EEA is Hachette Ireland, 8 Castlecourt Centre, Dublin 15, D15 XTP3, Ireland (email: info@hbgi.ie)

Printed and bound by Clays Ltd, Suffolk, NR35 1ED

ISBN: 978-1-83799-440-3

Substantial discounts on bulk quantities of Summersdale books are available to corporations, professional associations and other organisations. For details contact general enquiries: telephone: +44 (0) 1243 771107 or email: enquiries@summersdale.com.

IAN MOORE

Vive le CHAOS

My So-Called Tranquil Family Life in Rural France

summersdale

For Natalie, without whom nothing would be possible

CONTENTS

A MOORE IN THE LOIRE

It was one of those moments that a stand-up comedian dreams of. That moment when you are on stage and you have the audience in the palm of your hand; you can lead them anywhere you want; you can tease them, raise them up, lower them down. You have total mastery over the room and your view of the audience and of yourself is almost from above the stage, like an out-of-body experience.

There is no better feeling.

I looked out at the room and at the faces convulsed with laughter; 450 people all dancing to my tune, I felt – hang on! What's that bloke doing? That bloke in the second row with the goatee beard and the leather jacket – what's his problem? Why is he not laughing like all the others? What's wrong with him?

I tried everything. I brought out the big guns, the infallible old material. My rhythm changed, my tempo increased; the rest of the audience looked like they may die from laughing, but 'goatee face' in the second row...

nothing. Maybe he has locked-in syndrome, I thought. Then he yawned.

The red light came on, showing my time was up. I thanked the audience and left the stage to deafening applause. 'That was Ian Moore!' shouted the MC, struggling to be heard as the noise increased, 'Ian Moore!'

'Wow!' said Chris, one of the newer acts, as I stomped back into the dressing room. 'That was brilliant. You must be really pleased with that?'

I took a long drink of water as Chris, obviously really new to the game, waited for my response – maybe some advice, some words of comfort, before he went out there himself.

'There's a bloke in the second row,' I said, 'real attitude problem. Watch him, he might be trouble.'

'But they loved you!' he said, almost shouting. 'They LOVED you!'

'Four hundred and forty-nine of them loved me,' I replied, looking at him like I was his sensei or something and he was my protégé. 'That bastard ruined it for me.'

'Well, I'd be happy with that!'

'Ha!' There was a derisive snort from the corner of the dressing room. John, another old hand like me, was sitting on a leather sofa with a bottle of beer in hand. He was due on next, but he was in no hurry; unlike the excess of nervous energy that prevented Chris from sitting down, John may even have to be woken up before he went on. 'Look at him,' he said to Chris, pointing at me, 'look at him. Look at the way he's dressed! If his tie was crooked or he had fluff on his sleeve it would ruin his gig for him. He's a mod. Have you not seen *Quadrophenia*? They're never happy!'

He had a point.

While mods have a well-deserved reputation for impeccable dress sense, with very English sharp suits and matching patterns, they also have something of a reputation for po-faced, standing-in-a-corner-trying-to-look-cool detachment; possibly also very English. If mods are anything, they are stiff upper lips in well-ironed trousers.

'Nothing wrong with perfection, John,' I said, putting on my 1960s Michael Caine *Ipcress File* mac, 'you should try it some time.'

Striving for perfection eats away at you though and the yawning, goatee-bearded man in the audience bothered me, and what bothered me more was that it bothered me – and a four-hour, late-night and solitary drive home is no place to try and shake the demons.

I was in a hurry to get home. I'd been away performing in Manchester since Wednesday and now it was the early hours of Sunday morning. I wanted to get home and wake up in my own bed, next to my wife Natalie; to feel the warmth of my beloved Jack Russell, Eddie, at my feet and hear my three-year-old, Samuel, quietly breathing in the next room.

Only... did I? Did I really?

Firstly, the constant driving was beginning to get to me. I had been up and down the motorways of the UK as a club comedian for six years now – that's 40,000 miles a year, mostly driving bleary eyed through the night. There were times when I had got on a motorway in the North and a few hours later would suddenly realise that I was nearly home, the drive having been done almost subconsciously while my mind was elsewhere. Like a fighter pilot who had been on too many missions, I felt lucky to be alive, but also convinced that disaster was just around the corner. It had got to the point where Natalie almost had to talk me into the car to go to work.

And secondly, where was I actually going? Yes, I was going home to my family, but we lived in Crawley in West Sussex, and even if you love your family (which I do) and you are used to travelling (which I am), if your final destination is bland, concrete 'New Town' Crawley there's always going to be a part of you dragging its feet.

We'd moved there from South London seven years previously 'to get more for our money' and to help me to turn professional as a stand-up – for a couple of years Natalie commuted to London every day, supporting us as I built up my career. It didn't take long for me to get the lie of the Crawley land. A local pub was advertising a 'comedy night' and I went in to offer my services.

'Oh, sorry, mate,' said the landlord, 'we knocked it on the 'ead. Got too violent.'

It was half three in the morning by the time I drove past our house. I wasn't driving past because I had a reluctance to go in, but because – as usual – I couldn't park outside the place. We lived in a row of terraced and semi-detached Victorian cottages near the centre of town; there were no driveways, no off-street parking, but plenty of cars. Interlopers used the street as a source of free parking while they sauntered into town pleased with their discovery. It was one of my many bugbears.

Twenty minutes later I was opening our front door, having parked up a couple of streets away and struggled back with my luggage (mods don't travel light). I was being as quiet as I could be, though obviously not quiet enough. As soon as the door shut, Samuel started screaming the place down. I panicked and tripped over my case, falling into the kitchen in an undignified heap and banging my head on the oven. Natalie came charging down the stairs, clearly thinking a burglary was in progress.

'What are you doing?' she hissed, pointlessly as Samuel was now very much awake.

'I fell over. I've hurt my head,' I replied pathetically, also whispering.

'You've woken him up!'

'All I did was close the front door!'

'Well don't!'

'What?'

Every parent of small children knows the scene. You've been through months and months of trying to get the little sods off to sleep and then, when they finally are, you almost daren't move or speak in case you wake them up. You creep around your own house, glare at each other accusingly if one of you makes a sudden noise and you watch television with the sound so low that you're constantly turning to each other whispering, 'I missed that. What did he say?' This goes double for a very small house, and as I lay there with my 5 foot 10 inch body partly in the kitchen, partly in the 'hall' and partly in the living room, after a four-hour drive, a gig I didn't enjoy and in a town I didn't want to be in, I just closed my eyes, rolled over and went to sleep.

At some point in the night I had made it to my own bed without either waking Samuel or being told off, and now as I hazily awoke in the late morning I felt slightly better disposed towards the world. I was home at least, even if home could be trying at times. Natalie came into the bedroom, a welcome cup of tea in her hand. 'I don't want to rush you,' she said, 'but someone's just left. There's a car-parking space right outside. I'd do it, but I don't know where you left the car.'

It was a depressingly regular game we had to play and as I hurried to get dressed I kept glancing out of the window to make sure the space was still there. I ran downstairs and out of the door, trying to remember where I had in fact left the car.

'Block the space with something!' I shouted over my shoulder.

'With what?' Natalie shouted back.

'Er, I don't know, Samuel's tricycle!'

'I'm not leaving his tricycle in the road! Hurry up!'

It was a fair point and I went haring off. Five minutes later I returned and of course the space had gone. I got out of my car and just stared at the 'foreign' object, a gleaming BMW. I closed my eyes, threw my head back and just howled, the frustration and fatigue combining to make it a primeval cry from the depths of middle-class, small-town-frustration hell. Neighbours came to their windows to see what could possibly have happened to tear apart their peaceful Sunday morning so violently, and what they saw was me standing in the middle of the road, my car blocking the traffic, my eyes closed and my head thrown back roaring at the sky. The fact that I was impeccably dressed must only have added to the 'man at the end of his tether' feel of the scene, and as someone in a blocked car started beeping his horn at me I just stayed frozen in that position, unwilling to move.

Natalie came out, waving nervously at the neighbours and apologising to whoever it was beeping their horn. She put her hand on my arm and said quietly in my ear, 'Go inside, my love, go inside. I'll put the car away.' I began to trudge off. 'And Ian,' she said firmly, 'we need a holiday.'

I remember, as a ten-year-old child, watching Ian Botham hitting six after mighty six over the heads of the Australian fielders; his mixture of swagger and belligerence was utterly captivating. It was the summer of 1981 and 'Botham's Ashes', and I was stood outside a Radio Rentals in Truro unable to move. I was spellbound and despite my dad, not a fan of cricket in the slightest, imploring me to move so that we could get on with what had hitherto been a pretty dull Cornish holiday, I couldn't. My love of cricket started there; a lifelong passion that would lead to days glued to the television or radio and nights poring over statistics. I knew even then that this was life-changing, not just for Ian Botham, but for me.

Over twenty years later and I was standing outside an estate agent's in a small town in the Loire Valley, going through a similar shop-on-the-high-street life-changing epiphany.

'Have you seen how much places cost around here?' I asked rhetorically, Natalie having wandered off down the road with Samuel. She knew the score. Natalie's parents, despite being the main reason that we had moved to Crawley, for which I will never truly forgive them, also had a small holiday cottage nearby. We had been visiting every year for the last ten years. We loved the place. Danielle, Natalie's mum, is French and some of her younger siblings grew up in the town and her father was Post Master there; Natalie's grandparents, who were coming for lunch, still lived locally.

The town is everything you imagine a small, rural French community to be. It has a large, dominating church, a small chateau on the riverbank, a couple of nice restaurants, two or three bars, a number of *boulangeries*, *charcuteries* and *alimentations*, a grand-looking Hôtel de Ville, a weekly farmers' market and, as with every small French town, about half a dozen opticians. It is kept scrupulously clean, vast amounts of money are thrown at floral displays and again, as with all French towns, parking is free.

'Seriously, Natalie, come and look! Look at what we could afford over here. We could buy a village!' OK, that was something of an exaggeration, but at the time the pound was massively strong against the euro and I was just making a point. Natalie carried on walking. The plan had always been that we would retire here, settle down later in life and just soak up the pastoral tranquillity of the Loire Valley; I would write light, undemanding comic novels and Natalie would tend to her horses. It was a pipe dream; an ambition, but one that seems so far off when you're in your early thirties that you may as well lay claim to a rural idyll on Mars and set about designing your own personal spaceship. Natalie sensibly kept walking.

'Come on,' she said over her shoulder, 'we'll be late for lunch.' I picked up the magazine from the rack outside the agency and ran off after her.

The hazy afternoon sun beat down as Natalie and I, along with her parents and her French grandparents, sat around lazily in the small garden. Samuel was asleep indoors, so the rest of us were taking advantage of the chance to rest; the only noises were the bees on the deep mauve hibiscus and the crickets in the next-door field. I could contain myself no longer.

'I think we should move here,' I said, breaking the silence as we lay in the garden.

'Yes,' Natalie replied, 'it would be lovely, it—'

'Now. I think we should move here now.' I sat upright as if to indicate that this wasn't some idle thought or that the lunchtime rosé had taken a mischievous hold.

'What did he say?' asked Natalie's grandmother.

'He wants to move here,' Brian, Natalie's dad, translated. Whereupon her grandmother just rolled her eyes and tutted.

It wasn't that I didn't get on with Natalie's grandparents, but the language difference was a big barrier for all of us, and they could never properly hide the disappointment that their eldest granddaughter hadn't married a Frenchman. That she'd married an Englishman was just about tolerable, but one that dressed as some kind of anachronistic dandy was a constant source of bewilderment for them. I wasn't going to drop the subject.

'Give me one good reason why we shouldn't?' I was asking Natalie specifically, but throwing it open to the group.

'You don't speak the language,' said Brian.

'Natalie is fluent and I can learn,' I countered.

'What about Samuel's school?' asked Danielle, though I could see her heart wasn't in the objection.

'He's just started nursery, it's hardly an issue,' I replied.

'What would Natalie do for a living then?' Danielle continued. Natalie had gone back to work part-time as a recruitment consultant in Crawley and wasn't enjoying it. Though she liked her job, she found it difficult to adjust to the part-time nature of the work and it also took her away from Samuel, leaving her, in her own eyes, as a part-time parent as well.

'I'm sure I could find something with my qualifications and languages,' Natalie said.

Interesting.

'OK,' Danielle said, nodding at me, 'What will *you* do for a living?' There was a brief silence as everybody, except me, gave this some thought. Then, like a well-briefed barrister, but in floral shorts and a buttoned-up polo shirt, I took to the floor.

'I've been doing a little research…' I began.

My case for the defence was this: I would commute, simple as that. This place, I explained, is within an hour and a half's driving distance of three airports (Tours, Poitiers and Limoges), all served by dirt-cheap budget airlines and flying direct to London. Failing that, it would take two hours to get to Paris by train and either fly from Orly or Charles de Gaulle or even take the Eurostar. Yes, I would be spending far more money on travel than at present, but we could sell our house in Crawley, pay off the mortgage and still buy a sizeable property here mortgage-free. I wouldn't need to work as often because of the lack of mortgage, so I would concentrate solely on the weekend gigs, Thursday to Saturday. I would leave Thursday morning and be back home again for Sunday afternoon.

They all looked at me. Clearly I was better prepared for this argument than they were, but it was Natalie's opinion that counted most and I could see she was tempted. She loved this place as much as I did, and although she also loved being near her parents in Crawley, deep down she knew that if she wanted more children we couldn't do it in the house we were in.

'But you hate the travelling,' she said. 'You'd be doing more of it.'

I was ready for this.

'I hate the driving,' I replied. 'I hate the M25, the M1 and all the other Ms in between. I hate how tired and irritable it makes me, but I won't be flying the planes or driving the Eurostar; I can be relaxing. And anyway,' I continued, about to deliver my clincher, 'in five years' time I'll be off the comedy circuit and just writing from home.'

'But the travel – surely not?' Danielle asked reasonably, though her French accent as always came to the fore as she got more vexed. 'It will be too much.'

'Look,' I said, addressing the group with my closing arguments, 'the travel at the moment is too much. I can't go on doing that. Yes, this way will be equally tiring, maybe more so. But I'd be coming home to here, to peace and quiet, not to a box in Crawley and that makes a huge difference. Natalie wants another child, but I'm not happy mortgaging ourselves up to the hilt somewhere we don't want to be on some faceless estate with a rough school just to do that. Natalie wants horses too. In Crawley, if you had a horse you'd come down in the morning and find it on bricks!'

'What is he going on about now?' asked Natalie's grandmother.

I'd planted the seed and my strategy was not to labour the point, but to see how Natalie felt at the end of the summer; I was going away that weekend for a run of shows in Birmingham while Natalie and Samuel stayed in the Loire, which would be a good test for all of us. I could see if my travel theory actually stood up in reality and the others could think about the practicality of it all without me butting in and fighting my corner, banging on about horses and bricks and making Crawley, mostly unfairly, out to be a cross between Sodom and Gomorrah and war-torn Beirut.

The last thing I expected, twenty-four hours after returning to the Loire on Sunday afternoon, was to be signing a *compromis de vente* and paying a sizeable deposit on our dream home.

2

MY ANIMALS AND OTHER FAMILY

It wasn't meant to be like this. I distinctly remember the reasons for moving out here and they were exactly what Lenin had promised the Russian people in 1917: 'Peace! Bread! Land!' Five years after signing on the dotted line I was now supposed to be enjoying the fruits, that is sitting languidly under a tree, chewing on a length of straw and occasionally muttering the word 'suckers' under my breath as my thoughts wandered smugly back to England. We, the Russians and I, had been duped.

What very much wasn't part of the plan was to be breaking my back erecting an electric fence and then having to be the poor fool who had to test every inch of its 400-foot perimeter – a process which involved touching the thing at regular intervals, shrieking (to the delight of your family, who are watching) and doing the whole thing again a few seconds later. We had land alright, we had bread, but whatever peace was to be found was being constantly disturbed as a grumpy, loudly swearing mod went about his equine husbandry duties.

'You're very brave,' people had said when we told them we were moving to France. 'That's a very courageous thing to do.' Really, we thought, brave? If for one moment I had thought that it was a 'brave' thing to do I probably would have had second thoughts, but Natalie, though reluctant to leave Crawley, was just as convinced that it was the right thing to do. There were times in between signing the contract and actually moving in when we wobbled a bit – not because we were having doubts but because, even at that stage, obstacles kept being thrown in our way.

Immediately on signing the 'contract to buy', the pound fell. Our budget, if we were to remain mortgage-free, was pretty tight, so when the exchange rate fell over the next few months from €1.50 to the pound to €1.25, that left a big hole. It doesn't sound much looking at that, but £200,000 at €1.50 is €300,000; at €1.25 it's €250,000; and we didn't have a spare fifty grand knocking about. Every day we would check the exchange rate, but were powerless to transfer any money until we sold our house. We had until 11 January to pay the remainder of the purchase price or lose our deposit and our dream home in France. Natalie was also now pregnant and the stress wasn't helping. We finally exchanged contracts just before Christmas, left England just after the New Year and were due to move in on the fourth which, coincidentally, is both Natalie's and Samuel's birthday.

The night before we moved in we were to stay with Natalie's grandparents, but before we went there we decided to drive past our new house; we hadn't seen it in months and like children on Christmas Eve we were impatient and just couldn't wait for the next day. It was dark by the time we arrived in town and as we began the 3-kilometre drive out into the countryside a fog began to fall. The country road to the property, which surely hadn't been this narrow last summer, also seemed much longer than the 3 kilometres that we remembered, and as the car headlights picked out the eyes of darting creatures and swooping owls, it all seemed very cold.

'Are you sure we're on the right road?' Natalie asked, though she knew we were. Eventually, after what seemed like half an hour, we reached our house – dark, cold and smaller than I'd remembered it. We didn't even get out, partly because we didn't want to wake Samuel and Eddie who were sleeping soundly in the back, but also it just didn't look very welcoming.

Neither of us slept well that night.

Monsieur Norbert, owner of the estate agency, was there to greet us at the *notaire*'s office the next morning for the final contract signing, though 'greet' would be over-egging it somewhat. A surly individual, what he lacked in warmth he made up for with laconic aggression, but as his family owned pretty much everything around here from hotels, restaurants, estate agencies and a haulage company, he was best not crossed. Not that we were in a mood to anyway – we just wanted the keys; we wanted to see exactly what we had let ourselves in for.

What a difference a day makes! Whereas the evening before the drive had seemed long, the darkness and the fog oppressive, the house cold, the next day was glorious with warm winter sunshine. The fields were wide and seemed to go on forever, and thousands of black and white lapwings were chattering to each other as we drove serenely down 'our' road. We opened the gate and drove in. Straightaway Samuel and Eddie went running off exploring the two and a half acres with outbuildings, an orchard, a pond and a hayloft. 'Our' two and a half acres with outbuildings, 'our' orchard, 'our' pond and 'our' hayloft.

Natalie and I opened the huge, windowed, stable doors that formed the entrance to the main house and turned around to look at the land. We stood, almost breathless, soaking it all up as Samuel and Eddie played in the distance, 'our' distance...

'Well?' I said, stroking Natalie's pregnant stomach, 'Happy Birthday!'

It had all seemingly happened in a blur, but at that moment as we soaked up the surprisingly warm winter sun on the *terrasse* all doubts, money worries, house-moving stress, pregnancy fears, travel concerns, everything just melted away. All we could hear was Samuel laughing somewhere; there was no other sound, nothing at all. It was exactly the peace we had both been looking for.

'Argghh! Bloody hell!' I screamed again, another electric shock shaking me from my reverie and bringing me back to reality five years later. I was only halfway around the perimeter of the fence and I could now feel myself twitching – so much for 'peace'. And so much for dignity. My fence antics had drawn a crowd – my three sons Samuel, now nine years old, Maurice, five, and Thérence, two, followed me around finding the whole thing highly amusing.

In my defence, it had been a tough week.

For the second time in a fortnight Natalie had found yet another abandoned kitten, and it took an awful lot of persuading to stop her adopting it. For hours afterwards I caught her staring wistfully at the point in the hedge where it had been miaowing mournfully. The one she had rescued the week before had to be bottle-fed every few hours and therefore took up far too much time. Plus, and I have this on very good authority, cute little kittens grow up to be cats, and I've never got on with cats.

Toby, our collie-spaniel cross, had fallen mysteriously ill and I woke earlier in the week to find the EU dog-diarrhoea mountain in the hall. I'd got up extra early, about half six, so that I could do a bit of work, but instead spent the hour before the older boys had to be up for school on my hands and knees mopping up dog poo and retching uncontrollably, while Natalie and Thérence slept on. It was deeply, deeply unpleasant. And it's unlike Toby. When we first got him from the rescue centre he was a bit of a tearaway, but this wasn't a naughty gesture, this was clearly a very nasty stomach upset. He's just not naughty anymore; he occasionally takes himself off for a walk but that saves us a job. He's a good dog.

His predecessor, Volcan, a Brittany spaniel, was not a good dog; he was constantly trying to challenge me – nobody else, just me. One day he beckoned me, Lassie-style, to follow him; I did so and he took me into the workshop whereupon he turned around, looked me straight in the eye and urinated all over my original fishtail parka which was hanging up. Now that is more than a gesture; that is a statement of aggression and he was out by the end of the week. He was, however, gladly taken in by Natalie's uncle, the cow inseminator. I know, the mind boggles.

Our other dog, Pierrot, I feel a bit sorry for. My beloved Jack Russell, Eddie, had died at the age of sixteen (four years after we'd moved to France) which left me bereft and needing a small dog to take her place. We'd had Eddie since she was about a year old, a tiny little waif abandoned on the streets of London, clearly abused in some way and nursed back to health at Battersea Dogs Home where we found her. They had named her Edelweiss because of her white coat, a name which we shortened to Eddie because at the time we lived in South London and wandering around the mean streets of Stockwell shouting 'Here, Edelweiss!' could only ever end badly. So poor Pierrot, I'm afraid, was rescued on the rebound.

As seems befitting for an ageing King Charles spaniel, Pierrot had descended into debauchery and moral decay and had taken to pleasuring himself shamelessly. He'd developed a passion for frottage. Now, all dogs like a good tickle or a scratch, but he'd started rubbing himself on furniture and the look in his eyes was, well... there's no easy way to put this... his orgasm face. He had become like a dissolute great uncle: charmingly drunk but without any shame whatsoever, and tolerated because of his age, the dirty old man. We'd be eating dinner, hear a groaning noise and realise that Pierrot was under the table happily rubbing himself up against a chair leg. It was, needless to say, quite off-putting. The rescued kitten, naturally curious anyway, just stared at him with a look of complete disdain on her face, like a rich woman in a fast-food restaurant: fascination and disgust in equal measure.

The next day I had decided to repeat my 'get up early and do some work' folly only to be greeted by Junior, our horse, standing, snorting at the lounge window, and another massive puddle of doggy arse-vomit in the hall. Junior had broken through the fence (the part that hadn't yet been electrified) and had decimated one of my precious apple trees. He looked decidedly peaky, which served him right frankly, but I took him back to his stable in the pouring rain while Natalie dealt with Toby's mess; a fair deal I thought.

Then Natalie found another three kittens.

We rang the local Animal Rescue Centre, the SPA, which apparently isn't at our house as I had begun to believe it was, and were told that they couldn't take the kittens because we live in the wrong *département* (county, that is); but make sure, they said, that we get them all sterilised, including the mother if we found her. Sterilisation is very expensive, they added. Thanks, keep up the good work.

One of the local vets, taking something of a harsh line, said that the cats had to be 'removed' or we would be overrun in the next few years by in-bred moggies. How do we do that, we asked? You don't want to know the answer – and anyway we'd run out of bin bags.

The hunting season was due to start the following week and I really couldn't see them surviving the carnage that is created by local *chasseurs* and droves of middle-management types coming down from Paris for a couple of days, all blasting away at anything that moves. Samuel hated it so much when we first arrived that he went charging into the field with his toy lightsaber, ready to kill them all, and I had to go chasing after him and bring him down with a rugby tackle while pheasants plummeted to the earth around us.

I had to go back to the UK for a couple of days to work, but I made it very clear that on my return I expected the kittens to have moved on. I wasn't interested where they went, but a line had to be drawn, I said. Enough is enough, I emphasised. No more animal adoptions, I said, 'Unless' – and I made this absolutely clear – 'it's a billionaire bloody unicorn.'

Who was I kidding? Natalie and the neighbouring farmer's wife, Dominique, were deciding what to do with the kittens when a car pulled up and asked what was occurring. Now, whether he was a cat lover, a good Samaritan, a madman or just plain hungry I don't know, but he took one of the kittens. And then there were two. Natalie and Dominique decided between themselves it would be safer to move them. Move them into my house, as it turns out, until – and I quote – 'They can be rehomed'.

I mean really, do people think I'm stupid or something? Samuel and Maurice had already named the two 'temporary' newcomers Fox and Stripe, and taken one each to look after. So of course, when someone comes calling for either Fox or Stripe it's going to be beautifully straightforward just handing them over, isn't it? That won't upset the boys at all, will it? That won't scar them for life or anything. Years from now, as Samuel pours his heart out in therapy, he'll be asked what his abiding childhood memory is. 'When I was nine my daddy took away my little kitten, she was called Fox, and he gave her to a stranger. It has consumed my every waking moment since. That is why I hit him with a shovel.'

All of this became apparent immediately on my arrival home and there was no point fighting it. Checkmate, Natalie, you diabolical, evil genius.

Resistance is utterly futile. I may under French law be laughably termed the 'head of the household', but I am a constitutional monarch – I have no real executive power at all; I'm just wheeled out occasionally for ceremonial purposes and I'm useful at testing electric fences.

I shrieked again as the testing continued.

If you were to define the word 'stubborn' at a level that everyone understands then 'adjective: behave like a French horse' would pretty much nail it in my opinion. We had owned Junior for about two years and he was still as truculent as the day we got him: wilful, moody, almost unrideable and seemingly determined to escape at any given opportunity. Our relationship is on the cool side; we are not close.

He was welcomed with optimism on my part. Since we'd moved in I'd been mowing the land on a *tondeuse* (a sit-down mower) which is every boy's dream, until you actually use one. They are, in practice, bone-shakingly awful things that throw you about so much that by the time you've finished, in my case four hours later, you feel like you've been in a cocktail shaker in the hands of a jittery barman on a kicking bull. When the *tondeuse*, due to a lack of upkeep and maintenance from me, finally gave up it seemed the 'green' thing to do: give over most of the land to a horse, then sit back on the *terrasse* and watch Mother Nature mow the lawn.

The first time I met him I knew there would be trouble. He bit my arm.

'He bit my arm!' I squealed.

'He's just being friendly,' Natalie said.

'But, he bit my arm!'

'You probably upset him.'

'How? By having arms?'

I knew then that whatever this creature did, whatever damage he wrought, whatever mayhem he caused, he was staying. In Natalie's eyes he could do no wrong.

I built him a stable and he ate the grass – that was the deal. But he never relented in eating the grass. Then he ran out of grass and wanted the grass on the other side of the fence. Then he demolished two apple trees and a walnut tree. He just would not stop eating. Nothing seemed to satisfy his hunger, and he couldn't be exercised because he didn't want to interrupt his constant eating. And he was always getting out of his paddock; he learned that if he rolled a certain way he could slide under the fence. Is that natural horse behaviour? I was beginning to suspect that he wasn't a proper horse at all, but two escapologists in a pantomime horse costume.

Natalie and I were in bed one night and we both heard a noise that seemed to come from downstairs.

'Did you hear that?' Natalie hissed.

'Yes,' I replied.

'What was it?'

'I don't know,' I said, 'violent intruders?'

'You'd better go and check.'

I ventured nervously downstairs, creeping on tiptoe and offering a meek *'Bonjour'* to anyone who may have been there. Then I nearly had a heart attack. There, at the large lounge windows, was a ghostly apparition, an image straight from a horror film that frightened the bloody life out of me. Junior, with the full moon right behind him, was snorting at the window; the vapour from his nostrils had formed large circles on the window pane, adding to the eerie, ghoulish nature of the scene.

'Well, what is it?' Natalie whispered from the top of the stairs.

'Ghost Horse,' I replied.

'What?' she said loudly and came down the stairs to witness the horror. 'Ah, bless him. He's lonely.'

Of course he is.

So over the next year no matter how many times he escaped or demolished fruit trees, no matter how many new fences needed to be erected and electrified it was all because he was lonely and not, apparently, because he's just a horse-git.

Technically speaking, Junior is a pony and not a horse; I'm not sure what the difference is and frankly I don't care – he's big and looks like a horse which makes him, in my opinion, a horse. He's a Norwegian Fjord by breed, a Viking horse, which would account for some of his more aggressive behaviour and the fact that he loves bad weather. Hardy doesn't come into it; if there's a violent thunderstorm he stands out in his field facing the thunder and lightning, pawing at the ground and snorting his encouragement for the elements like he's possessed or something. So when I got back from work one Sunday and was confronted by a donkey, I didn't fancy the donkey's chances. The donkey, about half the size of Junior, was called T'Thor, or 'Little Thor' after the Norse god of thunder, which seemed a cruel joke in the circumstances and he was a nervous character from the off – far too weak to stop Junior from mounting him in an equine twist on *The Shawshank Redemption* 'prison pecking-order' scenario. It's Norwegian Fjords, you see, raping and pillaging is in their blood.

T'Thor lasted a fortnight before he had to be returned to the rescue sanctuary whence he came. The lady from the centre came to assess him before taking him back and declared that he was depressed, which I thought was just a donkey trait to be honest, and that he needed to be back amongst his own kind. Yes, and not be rogered repeatedly by a Viking re-enactment enthusiast either, I suspect. Samuel and I would have preferred to have kept T'Thor and got rid of Junior instead but it wasn't really an option; T'Thor was by this time a broken man, a mere shell of a donkey.

'I don't think we should get another companion for Junior,' I said not long after T'Thor had left, 'he's clearly not that easy to get on with. It's not fair to experiment with another animal really, is it?'

Ultime, a two-year-old Connemara filly who had been badly mistreated, duly arrived a fortnight later while I was away working. A sneaky operation and practically a conspiracy by Natalie and the three boys.

'I couldn't exactly say no, could I? Poor little thing,' Natalie told me over the phone.

'No, not really,' I agreed. 'How is she getting on with Junior?'

'Great! He's only bitten her once.'

The bite turned out to be nothing more sinister than rather aggressive foreplay, because almost since the moment she arrived, Ultime and Junior had been 'at it' constantly. She clearly took a shine to the old reprobate early on, quite blatantly giving him the come-on. Unfortunately for Ultime, this new-found abandon had its consequences and she developed genital herpes. Well, I mean, if you will go at it like – well, like two horses who haven't had it in a while – what do you expect? I didn't know animals could get STDs, to be honest; I must have missed that episode of *All Creatures Great and Small*.

'What's wrong with her, Mr Herriot? I need her to pull t' cart t' market the morrow.'

'She's got chlamydia, Seth. What a hussy.'

Anyway, she did look very sorry for herself.

I tested the last bit of fence and decided to call it a day. Tired, beaten, charred and feeling like I had the hands of an arthritic ninety-year-old, I'd had enough. It was getting dark anyway; time to relax on the terrace with a chilled glass of local rosé and get a bit of that elusive peace and quiet that I keep being promised, a bit of 'me' time, especially after the animal-inspired madness of the week we'd just had.

Fat chance.

Thérence, who really should have been called Napoleon (such is his attitude to life), had hidden my slippers and was now pulling Toby's tail in an aggressive attempt to persuade him to take him for a ride. Toby looked at me for help, which I was too tired to offer. 'Where can you go to get a bit of peace around here?' he seemed to be saying to me. No idea, chum, no idea.

LIBERTÉ, ÉGALITÉ, REALITY

'I'm really glad you moved here, the gene pool could really do with some shaking up!'

I'm not sure what we expected when we took Samuel for his first day at the local school, but a tacit admission from one of the other parents that perhaps some local families were a bit too close wasn't up there.

Though I like to think that we've added a certain exoticism to the area – well I have anyway, I'm certainly the only mod around here – we didn't move to be the 'English family in the village'. Natalie and the boys all have French citizenship now; they are to all intents and purposes French; but that doesn't mean that the boys don't have their English traits and sometimes they stand out like, well, like a mod in a *boulangerie*.

That said, I love the fact that my children are part French, part English. There are things I'm not happy with, of course: Samuel doesn't like Yorkshire pudding, and Maurice, to stress his Frenchness, will eat baked potatoes but not the skin. But the point is that they fit in.

Samuel was a little reluctant at first. He started school very soon after we moved in, and we went to see the headmaster – Monsieur Vernon – to ask if he could just do some mornings for a while so that he could adjust. Monsieur Vernon was having none of it. While quite obviously loving the children in his care, he seemed to have little or no patience with their parents. He peered at us over his heavy-rimmed glasses; if this was the kind of weak, lily-livered attitude that British education produces, he seemed to be thinking, no wonder they're all coming over here.

'*Non*,' he sighed, more in disappointment than anything else. '*Non*. If you start school, you start school. It is not a hobby!'

Poor Samuel – he was only four! It was like he was being initiated into some highfalutin Academie Française, not the local infant school. We had the option of waiting until the new school year started in September, but that was eight months off and we felt that if we left it too long he would find it even harder. He only had a smattering of French and for the first fortnight or so clearly found it very difficult indeed, saying that he wanted to go 'home' and that he didn't want to learn French anyway.

I've learned over the years that parenting, more often than not, is about knowing when to bribe and what to bribe with; and the promise of various *Star Wars* related tat if he made more of an effort to speak the language did the trick. A switch flicked in his head and within another fortnight he seemed almost fluent and on a par, 'academically', with his classmates.

Samuel, having been born in England, is the most 'English' of our three boys, by which I mean he bottles his emotions up and says 'Bugger' a lot. Maurice and Thérence were both born in France and Thérence, the youngest, is to my mind the most French; he has strong opinions which he's prepared to stand up for and if he doesn't get his way he'll down tools. Maurice, on the other hand, is a sensitive soul, an artist, a 'creative' who wears his heart on his sleeve but who has, on occasion, a streak of Anglo-Saxon in him that very definitely marks him out as being different from his peers, insisting on wearing an England football kit to his football training being one example.

Maurice was born a few months after our arrival and it was a glorious summer. I was able to take almost a month off work, Natalie's parents stayed in France until the autumn, her grandparents were around the corner and the new arrival attracted a multitude of family visitors. It was only when I was back working, and twice as much to pay off the month's parental leave, that Natalie started to feel cut off. Her parents returned to the UK, her grandfather, Papy, became ill and couldn't easily drive himself and Mamie out to see her and the boys. The nights drew in and it quickly became a lonely existence, as I was away more and more. The support network that was around when we first had Samuel was not in France and we hadn't yet made firm friends in our new home, just acquaintances who couldn't fill that gap. She was feeling lonely, isolated and, despite the demands of two young children and a large house, unoccupied and bored.

So we began a search for a part-time job and a child minder, *une nourrice*, who could look after Maurice for the day and Samuel as well after school. The *nourrice* bit was easy. A brief search in *Les Pages Jaunes* showed one living just a couple of minutes' drive away, a lovely woman named Brigitte who had three daughters of her own, two of whom were similar ages to Samuel and Maurice. More importantly, she had room for our boys, as there is a legal limit to the number of children a child minder can look after at any one time. Brigitte and her husband, Eric, quickly became friends of the family, which immediately took the pressure off Natalie a bit.

As if to underline that we had done the right thing by moving out here, a job fell into Natalie's lap. We certainly hadn't been confident of that. We had actually moved to a very poor part of France, just off the main chateaux tourist trail and apart from agriculture there really isn't very much going on. Back in England Natalie had been a successful recruitment consultant and she didn't just want a job so that she could get out of the house, she wanted something that would stretch her a bit.

She got far more than she had bargained for.

Initially, when she started work as an estate agent, *une négotiatrice d'immobilier*, in town, it seemed like the ideal job. She was able to work just on Tuesdays, Thursdays and Fridays, it was local and for someone who could happily sit through television programmes like *Escape to the Country*, *Location, Location, Location* and *A Place in the Sun* without wanting to self-harm, it was perfect – almost too good to be true. And it was. Natalie liked her job, she enjoyed meeting people and seeing different properties, but there was a problem, an impediment to her potential success as an estate agent: (apologies to any estate agents reading this, but) Natalie isn't a heartless, devious worm.

It became clear very early on that the estate agency business, especially at this unfashionable end of the Loire Valley, was and probably still is a cut-throat affair. Monsieur Norbert, who had been pretty gruff and unpleasant when we were his clients buying our house from him, was even more unpleasant as Natalie's boss. There are three estate agencies in town and a limited number of clients, either buying or selling, so the chicanery and emotional blackmailing that went on in order to secure a sale or even just to get a house on the market was considerable. On top of that, Norbert seemingly liked to bully his staff and set them against each other, making the office an unpleasant place to be.

Most of Natalie's 'clients' it seems just wanted to chat anyway. How depressed you must be, or what circumstances must have led to the kind of loneliness that can only be leavened by the presence of an estate agent one can only guess, but Natalie's job soon took on the role of social worker and companion. She became hugely popular around town (she still is); a source of comfort to some people, always happy to lend an ear. And of course Natalie always did like nosing around other people's houses, so it was an even better deal for her and she would quite often return home with a gift, a plant here or a piece of furniture there and on one occasion a mod-hating Brittany spaniel, but not many sales as the market was predictably sluggish. She just couldn't lie to people to convince them to buy something that wasn't suited to them, or to sell something they didn't want to sell.

Even so, Natalie toughed it out for three years; the market was practically dead, staff quickly came and went, most of them unable to bear Norbert's bullying management and all on a pitiful minimum wage with no allowance for petrol or other expenses. She got virtually no commission from any sales she made, as Norbert would often claim that the sale was his anyway. To receive commission, the 'sale' had to be from a client that you had introduced to the agency, but Norbert's family had been in the area for generations so he would always comically claim to have introduced them himself. On one occasion he claimed commission on a sale because he had once played tennis against the clients' nephew!

Obviously living with me for so long it goes without saying that Natalie has the patience of a saint, but I don't know how she managed three years of that when all the odds were so stacked against her; I certainly couldn't have done it. So when Natalie became pregnant with Thérence it was something of a relief all round, not just that she could go on state-funded maternity leave for a maximum of three years, but that she would be away from Norbert. She would never openly admit it, but his harrying management style was having an effect on her health, as more often than not she would come home from work emotionally shattered, and would then have to look after Samuel and Maurice because I was away. It was a draining existence for her.

One of the plus points of her three years, though, was that she got to know so many people in the area. We walk around the market even now and have to stop every few minutes as another one of her 'clients' wants to say hello to her. This is something else that I've yet to fully come to terms with: kissing or handshakes? It's a bloody minefield.

I get the sense that the English have this idea that in France total strangers will meet in the street and lots of hugging and cheek-kissing will ensue. We just don't like that level of privacy invasion. In truth, though, the whole meeting and greeting thing is far more subtle, far more complicated than that, and as such the potential for social faux pas is enormous. You don't kiss strangers of either sex; if you are introduced then you shake hands and graduate to kissing later on if some sort of relationship (however flimsy) develops.

The day after we moved in, Monsieur and Madame Lebrun, the couple who we had bought the house from, threw a little welcoming soirée for us and invited the Giresses and the Rousseaus, two large farming families and our immediate neighbours. We arrived and were greeted at the door by the Lebruns. I shook Monsieur Lebrun's hand and kissed Madame Lebrun twice, once on either cheek, before she introduced us to the others. I shook the men's hands warmly, but it was clear, by subtle body movements, that the first farmer's wife was open to a warmer welcome and I kissed her on the cheeks also. The second farmer's wife, a short, stocky woman, wanted no truck with such an obviously louche attitude to social etiquette, and she gripped my hand firmly, started crushing it and began to push me backwards. It was like shaking hands with a wrestler and I was convinced that she was going to throw me over her shoulder and pin me down on the kitchen floor.

It was a confusing message. When we had arrived we had shaken hands, but by the time we left a couple of hours later we had exchanged cheek-kisses, even me with Monsieur, apparently thereby showing respect for his age and position. We had drunk a fair bit of local hooch and had a good time, a friendship had been forged and therefore kissing, in this context, was entirely appropriate.

What is not appropriate, however, is when an enthusiastic effort to do the right thing in the right situation ends up looking like some kind of sexual advance. We had gone round to introduce ourselves to our closest neighbours, Monsieur and Madame Le Boeuf, a lovely old couple who had moved down from Paris some years before. They were enchanted by four-year-old Samuel, saying how nice it would be to hear the sound of children in the area, and promptly introduced us to their nieces who were staying with them, two very attractive, very chic, confident young women in their early twenties.

Maybe I was taken up by the bonhomie of the whole thing, the affectionate welcome we had received was genuinely heart-warming and it may have got to me. Combine that with at least half a bottle of the kind of alcohol that would floor one of the Easter Island statues and you have a heady mix and the kind of fuzzy thinking and lack of limb-control that starts wars, never mind putting a halt on burgeoning neighbourly friendships. I went to shake the hand of one of the nieces and then for some reason got it into my head that I then had to kiss her as well, so started leaning precariously over the table, losing my balance and falling on her as she let out a scream.

I picked myself up, apologised profusely and, in lieu of having any actual French language in which to explain myself, acted out the fall again in order to illustrate that it was a genuine accident. Unfortunately, this just had the effect of making the poor girl think I was going to jump on her again, and she cowered back into her chair, clearly terrified. Monsieur Le Boeuf thought the whole thing was hilarious and poured more drinks, but the nieces obviously felt uncomfortable in my presence so when we did eventually leave a full hour later, I wasn't even offered a handshake. She could barely look at me.

It's like walking a kind of social tightrope and I can't be the only one to have inadvertently mixed alcohol and etiquette to such a disquieting effect.

Some people even use it to play politics. The mother of one of Samuel's friends, well at least he used to be a friend, doesn't like me. I don't know why; maybe she has a female relative left traumatised by falling Englishmen. But we see each other often enough to have to go beyond a handshake and she keeps changing the rules. We meet at least twice a week at the school bus drop-off point – one day it's one kiss on either cheek, the next it's one kiss on the left, two on the right; the day after it's the other way around. Then it was two on each. 'Four kisses!' she said, admonishing me for my lack of manners.

The next time I went to do four kisses and she leaned back out of the way like a batsman avoiding a bouncer, two kisses clearly being sufficient on a Tuesday afternoon as any fool knows.

I consider myself a man of the world, I've entertained foreign ambassadors, eaten with Bedouin tribes in the desert, played pool with the Russian Mafia, lived rough and stayed in the finest hotels on the planet. Never before has my protocol even been questioned, let alone challenged, yet after nearly six years in the Loire Valley I've become, socially at least, a gibbering wreck.

As if that weren't enough, my language skills were still not what they should be. I can handle linear situations – conversations with doctors, insurance people, mechanics and the like, where you have some idea of where it might all lead and where you can brush up on the vocabulary beforehand – but the subtlety, nuance, slang and sheer pace involved in a lively French discussion over dinner or at the school gates for the most part elude me. Part of what holds me back is that I can always rely on Natalie, or even the children, to translate for me and when they do so, I tend to just nod like I definitely understood anyway, but I just wanted confirmation. Nobody is fooled.

I've tried tapes, books, lessons, dubbed Michael Caine films, watching French television (surely the hardest, cruellest of all ways to learn French) and reading the local newspaper. It's all in there apparently, it just stubbornly refuses to come out in any coherent form whatsoever, and then I lose confidence. As a stand-up comedian, my job is all about communicating with people quickly, so if I'm talking to a French person and they start to look at me like a budgie looks at a mirror, a mixture of fascination, confusion and a total lack of comprehension, I start to stutter and panic and the whole shaky construction of my conversation begins to collapse. I even said to Natalie and the boys that we should set aside one day a week at home as 'French Day' so that I can learn more.

'But Daddy,' Samuel said, 'when you're here we want to be able to talk to you.' Yeah. That hurt.

The fact that both Samuel and Maurice are completely fluent in two languages without a hint of an accent in either (and that, shortly, Thérence will be also) is a source of immense pride to Natalie and me, and people often congratulate us on our children's abilities. Really, though, it's their work, their desire to communicate. They switch effortlessly between being English boys who can speak French and French boys who can speak English, and most of the time the only way you would know that they have an English background is when their 'eccentrically' dressed mod-dad comes to pick them up and they have to translate something for him.

'Your daddy is funny,' one of Maurice's school friends said once. I don't think she meant it in a good way.

FEELING A LITTLE CHATON

If I have garnered a well-earned reputation for being a little gauche socially, then it's fair to say that Natalie has earned an equally justified renown of her own. Where animals and their welfare are concerned, she is a soft touch.

As usual for a Sunday I had got home at about three in the afternoon, following the customary harrowing journey home. Though I was no longer driving nearly as much, I usually had to skip sleep on a Saturday night to try and meet all my travel connections. I had been working in Leeds the night before and in order to make my earlyish flight from Stansted Airport to Tours I had had to take an all-night coach from Leeds to Stansted. If ever you feel like you may be a winner in life and that maybe you just need bringing down a peg or two, I can heartily recommend an overnight National Express coach. As is often the case, I was the only one on the bus (going via London) whose belongings weren't in a black bin liner, and as usual the only one wearing a cravat. The overnight coach is undoubtedly convenient, as trains don't run through the night, but they are uncomfortable, generally crowded and sometimes quite menacing; they are not for the faint-hearted, though it has to be said, arguably preferable to the brutality of the budget airline flight that follows.

The drive home from Tours Airport through the vineyards and rolling fields via Amboise and Montrichard acts as my decompression chamber, before the boys quite rightly demand attention; though it's fair to say that I'm quite often in a fragile state having not slept for twenty-four hours. The boys, however, were playing their own games this time when I got back, so I was allowed to grab a cold beer, lie on my under-used hammock in the orchard and enjoy the late autumn sunshine.

Natalie was out at the front of the house walking Ultime (who appeared to be dealing stoically with her STD) up and down the verges on the roadside so that she could eat and cut the grass. I began to doze off, the soporific rural idyll washing the bestiality of my flight and all-night coach journeys out of my system. Five minutes I had. Five minutes, then reality came stomping through the grass and poked me in the eye with the pooey end of a stick.

Natalie was deep in conversation with a couple I didn't recognise, who had stopped by with some news. Now wide awake I wandered over, sensing trouble.

An old woman who lived a kilometre or so down the road had had a stroke and died. All very sad, obviously, and this particular woman was something of a character. She'd lived on about an acre of land on which stood various old caravans, a couple of ancient Citroëns and various other shacks; it looked like a shanty town. She also lived with lots and lots and lots of animals, all of which were now homeless, all of whom now needed care. All of them. Dozens of geese and chickens, some mangy old dogs, a horse, goats, cats.

'Had we known her?' the occupants of the car asked.

'Not really,' we answered.

'She was our aunt,' they said. 'It's a shame.'

'It is,' we agreed.

'Especially for the animals...'

No! Come on! What the hell is going on here? I thought. What are you people, salesmen? Don't you know that I'm married to Noah's female reincarnation? Of course they did, they'd have heard. They'd have been at the old lady's place, wondering aloud what to do with the animals, and someone would have pointed out that there is an equally mad woman down the road who'll take all your animals off your hands for you. Ignore her husband, they'd have been told, she does. That's it, I thought, we've become a mecca for anyone wanting to offload livestock. It's going to get like an animal Oxfam shop around here – we'll come down of a morning and find 'donations' on our doorstep.

'Would you be interested in...?'

'No!' I said.

'We have these three lovely *chatons*...' said the lady, completely ignoring me and pointing to a box of kittens on the back seat.

This is how drug dealers work, isn't it? You start off with a few kittens and next thing you know you've got a couple of goats, three pigs, a shire horse and your life is no longer your own.

'We've just taken on three kittens, I'm afraid,' Natalie told them. Phew!

'Well, we've also got two goats and a pony.'

Seriously, what's going on in a world where any Tom, Dick and Harry can pitch up and start handing out animals to the vulnerable and the weak? That's how they sell cigarettes in Burma and it's bloody unethical. Not to mention the fact that we simply might not be able to take care of the animals properly; we were using a horse with genital herpes as a lawnmower for God's sake! We should have been on a blacklist.

Natalie managed to resist, I think partly because I was smacking my head repeatedly on the bonnet of the 'dealer's' car while wailing about injustice and fate, but they'll be back at the end of the month, they said; give us a chance to talk things over, see if 'we' change 'our' minds. It all sounded much like a threat to me and I went storming off muttering expletives and generally behaving like a man who hadn't slept for a day or so and then been abused in transit. I flopped back onto the hammock and almost squashed a kitten which then spat at me, waved its backside in my direction and put me firmly in my place with typical cat haughtiness. They'd been here five minutes these cats and they were already bullying me.

Of all the animals I thought we'd ever own, I'd certainly not banked on cats. I'd never even liked cats, and it became increasingly obvious over their first few weeks that Natalie and the boys didn't feel I could be left alone with the kittens. In order to keep me and the kittens apart therefore, I was assigned tasks that kept taking me outside, though I am not, by any stretch of the imagination (and hammocks apart), an outdoor person. I don't do outdoor stuff; I am not capable. I don't even own a pair of wellington boots, my logic being that if I owned a pair I'd be asked to do things which involved having to wear them, and that's surely to be avoided. Some men may still see themselves as hunter-gatherers; but some of us sadly are best left with the admin.

The first year we were here I had to build a big bonfire for garden rubbish, which in itself is easy enough, but I just couldn't get the thing lit. Every time I got a spark going it went out. I tried rags soaked in petrol, barbecue firelighters, magnifying glasses using the sun's rays – I even rubbed two sticks together for about half an hour because I'd seen it in a film, but nothing worked. In the end I ran out of patience and just emptied the petrol canister on it in a manic arsonist-style frenzy, stood back (I'm not an idiot) and threw a lit box of matches at it. The resulting fireball threw me to the ground and as I lay there thinking that that was a bit too close for comfort I saw the fire snaking along the grass towards me and the petrol canister that was next to me. I got up and ran away shouting 'She's gonna blow!' and jumped into a hedge.

Yet despite this dubious track record with the great outdoors, rather than be trusted indoors with the kittens, I was, one sweltering autumn day, to be found waist deep in odious, rotted bio-matter, while wearing someone else's waders, all on the pretext of pond clearance. It is not a situation I thought I would ever find myself in and I don't want it repeated, but apparently ponds don't clean themselves and I had been earmarked to remove all the reeds.

'Didn't we plant these reeds?' I asked.

'The fish need to breathe,' Natalie said.

'Yes, but didn't we plant these reeds?' I persisted petulantly.

'Take those things off before you go back in the house, won't you?' And with that she was off.

Firstly, wearing someone else's waders just feels wrong, like using someone else's toothbrush. Oddly enough I don't own a pair of my own waders, largely for the same reason that I don't own a pair of wellies but also because, and I'm ready to be corrected on this, Fred Perry hasn't yet moved in to the 'Swamp Husbandry' market. If being a mod is about anything, it's about looking your best at all times and about dignity, both of which are sorely tested when you're wearing an agricultural gimp suit, covered in a tar-like substance that appears to have oozed up from the Earth's core and that smells like a landfill site on a hot day. It's difficult to describe the stench and texture of the stuff; it's fetid, ebony black and gloopy; like Dublin's sewers the morning after St Patrick's Day. And it doesn't give up its reeds without a fight either. I emerged from the pond an hour later looking like I'd struck oil, but smelling like oil that may have been formed in a Portaloo at the Glastonbury Festival.

In the end, though, it couldn't be avoided. I had to be left alone with the kittens. Natalie had to take Samuel and Maurice to the dentist and it was my turn to babysit while Thérence had his afternoon nap. Seriously, I thought, what's the fuss? How difficult could this possibly be? Yes they're frisky and in and out of cupboards and plant pots and they tend to crawl over you when you sit down and they bring chaos where previously there was order – but I can put my inherent OCD neatly in a drawer for an hour or so and just relax, can't I? You know, go with the flow. Chill. No? Apparently not.

Natalie and the children left reluctantly and I decided to lay down some ground rules. We were in the large open-plan kitchen-diner-lounge, with me in my customary position behind the breakfast bar, standing like a surly barman. The kittens were at the opposite end lying on the rug and enjoying the afternoon sunshine as it came in through the window. 'Right,' I said to them from a distance at the other end of the room, 'you stay in your half of the room, and I'll stay here and just keep an eye on you. Don't go jumping on the work surfaces, don't go scratching and pulling at the rugs and sofas and most importantly stay away from my shoes and my coats. You may look cute on a black and white Athena poster, but I'm no pushover, OK kids?'

Who was I fooling? I turned my back briefly and almost immediately there was a gut-wrenching, ear-piercing feline scream that chilled me to the core. I spun round to see one of the cats dangling from Maurice's wicker toy box! The cat had got one of its paws stuck in the handle and it was struggling violently. The paw looked like it was facing the wrong way, like one of those horrible football injuries that they don't show on television anymore; it sounded bad and it looked worse. I disentangled the cat and put it on the floor where it whimpered pitifully and tried to limp back to its bed, dragging its leg behind it.

I'm afraid that this is when I lost it.

'Well that's just bloody typical, isn't it? I turn my back on you for one bloody minute while Natalie and the others turn their backs on me for one bloody minute and you go and do this! What were you thinking?' All three of them sat there in front of me, just looking at me as I towered over them and went into a full-blown Basil Fawlty-style meltdown. 'What were you thinking?' I shouted, waving my fist in their little faces. 'You know who'll get the blame for this, don't you? Eh? Me! Me! That's who.'

All of a sudden they rushed at me simultaneously apparently 'limpless' all of a sudden. They're going to attack me, I thought – but they ran past and I turned to see Natalie, Samuel and Maurice standing there, mouths open, their faces a mixture of horror and, worst of all, disappointment.

'What are you doing, Daddy?' Maurice asked, not unreasonably under the circumstances.

'Playing,' I said, 'just... just playing.' There was an uncomfortable silence while they all looked at me and the kittens, none of which it seemed were even slightly injured, curled around their legs and purred. 'I'll go and see if there's anything that needs doing outside,' I muttered and scurried off.

That incident was used as the final reason why the cats couldn't possibly be re-homed. Some flim-flam about trauma was offered, but only half-heartedly and no-one was buying it. So, the decision having finally been made, rather dubiously to my mind, I came into my own with a to-do list: bowls, proper beds and collars were needed, I said, let's get these cats organised.

The pet shop is actually in a garden centre and is somewhere I usually try and avoid, because if Natalie has an obsession with collecting animals it is matched only by her addiction to gardening. There have been times when I have spent so long in garden centres I have seen plants grow, flower and die before we have made it to the checkout. I once, and I'm not making this up, collapsed in a garden centre in England, due to some long-standing inner ear balance problem, and Natalie carried on shopping while we waited for the ambulance. The combination of garden centre and pet shop is therefore potentially quite a dangerous one.

We got off relatively lightly in the plant section, with just a few lavenders finding their way into the trolley while I was off choosing collars and practising the word 'no' in preparation for the pet department.

'Daddy, can we get a mouse?'

'No.'

'Daddy, can we have a parakeet?'

'No.'

'Daddy, can we…?'

'No.'

'Daddy?'

'No.'

The chinchilla was the one that did it for me. A sad little South American fur ball cruelly out of place in a cage in Central France, with its big doe eyes and depressed manner. I have to admit it was very tempting to rescue it, to give it some kind of life.

'Daddy, can we have a chinchilla?'

'Er…'

'Yay! Mummy! Daddy said we could have a chinchilla!'

I was shaken from my temporary reverie. 'What? No I didn't! We don't know anything about chinchillas. No way! Have you seen *Gremlins*? Those things will ruin the sofa!'

Then it started – the wailing and moaning and gnashing of child teeth; even the chinchilla had a look on his face which suggested he'd probably be better off staying put. I'm proud of the fact that my children love animals so much – it is a civilising influence – but keeping a lid on it, especially when they are encouraged so much by their mother, was proving quite difficult.

Their love of animals is a by-product of the outdoor life that we were leading, but even they have their 'outdoor' limits. Nothing could persuade them to join Natalie and me in foraging for and eating wild mushrooms, and you can't really blame them for that. I wasn't all that enthusiastic either. There are mushrooms everywhere in the autumn, and while we were out on a bike ride one day we found a whole pathway of them in a little copse. Natalie wanted to pick them there and then, but Samuel and I, both naturally suspicious people, weren't convinced, as we know less about wild *champignons* than we do about chinchillas. We decided to be cautious and consult our book of French mushrooms when we got home.

Our particular book of French mushrooms, however, is one of the world's most useless guides, up there with *Fell Walking for the Agoraphobic* or *A Politician's Guide to Probity*. It's a thick book and 'details' hundreds of mushrooms and fungi, carefully separating the poisonous from the edible with each entry supported by a picture. The problem is that the pictures are all drawings and they are all exactly the same! Whether they couldn't afford a photographer and the illustrator only knew how to do one kind of mushroom I don't know, but it only serves to muddy the waters of the business frankly. This singular drawing, which (don't get me wrong) is very good, was seemingly of the exact mushroom we had found, so now we couldn't tell if it was poisonous, edible or just one of the charmingly entitled 'Mild Irritants' (making it sound like some mushrooms may try to sell you double glazing over the phone during dinner).

It's always best to consult experts in these situations, however, Natalie became convinced that the mushrooms were edible because Sandrine, the hairdresser, told her they would be. Firstly, I remonstrated, she's a hairdresser – she will say anything! And secondly, she's a French hairdresser – she'll say anything and wave scissors in your face if you disagree. At the time it was me having my haircut, and I'd rather she'd have concentrated on my late-sixties Steve Marriot haircut than convince Natalie to risk poisoning her family.

We picked the mushrooms on the way back from town (that's how convincing French hairdressers are), but I was still uneasy about the whole thing.

'Are you sure we should do this?' I asked, as if it was illegal or something.

'Well, Sandrine said it would be fine,' Natalie answered, though I could tell she was wavering.

'But she's French!' I tried one final time. 'They eat anything.'

'Oh, stop it!' The fifty per cent French blood in Natalie started bubbling to the surface like lava as she picked a couple of hub-cap-sized mushrooms. 'What's the worst that can happen?'

'Oh, I dunno, death?'

I cleaned the mushrooms with a damp cloth, having read somewhere that you should never wash mushrooms because you lose the flavour (or in this case maybe poison), covered them in chopped garlic, parsley and butter and put them under the grill. They looked magnificent placed on top of thickly sliced *pain de campagne*, the glistening melted butter and the aroma of garlic adding to their lustre. We sat there with our plates in front of us feeling like proper country folk, but we didn't eat them straight away.

'You first,' I said bravely.

Natalie hesitated and then dived in. 'Mmmm,' she said, overacting I thought.

We ate the mushrooms and I'm happy to report that there were no side effects, no sickness, stomach upsets or death. Or, most disappointingly, taste. They were incredibly dull. I'd expected a hearty, almost steak-like texture and a strong, woody flavour, but this was like eating soggy foam. The thing about France, you see, is that food is a kind of death or glory experience: food can be great or terrible, but should always be interesting. These mushrooms were neither of those things, in fact they were worse than death; they were bland mediocrities, sullen and insipid. They were the French countryside equivalent of a midnight hot dog in Leicester Square.

To us that didn't really matter though – we had picked and eaten wild mushrooms. And we'd not only survived the experience, we were living the dream.

'This is what country living is all about,' I said to Natalie. 'Freedom, peace, living off the land.'

'And animals,' she replied, though avoiding eye contact. 'And animals.'

5

UPSETTING THE APPLE CART

The autumn and winter are the busiest time for jobbing club comedians, and whereas I had only planned to be away Thursday to Sunday for work, the nature of the comedy circuit had changed. Not long ago every big weekend club (and there were at least two in every major city and town) would have a Thursday night gig, but a contraction of the circuit had meant that not only had some clubs disappeared altogether, but those that remained no longer had a Thursday show. Fortunately, I had by now started on the corporate circuit and was working as an after-dinner speaker or as a host at corporate awards ceremonies, which were not only more lucrative but which I actually enjoyed far more than a heaving club night, acting as crowd control for stag and hen parties.

The only snag in this was that my working pattern became far more unpredictable; I could be away at any part of the week or away for weeks at a time. I had worked pretty much the same schedule for over five years now, but things had necessarily had to change. I was earning more money but was spending more and more time away. And whereas before I would only ever be away for work, now I might be away for five days but only have two or three gigs. It wasn't practical to come home to France for a day, either financially or logistically, so I was spending time away from home and having nothing to do. It's hard enough being away from your family so much, without also having the nagging feeling that the family may actually be growing in your absence. Brief conversations were grabbed by telephone or Skype and the paranoia increased if I heard hitherto unrecognised animal noises in the background.

'What was that noise?' I would snap.

'What noise?' they would all chorus, alarmingly harmonised.

'I heard bleating...' I'd take a deep breath. 'Have you gone out and got a sheep?'

'It's just the telly, Daddy,' one of them would say.

'No sheep here, Daddy,' another one would offer as confirmation.

I'd spent most of the previous week doing shows to English expats and assorted other Anglophones along the French Riviera: Monte Carlo, Cannes, Antibes and Nice. It is one of my favourite places in the world, combining stunning coastline, classic architecture, fantastic food and some of the silliest-looking rich people you're likely to find anywhere. I first went to Nice nearly thirty years ago and it hasn't changed all that much in that time; yet despite all the magnificent things the city has to offer, its walkways are still paved with dog poop. This is by no means a Niçois phenomenon but most other places seem to have cleaned up their act. I find it astonishing that France, a country that cares not only a great deal about what it looks like but how it's perceived, would allow one of its more spectacular spots to be covered in dog crap. It's like they're in denial about it.

There are so many dogs in Nice, none of which seem to get about under their own steam – they are carried under the arm like a living handbag; they are, in effect, an accessory, but an accessory that poos. There are very few dog poo bins to be seen, and although there are a few dispensaries for poo bags, they are all empty. In the end you spend most of the time wandering around Nice not admiring the buildings, the light, the beach or the people but looking at the floor and making sure you don't get *merde* all over your loafers. Some cities, like Toulouse for example, have tried TV campaigns to force a change of culture among dog owners, but it's a slow process.

Personally I think the problem will get worse, and not just in Nice. In France, as in many other countries with a 'sensible' Green policy, supermarkets no longer have boxes of free carrier bags at the checkouts; it's all about 'Bags for Life' these days and while that's all very worthy, it's bad news for your dog owner because we've all run out of poo bags. It used to be that when I came home from working in the UK my case would be full of the kind of things that French cuisine simply isn't capable of reproducing, things like Wotsits, Marmite, brown sauce and sausages made of sawdust, water and fish testicles; you know, staples of the English diet. Now it's full of carrier bags. On any given weekend, if I stay in a hotel and shop individually for each meal I can get about a dozen bags. And we need them too, or at least Natalie does as this is very much her department. Honestly, her day revolves so much around the collection of animal excrement she could take a PhD in Scatology. She patrols the garden picking up any dog mess, so that the boys don't play in it, then she mucks out the horses and rounds up all the manure in the paddock to sell or use for bartering, and in between times she's emptying the cat litter trays and changing Thérence's nappy. (All of that changes when I'm at home of course; I occasionally change the nappy.) However, our shortage of poo bags had become so dire that I had started hanging around the fruit-and-veg section of the supermarket and, when no-one was looking, grabbing handfuls of the clear plastic bags and hiding them under crates of beer. It is very undignified and just one of the many unreported consequences of being eco-friendly.

In my absence the cats had grown at an alarming rate, to the extent that I was almost convinced they weren't semi-feral, semi-domesticated cats at all, but actually a family of abandoned black panthers. Walking into the living room was now like being in a scene from a *Born Free* spoof, as three quite large cats prowl round the place or lie in a postprandial daze on the rug next to the remains of a zebra carcass. I'm convinced that they will inevitably rip me to death one day, while Thérence will go on to make a fortune in the circuses of Las Vegas sticking his head in their mouths.

Having discovered that in fact we had the gender wrong for at least two of the beasts, we decided that it was, by now, time to name them properly and naturally the French have a system for the naming of animals. The reasoning behind this has been traced to the Gallic requirement that everything, without exception, must carry some form of bureaucratic burden. The system is this: animals born in a given year must all have names that begin with the same letter – so, for instance, the letter for the year 2011 is 'G'. What is the point?! Nobody stops you in the street and says, 'Oh what a lovely dog, what's he called? Aristotle? Oh, he must be five years old!' I don't understand the need for this unnecessary uniformity. It stifles creativity; unless of course it's the year of the letter 'F' – and then there's endless fun!

'Fart!' Maurice giggled repeatedly.

'Which one, though?' Samuel would say.

'We're not having a cat called Fart!' I'd say, attempting some form of parental control.

'All of them!' they'd both shout. And round and round it went in an endless cycle of giggling and the word 'fart', until eventually, after a few choice 'F' words of my own, we settled on Fox, Flame and er, Vespa. Vespa, of course doesn't actually begin with an 'F', but because Natalie has a fear of scooters and motorbikes (and because I'm a technical dunce) it was pointed out that having a cat called Vespa is as close as I'm actually going to get to owning the real thing, so the name stayed.

It was a small victory, but a precious one and it feels good now and then to be able to put two fingers up to bureaucratic restriction. France is seen from the outside as both heavily regulated and almost constantly on the verge of anarchy, but I think that they're very much two sides of the same coin. Like a teenager who feels hemmed in by parental control, just occasionally French society needs to let it's hair down and rebel; sometimes it's a grandiose gesture like a general strike, but mostly it's the small victories that keep the community together in a kind of 'them and us' way. Naming one of the cats 'Vespa' as opposed to 'Fespa' may seem like a pitifully minute gesture in the grand scheme of things, but to me it represented that we were in fact becoming 'French'. We'd taken your laws, Madame La République, and blown a very Gallic raspberry at them.

Of course, that's as lawless as I get. I suffer from a certain level of OCD; I need the cutlery in the correct part of the cutlery drawer, tins on the shelf should be facing forward, as should creases on trousers. DVDs should be in alphabetical order, pens need lids and pasta varieties shouldn't be mixed. I don't like chaos or surprise or anarchy. I'm obviously in the wrong family.

Before travelling to the South I'd been in London, where there were reports of fuel shortages in France, but I was sceptical. This is just another example of anti-French bias from the UK media, I thought, another opportunity for a bit of Frog-bashing what with their quaint, antiquated values like workers' rights and community; bloody cheese-eating communists. I was wrong though, there really was no fuel. Panic-buying, a peculiar human condition that leads otherwise sane people to buy ten pints of milk on Easter Sunday because the supermarket may be closed on Easter Monday, had emptied the petrol stations, meaning that all non-essential usage of fuel had to be curbed. Activities like mowing the lawn, for instance, were a definite no-no, and yet as winter approached it needed doing, otherwise the garden would look like it had an ugly stubble all winter. I could live with that – my OCD doesn't stretch to anything that involves physical endeavour – but Natalie couldn't.

'We'll let the horses out,' she said, as if it was the most natural thing in the world.

'What? You mean including the horse we're trying to cure of an escaping habit?' I said, not liking the idea one jot. 'You're going to let both horses wander around the garden with the cats and the dogs and the kids? Isn't that a bit dangerous?'

'No.'

'If you need me, I'll be inside,' I said.

It all seemed like a good idea on paper, a family communing with its animals on the lawn, bathed in late autumn sunshine; like a scene from an impressionist painting. Unfortunately, it failed to take into account the rather highly strung nature of Ultime, who clearly likes the safety of her paddock and once out of it becomes a little skittish, the slightest noise setting her off. And once she's off, Junior gets all 'protective boyfriend' about the whole thing and chases after her, which sets Toby off too and the whole place goes mad. It's like the Pamplona run, as people dive for cover, only with horses and not in Spain. Anyway, it's dangerous.

I watched the whole thing from the safety of the kitchen and it was bedlam. First you'd see Samuel run past the window, laughing his head off and shouting 'Stampede!', only to be followed by Ultime and Junior and Toby in a crazy conga, Benny-Hill-theme-tuned-style chase that probably looked more dangerous than it actually was. And it just kept happening, like they were on a relentless merry-go-round: child followed by horse followed by dog. I ventured outside at one point and got caught up in the whole thing, but then a car went past and it triggered Ultime off, and while she went haring towards the patio this time Junior, instead of following her, made straight for me. The bloody animal was trying to settle scores!

'He's just being friendly!' Natalie shouted as I went running past her.

'He bloody isn't!'

I dived into the hedge and almost landed on Maurice, who apparently had been hiding there for most of the afternoon.

'What are you doing here?' I asked, trying to sound brave.

'I don't want to get run over,' he said.

'Good point.'

Natalie realised that we weren't going to come out of the hedge until the horses were safely locked away, which she eventually did while muttering to herself something about my cowardice, completely ignoring, not for the first time, the fact that Junior clearly has a vendetta against me. My theory is that he sees himself as the alpha male in our family and will aim to protect Natalie in the same way that he protects Ultime. I have to make sure that we're not left alone together because he's obviously harbouring some deep-seated jealousy towards me. Is it jealousy? Or does he just dislike mods?

Despite the potential for serious animal-related injury and my natural dislike for physical labour, I actually had things that I needed to do outside. I had to harvest the quince.

It is not a role I had ever envisaged having in life, quince harvesting. I'm not even – and I'm aware how ridiculous a statement this is – much of a fruit fan. It's a messy business eating fruit and you're liable to get a squirt in the eye or, worse still, stains on your shirt and as such I shy away from it. I do love my orchard, though.

The previous owners, Monsieur and Madame Lebrun, had planted twenty-one fruit trees to mark their daughter's twenty-first birthday – various varieties of apple, plum, cherry, pear, medlar, quince, walnut. It was a beautiful gesture if you're going to stick around to enjoy the results and watch them grow, but has a whiff of sadness about it if you then decide to sell up a couple of years later, which they had done. Much of what they did to the house when they renovated was with their daughter (and especially future grandchildren) in mind. They put a secure fence around the pond, the swimming pool is raised, and the upstairs ceiling-to-floor gabled windows have child safety 'balustrades'; they obviously had planned to grow old there and watch their grandchildren run around the place. But then their daughter had declared to them one day that she had no intention whatsoever of having any children and immediately, seemingly in a fit of pique, they had put the house up for sale. We turned up less than a week later putting paid to any 'second thoughts' and so they'd moved on before the trees, as if mirroring the person they'd been planted in honour of, had borne fruit. We were the lucky beneficiaries and had taken full advantage.

This was the first time, though, that we had had a crop of quince in successive years since we moved here, which either says something positive about my orchard management skills or that I'd been doing something terribly wrong previously. Anyway, not only did we have a crop, we had a bumper crop. At a rough guess I'd say at least 40 kilos of the stuff. Normally I'd make a few jars of chutney, some quince Turkish delight or even a quince cordial and that would be that but I was still working my way through last year's crop.

Quince is a brute of a fruit, like a slightly hairy cross between an apple and a pear. They can't be eaten raw and their cores are so tough they wouldn't break down in a nuclear holocaust, so to actually do anything with the things takes something of a run up. I'm aware that this all sounds like a bit of a hissy fit at the Women's Institute, but (aside from charging people to throw them at Junior) I was running out of ideas of what to do with it all. You can't rush a good chutney either, and making the Turkish delight is not only a slow, highly involved process it's bloody painful as the boiling hot quince spits at you from its cauldron. So I'd taken to wearing protective goggles and Marigolds – all mod-approved naturally! Not, it has to be said, an incredibly manly way of doing it, but I was once taken to task by a heckler in the front row who wanted to know why I had a burn mark on my forehead. I tried to convince him that I'd been kidnapped and tortured with lighted cigarettes, reasoning that 'I got burned making fruit sweets' might not find favour with a hostile, late-night audience.

By carefully wrapping each quince in newspaper they will keep from autumn until about Easter, so you have a bit of time – but even so, quince with everything can drag a bit and even if I do make 3 tonnes of chutney with them I've then got to try and get rid of it. The French, apparently, aren't big on the stuff and when offered a jar at the dinner table most tend to sniff it, make positive gestures as to its bouquet and then ask about the background of chutney in general before replacing it on the table untouched. Also, current restrictions on how much 'liquid' you are allowed on board a plane makes bringing jars of chutney into the UK a risky business; I've been stopped once already at the airport and had a hard time convincing security that it wasn't some kind of aromatic explosive, just a preserve and very nice with cold meats. They confiscated the jar, probably because it was lunchtime, but clearly have me marked down now as The Chutney Bomber.

What I may do at some point is hire a van and import hundreds of jars that way. Instead of being one of those comedians who spends the last five minutes of their act trying to sell you the CD or DVD of the set you've just seen, I'll set up a little stall covered in a gingham tablecloth at the back of the club and flog chutney as people leave. I've become hooked on the process of making chutney; it's become my escape. Obviously moving to France in the first place was meant to be my escape and it still is, but what with Natalie and the boys and the animal equivalent of 'Open Day at the Borstal' I've found an inner bubble. When the stresses and strains of family life here increase and my world feels once again like it's teetering precariously on its axis, you can find me in the kitchen furiously peeling, cutting up and boiling all the goodness out of fruit like a crazy person.

(For those readers who are interested to try their hand at the sacred art of converting quince into something more obviously edible, I have given details of recipes for Turkish delight and chutney at the back of the book.)

VETS AND DOCS

I sat in the car unable to move, my hands gripping the steering wheel so tightly that my knuckles had turned white. I had finally made it home but I was so tired, so tense and so emotional at finally getting there that I couldn't actually move. I just looked out of the filthy windscreen at the gate and tried to will it open.

I don't often drive back from work, but sometimes the monotony of the Ryanair–easyJet–Eurostar merry-go-round needs to be broken, even if it's a more expensive option, even if it's more tiring. The first few months of the weekly commute had been fun; never short of a daydream, I convinced myself that I was some kind of one-man comedy SWAT team flown in and dropped behind enemy lines to bring mirth to previously mirthless communities. But even the most low-rent SWAT team doesn't have to argue about the weight of their hand luggage or occasionally sleep overnight in a freezing airport.

So this time I'd driven. I'd missed the earlier ferry despite driving from the Midlands pumped full of Red

Bull and ProPlus at a ridiculous speed, and so limped into Dunkerque at 5.30 in the morning to begin the six-and-a-half-hour drive from there back home. The car, an old Golf Estate we had had since Samuel was born, was suffering. The indicators, never the most overused part of a car in France, had packed up entirely, and one of the headlamps had gone which I didn't actually realise until I'd got home – I just assumed my eyesight was failing or I was suffering from mild hallucinations from the caffeine supplements. The weather all the way from Dunkerque had been atrocious; misty, low cloud and heavy rain. It wasn't much fun.

And so I sat at the wheel staring at the gates, hollow-eyed and frozen still, relieved and overjoyed to be home but a physical wreck, twitching as the last of the energy boosters wore off.

Natalie appeared at the gate. In her coat.

'The cats need feeding, Thérence needs changing and feeding and Pierrot needs to go to the vet. I'll be back in a couple of hours.'

For anybody who thinks that I exaggerate the level of anarchy that is the Moore household, then I can only say that I wish you were right. I wasn't exactly expecting a ticker-tape parade on my return – a cup of tea would have been nice – but there simply isn't time for any of us to stand on ceremony anymore. Things have to be done. Constantly.

Pierrot, while still exploring the darker areas of canine perversion, seemed to have turned himself into some kind of water feature. Slurping in gallons of water at one end while simultaneously relieving himself at the other, he was behaving like a fountain in a town square. So my first few minutes at home were spent mopping up urine while being eyed hungrily by a family of feline predators, at which point Thérence decided to dump something so heavy into his nappy it looked like he was wearing bungee pants. Home sweet home.

All dogs, it seems, have a sixth sense about vets. They know almost as soon as you put them in the car that they aren't actually going for a nice walk by the river, but to have their giblets prodded at by a man in a white coat. You can't blame them for being wary. We have a choice of two vets where we live. One, who we initially went to when we first moved here, is a tall, brusque man whose bushy, black beard always displays remnants of pâté and baguette and who, according to Natalie's grandparents, had shown insufficient care to their absurdly pampered poodle, to the point of murderous neglect. It is not a reputation most vets would cherish, but one that he clearly revels in as only the most needy and desperate owners make appointments with him, leaving him plenty of time for golf or something. The other vet is a scatty lady from Belgium whose French isn't very good and who the locals don't really trust, partly because she's foreign and partly because she's a woman. She also has a boyfriend who lurks around her surgery like Igor from *Frankenstein* and who quite clearly hates people. He is, I think, a disturbed young man, an attitude I put down to the fact that he only has one eyebrow which looks like an angry caterpillar above his piercing blue eyes – like Bert from *Sesame Street*.

He also fancies himself as some kind of dog whisperer and like anybody who thinks they have a 'gift', takes himself very seriously indeed. I once took Volcan, my mod-hating Brittany spaniel, there for an injection and the vet had delegated 'Bert' to perform the task; I needed to get Volcan to lie on his back, he indicated. I laughed and said it couldn't be done, Volcan being about as playful and obedient as a cluster bomb. 'Bert' looked at me and snorted, he put his hands either side of Volcan's head, looked into the dog's eyes for a full minute and then in a blur of movement that was part wrestling move and part origami had the astonished dog on his back and loving it! It was actually quite impressive. However, instead of taking the opportunity to inject the animal he righted Volcan and grunted that I should try the same thing. Normally one to shirk a challenge, but feeling slightly intimidated, I took Volcan's head in my hands, stared into his distrusting eyes and then for what seemed like five minutes I scuffled with the wretched animal like we were two drunken teenagers getting off with each other at a party. It was all very ignominious and in the end 'Bert' had to separate us before I was the one that received the injection.

Thankfully 'Bert' wasn't around this time, which was a relief to both me and Pierrot – although, to be fair, the poor animal was somewhat preoccupied anyway what with blood samples, injections and having a vet's fingers shoved up his backside. All of which proved fruitless, unfortunately, as the vet was left clueless as to what his current malaise might be. She checked for diabetes, she checked his liver and kidneys; she gave him a right going over but there didn't seem to be anything physically wrong at all, though we had to go back for more tests at a later date.

It was just his age it seemed; he had put on weight, he barely exercised, he was tired, he was drinking too much and he occasionally found it difficult to control his bladder. In fact, more and more we resembled each other as age was beginning to wither both of us, but from opposite ends of the spectrum, his from an increasingly sedentary lifestyle while mine from too much movement; too much travel.

'You look just like John Lennon,' the doctor said with a smile on his face.

I responded with a cold, hard look; not because I was affecting some kind of faux boredom or that I wasn't actually quite flattered, but that my sinuses had locked my face up to the extent that I was like an over-botoxed Hollywood starlet and incapable of showing any emotion whatsoever.

'The Beatles?' he said, taking my lack of response to mean that actually I didn't know who John Lennon was and pointing to my clothes, the military-style pea coat and Baker Boy hat in particular giving me a Beatles, circa 1965 *Help!* film look.

'I know who he is,' I said testily, 'and today I feel like him.'

In my defence I normally don't let the flu set me back. By that I don't mean I'll just suck it up, not mention it and carry on regardless, hell no; I'll moan like an injured seal, take it out on those around me, cram myself full of Day Nurse and resentfully go on stage anyway. I certainly never go to the doctor with it – not normally anyway, but after a week in bed Natalie had had enough of me texting downstairs for 'more Lemsip and a bit of toast'.

Now the French health system is quite rightly lauded as the best in the world, there is never any problem with seeing a doctor and I don't mind paying a fee at the surgery to make this possible. At the moment it's €22 and the fee is reimbursed later anyway, but it means that people won't turn up to the doctor's just to have a chat. You go because you have a problem not because you're a bit lonely. The poor, beleaguered NHS in the UK is being crushed under the weight of expectation that it and every service it provides must be free for an ageing population – it's unsustainable, particularly at the GP level where doctors have become so fearful of their time being wasted that it is now virtually impossible to see one and if you do you must run the gauntlet of Rottweiler Receptionist, Nurse and Bouncers.

The doctor examined me, pointlessly I thought as it was perfectly obvious what was wrong with me.

'I'm not feeling well either,' he said dolefully, obviously needing to unburden himself and in particular, I felt, looking for sympathy from Natalie who he normally chats to endlessly about horses. You'll be lucky there, I thought. I love my wife dearly but she has never, in my experience, exhibited any kind of sympathy to a man with a cold.

'There's a lot of flu around at the moment,' the doctor said airily, and I looked at Natalie in an I-told-you-so kind of way and held her gaze, not because she had doubted that I was ill, but because she has a way of making me feel guilty when I am. 'You've not got the flu, though,' he continued and I looked away from Natalie quickly. 'You're exhausted, completely run down.' It was a partial victory.

As it happens I'd planned to take the following weekend off work anyway because I felt I needed a break; I don't for a moment pretend that I have a tough, tiring job or that a few days hammering away at the coalface of show business is really that physically wearing, but every so often the travel takes its toll. I tend to lose at least one night's sleep a week because of travelling and the build-up of that over a few weeks inevitably has its consequences. Even Natalie recognises this, showing much more sympathy for exhaustion than she does for what she dismissively calls 'a bit of a sniffle'.

Despite telling me that I needed to rest, the doctor, being French, couldn't resist writing a prescription anyway. France loves antibiotics; in fact, it loves medicine of any kind and dishes the stuff out with wild abandon, this despite warning posters in every doctor's waiting room to use medicine, antibiotics especially, sparingly. There are two adults and three children in our house, so there might be about ten visits to the doctor every year between us, and each time we bring home at least five new boxes of medicine; we have so many prescription drugs in our house we could set up a black-market chemist. We have four medicine cabinets and they're all full. Doliprane, Bronchokod, Amoxicillin, Smecta, Spasfon, Adiaril, Advil... the list is endless, and all are expected to be taken at meal times, which practically means an extra course. While I felt somewhat vindicated for spending most of the day in bed, the doctor's diagnosis did present problems of another kind. We live in a very rural, very agricultural area and the locals have enough trouble trying to understand exactly what I do for living as it is, there being no culture of stand-up over here. They can just about accept that I'm in 'showbiz' and therefore are very tolerant when I dress the way I do. But to do a clearly non-physical job and dress eccentrically is one thing; to then describe yourself as 'suffering from exhaustion' is frankly beyond the pale. One of the local farmers nearly chopped his own arm off in a freak combine-harvester related incident a couple of years ago and he still got his harvest in.

Feeling genuinely exhausted is all very well, there can be quite serious health repercussions, but you try telling that to rough-hewn, agricultural men of the soil. It just doesn't wash. The parents of one of Samuel's school friends popped by one day to find me coughing, spluttering and lying down in front of the television and at first, they seemed quite concerned.

'He's tired,' Natalie told them and they both looked at me like maybe Samuel would suffer if a real man wasn't around to guide him; the dad especially, who is a huge man, a former lorry driver who now suffers from multiple sclerosis, seemed particularly and quite correctly short of sympathy.

The sudden death of one of Natalie's French uncles put my own physical weaknesses into their proper context. Thierry had been a very good friend to me ever since I first met him over twenty years ago; a big, smiling bear of a man, together with his wife Monique, he was a fantastic and generous host who could never do enough to help, whether it was making me feel part of the family or, as a widely travelled import/exporter, sourcing material to fence our horses in, a full-time job in itself. He had started going downhill very quickly during the summer, a serious liver problem ageing him ferociously, though it was never clear exactly what the problem was; a rare tropical disease picked up on his exotic travels they thought, or just voracious cancer. It was eventually diagnosed as the latter but far, far too late.

The indecent haste of Thierry's death was matched by the funeral service itself; he wasn't a religious man so there were no spiritual fillers to pad the thing out. Natalie spoke about what she remembered of her beloved uncle, a moving heartfelt few minutes which struck a chord with everyone and drew admiration from all present too as Natalie, fighting back the tears, reminded them all of what a big part he'd played in their lives. Samuel cried throughout, while Maurice watched him closely, unsure of his own feelings and too young to understand properly what was going on. Thérence remained silent in my arms watching his mummy a few metres away not only hold herself together, but have the entire room in the depressingly modern and clinical crematorium utterly rapt.

Back at the house for the wake, the talk was of Natalie's 'performance', how moving it had been. But there was laughter too and, this being a large French gathering with food involved, there were strong opinions thrown about, but generally the talk was of Thierry and the conclusion reached by most was this: 'He worked too hard,' they said. 'He did far too much travelling,' they agreed. 'It was bound to take its toll,' they chorused.

I caught my mother-in-law's eye. Danielle had been saying for months now that I had to ease up on the travel, that what I did wasn't sustainable.

'You hear that?' she said. 'You hear what they're saying?'

'Yes.' I replied, not wanting to get into this discussion. 'Too much travel, worked too hard. I hear it.'

'Well?' She looked me straight in the eye, demanding an answer that I couldn't give.

FOREIGN HOARDERS
AND BROCANTE DREAMS

When we first bought our place we were warned by parents, other assorted family and basically anyone we told that what we had taken on was too big. There would be too much maintenance they said; constant work. We thanked people for their concern, knowing they were right, but all the time thinking it a small price to pay for basking in the smug knowledge that for the same price as a two-up, two-down in the rough end of a 'New Town', we'd bought our dream property. In truth though, we had behaved like kids in a sweet shop.

Smugness doesn't do the upkeep either, and it was probably less than a fortnight before we approached the handyman/gardener who had worked for the previous owners to 'help us out a bit'. Manuel comes round at least once a week now. Whether he's been asked to or not.

He hadn't really got on with our predecessors; in his eyes, it seems, they were city folk and knew nothing of the countryside, hacking away at their fruit trees and storing the winter logs in a damp place. I think now, though, he'd regard them as a pair of professional gardeners compared to my outdoor efforts. Thankfully, he adores Natalie, loves the boys – particularly Thérence and Maurice who are both outdoor types – and is invaluable when I'm away. But like I say, he's not sure about me. He's a fair bit older than I am (about sixty years old), but he has fewer grey hairs than I do and though not really stocky or muscular is stronger than the Mafia and just as unlikely to talk. He has a slow, rolling gait as if all the strength he possesses needs to be controlled until needed, but could go off like a firework at any moment.

Manuel is Portuguese and part of a sizeable Portuguese community in the Loire Valley; the Portuguese are actually the largest immigrant group in France. Though he and his wife have been here for thirty years, his French is spoken with a very strong Portuguese accent, and as my French comes with a heavy Michael Caine twang, communication is something of an issue. Over the years, though, we have developed a way of communicating: I'll shrug and he'll tut. To be honest, communication between us isn't really an issue as he has little or no respect for my opinions and thinks I'm not to be entirely trusted with any of the bigger property maintenance decisions or upkeep. The last of which I'd probably agree with him on.

One of his many advantages is that he owns a *remorque* (trailer) which comes in very handy indeed. Every so often in a frenzy of OCD mania I will set about one of the outbuildings, ignoring Natalie's and the boy's cries of 'I could make something of that', 'I could put that on eBay' and 'I've been looking for that for ages', and I will have a right good clear out. Nothing, it seems, is ever thrown away and it's usually my 'workshop' (there is a bag of rusty tools in there) that it gets dumped in, the logic being that I'm rarely in there. On this occasion I had collected up quite a bounty: a fridge/freezer, a television, a rug, a goldfish bowl and a set of mouldy luggage being just a selection of the rubbish we'd accumulated. It looked like a haul from a 1970s game show, cuddly toys included.

But Manuel wasn't keen to lend me his *remorque*. His opinion of me is so low now that he actually follows me around my own property making sure I don't break anything or come to harm. As usual, then, we came to an arrangement: we'd load up his trailer, putting all the dirtier boxes in my car, and go together to the local tip, in convoy. It was his idea, and the only one on the table.

I love the fact that the refuse tip, the civic dump, in France is called the *déchetterie*. Of all the vocabulary that I have had to learn, *déchetterie* is the easiest; it's the closest to nominative determinism I think the French language gets: *déchetterie* to me is 'de-shittery', as good a description of a clear out as I can think of. But that makes light of the place and you can't do that, it's a very serious business indeed. When I first visited the tip there were just two skips, and when one was full you'd just chuck stuff in the other. It was a simple system, run by a lovely woman, Elisabeth, and it worked. Now, though, there are twelve skips, a sinister underground 'oil recycling' bunker, more rules than cricket and Elisabeth herself has been recycled and replaced by more evangelical recyclers.

But first we had to get there, and Manuel was clearly uncomfortable with me leading our convoy, presumably feeling that I could barely get to the *boulangerie* without then requesting the assistance of a search party. Now I like driving, when it's not for work, but I hate the boredom of regular routes – I need 'long' cuts, gear changes, junctions, back roads and new sights. I guess it's all to do with the amount of travelling I do, but I have to make even the shortest journey more interesting. I go where I want. I'm a free man.

I decided to take a circuitous route, much to Manuel's annoyance, and by the time we arrived at the *déchetterie* he was furious.

He didn't actually say anything, but I could see he was riled and he avoided eye-contact as we began to empty the rubbish. Coping with a truculent Portuguese man is one thing; adding an equally hostile Frenchman into the mix is trying in the extreme, and Elisabeth's replacement was in a cantankerous mood. It was after lunch and as he leaned in close to explain yet another change in the skip system, he smelled of wine and *saucisson* and his obviously now extinguished cigarette, possibly reclaimed from one of the skips, was still stuck to his bottom lip. It may have been there for months for all I know, it was shorter than his stubble. I took a step back from his breath and threw a box of assorted rubbish into the designated 'assorted rubbish' skip. His cry was gut-wrenching.

'Argh! Non! Qu'est-ce que vous faites? Mais non, Monsieur!'

I could see Manuel nodding sagely in the background and I realised my mistake. I hadn't just thrown the box of rubbish in, but the 'box' with the 'rubbish'. The rubbish may be fine, but the box itself should have gone into another skip, the box skip, and he was apoplectic; to my mind I'd put some cardboard in the wrong skip, but he was acting like I had attacked his family. He started to fish out the offending carton with a shepherd's crook, but then everything in the box came tumbling out, glass, plastic, floor tiles – all in the wrong place – and then, as a final insult, a broken electric pump fell out. He slumped over the side of the skip and took a moment before raising his head and looking at me with tears in his eyes. I had put electrics in a non-electrics skip, but by his reaction you'd have thought I'd urinated into a vat of the Touraine's finest Muscadet.

'I'm sorry!' I said, 'Where do you want the electric stuff?' pointing out that we also had a fridge and a TV to offload too.

Now his eyes lit up. 'Er, put them in my van,' he said, recovering his composure quickly. 'Over there.' What a racket! I suppose it's a perk of the job, and if he can make something of the stuff then that's recycling in its purest form – and in the man's defence, he's not the only one at it.

Twice a year the local council allows you to put whatever sized rubbish you like out the front of your house; it's called the *monstres* and obviously it saves having to hire a van or trailer, or begging your gardener to use his for the job, and it means that big rubbish, white goods, broken down TVs and old sofas aren't just dumped by the side of the road – or rather, they *are* dumped by the side of the road, just with an official stamp of approval.

It also offers a chance to the local Romani population to do a bit of recycling of their own. The children have a saying around here, a warning to others not to touch their stuff: '*Pas touche Manouche, si non ta mère te mettra une couche!*', which is slightly offensive in tone but roughly translates as 'Don't touch my stuff, Gypsy, or your mother will put you in a nappy.' Frankly I don't understand what it means either, just that the Romani here are renowned for their sharp practice. They have a 'reputation'. There are lots of them here too, possibly because it's quite flat, which is an important consideration if you live in a caravan, but they aren't feared as much or treated as pariahs like 'travellers' are back in the UK. There are few confrontations and the same families have been here for generations, which is something I've never really understood – I mean, are you travelling or not? Make your mind up.

They all have a very distinctive look, and yes I know how that sounds but bear with me. They are obviously all inter-related and having stayed in the same place for years now all look very much like each other; the men resemble a young, but swarthier, Elvis Presley, with jet black, greased-up quiffs and clothes like early rockers. The women, though stunning when younger, are clearly encouraged to beef up as they age and often resemble a later-period, Las Vegas Elvis, which at least gives the whole thing continuity.

It's true that an awful lot of scrap metal gets thrown away and some of the white goods might not be beyond-repair *monstres*. It's an ideal system in many ways, and those that have put the stuff out in the first place aren't bothered, they're just glad to see the back of it. It's quite an arresting sight, though. Dozens of young Elvis lookalikes scurrying about picking through piles of discarded furniture and electrical goods, with Natalie.

She really is utterly shameless and she's passed it on to Maurice. I hadn't realised that while we were on holiday last year Maurice had discovered that when people packed up to leave the campsite we were staying on, quite often they would leave behind deck chairs that they no longer had room for. Maurice, chancer that he is, would go around the campsite collecting discarded beach furniture and store it under our caravan. It was only on our last day that I noticed the piles of stuff hidden away, like a deckchair graveyard – all sizes and colours and all collected by Maurice who hoped to sell them on at a later date.

It's in his genes I'm afraid. Natalie cannot contain herself when the *monstres* is on, it's like a *brocante* (flea market) to her but without the overheads, and to give her credit in the front garden we do have a lovely sewing table, no home should be without one, and numerous baskets dotted about the place. The only downside to this carry-on is that I get roped in as driver and, I hesitate to say it, strongman; she tells me where to stop and what to put in the car, which I do as quickly and as surreptitiously as possible. It's the lack of dignity I can't stand. I know these things have been thrown away but really... I'm afraid that I'm far too English for all this, far too embarrassed and I hide my face if a car approaches. Not that anonymity is an issue when you're the only mod in the area. I can just about cope with grabbing something hastily, throwing it in the boot and making a quick getaway. But I really draw the line when I'm asked to climb into a skip.

I was out chauffeuring Natalie on one of the *monstres* runs and I saw an original 1960s hanging basket chair that would be perfect, if I were allowed any choice in the matter of interior decoration, for the office I someday planned to build. I had to have it. Without having to climb into the skip I managed to drag the thing out right from under the nose of a young Romani lad while Natalie rifled through some pottery across the road. I threw the chair into the car, dived back into the driver's seat, pulled my jacket collar up and put my sunglasses back on. I'd got what I wanted but it wasn't exhilarating in any way; it just felt wrong.

I stayed there for a few minutes waiting for Natalie and then there was a knock at the window, it was the young lad from the skip. Oh no, I thought, he's going to claim a prior stake and there'll be some unseemly toing and froing over the thing. He knocked on the window again.

I opened the window a fraction. 'Yes?' I snapped.

'You left the hanging hook behind,' he said, giving me the ceiling hook for the chair before taking an impressive standing leap back into the skip.

'Now you're one of us,' Natalie laughed as she got back into the car. Oh, the shame.

Of course, most of what's left out in the *monstres* is unusable rubbish, that's pretty much a given if Natalie or the Romani can't make anything of it, and so the majority of what's left is collected up to be deposited in, hopefully, the right skip at the *déchetterie*. There is the third option though, the *brocante*.

There is this romantic notion of a French street *brocante*, perhaps fed by the endless *Bargain Hunt*-type programmes that used to be afternoon television fillers but which now seem to pass as acceptable prime-time viewing, and the notion is that you can literally make your fortune by browsing through other people's tat. I think it's very unlikely indeed. It may have been the case a few years ago that what was fashionable in the interior design world of Britain was coincidentally exactly the kind of stuff that the French were throwing out, but largely those days have gone or, as seems more likely, the French have cottoned on to the real value of what they have and price things accordingly. Now, there are *brocantes antiquités* which are the expensive higher-end markets; there are the *brocantes* themselves, where you may find a bargain; and there are the *vide-greniers*, literally 'loft-empties', and to my mind horrific places just full of tat, basically a *déchetterie* without the order.

When the idea of having a stall at the local annual *brocante* was first suggested I made my opposition to the idea perfectly clear. It's a waste of time, I said to Natalie, and I knew this from experience. It's a long day, I said, where we sell nothing and you and the boys spend the time buying from other stalls, leaving me minding the shop and haggling with old women over the cost of shabby, discarded doilies and broken breadbins. It's undignified, tiring and fruitless, I stressed, and we are not doing it. I felt strongly about this and also thought that, just this once, maybe putting my foot down would have some effect. I was pleased with my reasoned argument and eloquence. That's that idea crushed, I thought naively; no *brocante* for us...

Six o'clock on a Sunday morning is no time to be setting up a trestle table covered in broken stuff, not that there's ever really a good time. The initial idea had been that just Natalie and Maurice would do the setting up and that Samuel, Thérence and me would turn up later; it didn't happen like that. Maurice was understandably nervous at having to fend off early morning crap-scavengers while Natalie parked the car and dawdled her way back to the stall, so I was roped in to act in a security role while Maurice sorted the stuff out. As it was, Natalie disappeared with the car and Maurice fell asleep under the table, leaving me to deal with the kind of people normally found passing off car stereos in pubs or loitering by people's bins.

'How much for the…?'

'I haven't bloody unpacked yet!' was typical of some early exchanges, me not being particularly suited to the early Sunday morning, sell your own 'tat' combination.

Eventually Natalie returned – with a lampshade. Brilliant, I thought, we haven't sold anything yet and already she's bought stuff; this early into the game and we're already one–nil down, this could be a hammering. I left her to it and promised to return later with Samuel and Thérence, by which time I presumed that her stall would have expanded as she bought up everyone else's stock in a *brocante* version of Monopoly.

The plan had been to arrive late morning with the others and have lunch with Natalie and Maurice, but I hadn't bargained on Samuel's hereditary desire to buy other people's discarded dross and we were back within the hour to see the place in full swing.

What became particularly apparent as Samuel, Thérence and I walked through the market was that everybody seemed to be selling the same stuff; every stall, including ours, had a pram, a baby-walker and/or high chair, a selection of baby clothes, naked Action Man dolls and a broken first bike. It was like a car boot sale the day after King Herod's rampage.

'Have you sold anything?' I asked as we approached Natalie and Maurice. They looked at each other conspiratorially.

'We've had some enquiries,' Natalie replied, with what is presumably sales-talk euphemism for 'no'.

A man approached the stall at the same time we did and picked up my old wheelie, multi-compartment, international travel computer case and asked how much. Under her breath, Natalie said that he'd been there three times already but that she refused to go lower than €8.

'Eight euros!' I shouted, 'That thing is in mint condition and it cost me fifty quid!' I turned to the man angrily and was about to tell him to clear off when Samuel interrupted.

'Four euros,' he said.

'What?!'

'Done,' said the man coolly, totally ignoring Natalie and me.

'What the—' I began.

'We've got to get this thing started,' Samuel replied and skipped off with my €4.

I suppose he had a point, though his argument was somewhat undermined when he returned ten minutes later with a selection of *Star Wars* fridge magnets that he'd purchased for a 'bargain' €4. A friend of Samuel's then turned up and asked how much Samuel wanted for his *Dragonball Z* books.

'Two euros each,' Samuel said, enjoying his role as entrepreneur. There were eight books and his friend clearly didn't want to pay that much.

'Four euros, the lot,' I said and pocketed the money quickly as Samuel started to protest. 'Now you've got it started, son, we've got to keep the momentum going.'

It was a long, frustrating morning. The stall was in the full sun and it was draining our spirits; mine particularly, as I watched the 'must-have' toys of a couple of years ago be sold for 50c. I mean really, I searched high and low for that James Bond car, it cost me a fortune and I remember Samuel's face when I gave it to him; it was the world to him at the time and now 'It's just a toy, Daddy.' The Bob the Builder bicycle, both Samuel and Maurice's first bike, got a lot of enquiries but nobody would pay more than €5. Five euros! I mean it's a bloody bike, I thought, it works for God's sake, you tight bastards – and yet they'd just look at you like you were trying to rip them off and all the while clutching a mouldy old sandwich toaster that they'd bought for €2 next door. Yeah, good luck with that purchase, you fruitcakes.

The final straw for me was when Samuel, having been off on one of his forays, returned with a battery-powered robot that was actually bigger than Thérence and which then sat by our stall and gained more enquiries than any item we were actually selling. Tempers shortened as the day went on, and as the rain started at about four o'clock there was an almost palpable sense of relief from the whole market as everyone realised that they could legitimately start packing up; nobody was having a good day and many of them stated, quite categorically, that they'd never do it again. I would have done the same, but realised the futility of such a gesture, knowing that Natalie regards *brocantes* in much the same way as childbirth – the pain, inconvenience and exhaustion all quickly forgotten as the next one is planned.

And by the end we still had the pram, the baby-walker, the mountain of clothes, the naked Action Men, the lot. There seemed to be no dent whatsoever on our 'stock'. I only got rid of the bike because, after everything Natalie, Samuel and Maurice had bought, I couldn't actually get it back in the car.

'Why don't I just take all this stuff straight on to the *déchetterie*?' I suggested hopefully.

'No,' Natalie said pensively, 'we can try again in the spring.' Fortunately, spring seemed a long way off.

HUNTERS, GATHERERS, MODS

Though I like the idea of four properly old-fashioned seasons, each distinct from the other (as opposed to the new-fangled two-season years, which are both grey but with one slightly warmer than the other), the winters here are harsh. And bleak. Harsh and bleak. And long. Harsh and bleak and long.

Preparing for winter here is like being on a ship and expecting a heavy storm, it's all about 'battening down the hatches'. All outdoor furniture has to be put away, even the heavy stuff. In our first winter we left a large table out, a heavy iron-based structure that we had trouble moving ourselves and so, we thought, would be fine outside. I remember that Natalie and I were watching from our bedroom window as a very localised typhoon picked the thing up and threw it across the garden; everything that isn't nailed down is now put away.

The swimming pool has to be put into hibernation too which – and, yes, I am aware of what a ridiculous complaint this is – is also hard work. I hardly use the thing; my particular level of killjoy sense of order means that I tend to spend most of my time standing at the side with a net ready to trap any unsuspecting insect that has the temerity to land on the water, that and telling the boys not to splash too much. At the end of autumn, though, the pool has to be cleaned, the pump drained, pipes disconnected, steps removed and – this is the killer – the winter cover installed. It weighs a tonne, is 10 metres long, 3 metres wide and I wrestle with it twice a year. It is, as Natalie keeps pointing out, a four-man job, and I should ring friends up and ask them for help. I just can't do that though; I haven't yet reached the point in my life where I can comfortably ring people up and ask for assistance with my pool cover – who am I, the Sultan of Brunei?

There are also some jobs that should already have been done that, with winter around the corner, can be put off no longer. The firewood has to be stacked. Monsieur and Madame Lebrun had kindly thought to order our first load of firewood for us before we moved in, a tricky thing to do in midwinter apparently, all the wood having gone already. (You have to plan ahead you know, it doesn't just grow on trees.) Eventually, after a great deal of searching, Madame Lebrun found a local supplier who could deliver enough wood 'to see us through the rest of the winter'. The rest of the winter? I'd never seen so much wood! Just how long does winter last around here, we thought? Perhaps we were entering a new Ice Age.

Before piling up the wood, however, the *préau*, a kind of open barn affair, had to be tidied, which I insisted on roping everyone in on, seeing as in my opinion they'd made it a bloody mess in the first place. The *préau* is an important part of the property – wood store, hay loft, bird sanctuary – and on the central column there are two inscriptions scratched into the stone. It's always sobering rereading them, but both are quite faded now and difficult to make out. The first is either a call to arms as the Germans were sweeping through France, or a lament at defeat.

'*Les Allemand Son Antré A Chabris le 20 juin 1940 Apré une Resistanse de 7 heures et...*'[sic]

(The Germans entered Chabris on June 20, 1940 after a resistance of 7 hours and...)

And the second one is a similar rallying cry, just as the Normandy landings were taking place and signed Riolland.

'*6 juin 1944 les ameriquins ons débarquer pour chaser les allemans qui etet en france.*'[sic]

(6 June, 1944. The Americans disembarked to chase off the Germans who were in France.)

They are, as far as it is possible to say, in different 'handwriting' and to my mind the latter is an entreaty to avenge the death of the former and it makes me feel very humble. I feel like the owner of something very valuable; that the place where we now live has a noble history that we must preserve, a way of life that, my nomadic and bizarre lifestyle apart, must somehow be kept.

And as we had a family moment around the inscriptions and tried to explain to the boys their significance and a little of World War Two, the gunfire began.

I know! The irony of the situation wasn't lost on us either, as we hit the ground in blind panic. Not more than 15 metres away on the other side of the fence some hunters had gathered, about twenty of them, and they must have let fire almost simultaneously. It was deafening and terrifying. The animals, who follow us everywhere en masse, reacted in different ways: the cats dived for cover under a hay bale; Toby shat himself on the spot and then started chasing his own tail while Pierrot, too deaf to have heard the barrage even from this range but never one to pass up the opportunity of a bit of sexual gratification, started rubbing his backside on my head. Ultime began panicking in her stable and kicking the walls while Junior ran out into the field and gave it his best 'Come on then, d'you want some?' neighing, which actually seemed to abate the hunters, albeit briefly.

I hate the hunters; I know it's been a way of life here for centuries and I'm aware also that it's exactly the way of life that those who wrote the inscriptions in the *préau* wanted to maintain, but there is something not only barbaric but farcical about seeing twenty grown men (and they are all men) with their pristine, green hunting gear and their shiny guns enter battle with... well, what exactly? The fearsome partridge? The dread, fire-breathing pheasant? The slavering, swivel-eyed raper of womanfolk that is the rabbit? It's a truly ridiculous sight that is at once comical but also very scary; these people are on an armed jolly! This isn't paintballing, these are real guns, and in this weather you can bet that there'll have been a few warming Cognacs knocked back over lunch too.

We went back indoors and had an earnest talk about how we have to learn to embrace the countryside, to take its stings as well as its charms. We are part of this community now and if we're prepared to accept the odd game bird here and there then we should also be able to put up with how it's killed. We had a neighbour in Crawley who ran over a deer and we didn't get all prissy about the venison we enjoyed for weeks after that, did we? The blunt truth is that the French are less squeamish about these things – they don't just take an active part in the eating of and preparation of what goes on their dinner plate, they want to know where it came from, how it got there. And don't misinterpret that as meaning that all French food is organically reared or humanely killed because it isn't; this is the land of foie gras, and feelings, yours or the animals, don't come into it.

We, as a family, had to make adjustments. We had to take our middle-class, southern English, townie attitudes and put them aside. We could choose not to like what the hunters do, but we had to accept that they are what they are; that it is their way of life. Or, we could just buy our own weapons and shoot back, whatever. Junior, on the other hand, tends to fight fire with fire and, as if in response to the violence around him, took this opportunity to trash the chicken coop.

It was generally acknowledged, by Natalie and the boys, not by me, that it was only a matter of time before we actually had chickens; Junior, though, had put the whole thing on the backburner. Clearly spotting a blade of grass with his name on it, he destroyed the fencing around the coop, trampling it down and making a right old mess. He also, according to Natalie, left the fence in such a state that it was now causing a danger to Junior as it 'might cut his legs'.

'Serves him bloody right!' I said, thinking naively that that would be an end to it.

Two hours later I was still there in sub-zero temperatures with a barely up-to-the-job pair of pliers cutting back the damaged fence, all the time gunfire raging and Junior standing over me snorting at my back, mocking me. With his long winter mane he looked like a heated, malevolent Tina Turner. The last bit of the fence proved particularly troublesome; by now my hands were not only frozen, they were cramping up and the splinters I had got from stacking the firewood weren't helping. I gave one final almighty heave and the fence came apart but sent me spinning backwards, past a nonchalant Junior and into the electric fence where I briefly thrashed about before sinking to my knees.

I decided that was enough for the day. It was getting dark anyway; time to relax in front of a roaring log fire, and get a bit of peace and quiet. I am good at my job. I can cope with most situations, I am pretty unflappable. I have the skills and experience that means if you put me in a room with 400 drunk stags and hens I can deal with it pretty well, rarely losing my patience. But give me three boys, three cats, two dogs, two horses and a wife who seems to have found a way to make cushions breed and I am obviously completely out of my depth.

And the cushions thing was getting out of hand, frankly. Natalie has two hobbies when the weather turns: she picks up animal poo (actually a year-round occupation) and turns the humble cushion from a soft-furnishings accessory into an interior design plague. I swear, when I die I will be neither buried nor cremated but stuffed into a fabric case and just left on the sofa for all eternity. People will pop by and exclaim: 'Ooh, that's a nice cushion! Is it a Cath Kidston?'

'No. It's my dead husband.'

The place had become like the children's ball room at Ikea, only full of cushions and intended for use only by adult Laura Ashley fetishists. It had become impossible over the last few years to sit on a chair or settee comfortably; every seat had piles of cushions on it. It was taking half an hour to get to bed because of all the cushions that had to be removed from the duvet beforehand; and woe betide anyone who puts them back in the wrong place. I had to start taking pictures on my phone of sofas and beds before I used them, so that I could get the myriad of cushions back into their rightful spot before a straggler was spotted and blame was apportioned. We lived in fear.

And it wasn't just the cushions. My slippers, recently imported beautiful suede, paisley-lined moccasins, fell apart the minute I put them on. The cats, it seemed, had thought it would be a bit of a wheeze to just chew all the stitching off and then leave the things looking intact – but would they listen as I told them off? Of course not, because they were watching the football on the television. They were, all three, lined up in front of the screen watching the football until, at half time, they all marched off and started fighting. It seems we've got cats that in some strange twist on the Hindu concept of reincarnation used to be 1970s football hooligans! Thérence meanwhile was developing his own brand of chaos. He had started hiding things. He had hidden one of Maurice's slippers and though we turned the place upside down it could not be found – equally vanished without trace was the blue toilet cleaner contraption that sits in the loo. Where was he putting these things?

Pierrot was constantly sneaking into the kitchen and eating the cat's food; a refreshing change actually as, in a bizarre supplement to his not inconsiderable diet, he had taken to eating the cats' excrement. Filthy animal. I mean, where's the dignity in that? He's part King Charles spaniel for God's sake, is this how far royalty has fallen? Perhaps we'd misjudged him; maybe he was just trying to help Natalie by collecting up some of the poo on her behalf?

Either way, it was disgusting. You didn't mention that in the 'Circle of Life' did you, Sir Elton?

Toby felt harassed as well, as firstly Thérence would pull his tail and then the cats, momentarily taking their eyes off the television, would jump on his back and try to ride him. He's a sweet-natured dog (thick, but sweet-natured), so rather than harm the cats or even warn them off, he would just look at me like he's saying, 'What happened to us, man? We used to be in charge round here!'

I knew exactly what he meant. The place was feeling like bedlam. And the noise! Everybody, it seemed, was now playing with marbles. Samuel and Maurice had been playing in the field until Junior, unable to cope with seeing others enjoying themselves, ate one of their marbles. They were now playing inside. On a tile floor! And the noise went through me, it was like iron gauntlets scraping down a blackboard. Thérence would then pick up the marbles and throw them at the windows or the television and the cats were constantly chasing the marbles around the house. It was total anarchy and no matter how much shouting, threatening, swearing or begging I did, it just wouldn't stop. At times like this you have to take solace in the little things but it was so manic and noisy that I couldn't think of any.

In the face of all this pandemonium I responded with a proper, masculine, hunter-gatherer pastime: I built fires. If I'm honest, the first winter we were here Natalie had to show me how to build and light a fire, which is as pathetic as it sounds, but since then I've become something of an expert. I find it, disturbing as this may sound, both enjoyable and fulfilling. And make no mistake – the job doesn't end once the thing's lit. There's all manner of prodding, adding to, flume adjustment and control freakery to be employed. As someone who has to bring his 'just can't leave it alone-ness' to everything he does, it's manna from heaven to me. The winter evenings literally flew by.

The one problem, though, with a real log fire is temperature control; they don't control themselves, they're either on or they're not, meaning that if it's the first (and possibly only) job you do all day, and you start in the morning, by dinner time it is so ridiculously warm that despite plunging, sub-zero temperatures outside, it is too hot to do anything other than just lie about indoors in your pants.

There are two open fireplaces indoors; one more than is necessary, so we only use one, which is just as well because in spring we had owls nesting in the unused chimney. A *Springwatch*, Bill Oddie-type privilege you might think? Well, sort of. They are majestic beasts to be sure. There were four of them, all adolescent but big nonetheless, and they would perch on the chimney itself as darkness fell, the light hitting their wings as they flew off in search of prey; and in that respect it really did feel like a privilege to have them nest so close. But seriously, the noise! Whoever it was who first suggested that owls go *tu-whit tu-whoo* was either a soppy git, a drunk or deaf and possibly all three.

They do not go *tu-whit tu-whoo* at all, at least barn owls around here don't. Far from being the kind of noise which makes you pause, go misty eyed and say to your children, 'Did you hear that children? That was a wise old owl', this is the kind of noise that makes grown men crumble, piercing your soul as you rush screaming from the scene shouting, 'The Devil cometh! Repent!' It is not *tu-whit tu-whoo*. The book we have describes it as a shrill *khrihh*, which is best summed up as either two cats fighting a violin in a metal box or Joe Pasquale being beaten to death with a set of bagpipes. A truly, truly horrible noise. Oh, and they snore too.

The chimney-perching owls added a certain eccentricity to the place, which seemed fitting as the locals were still coming to terms with my out-of-the-ordinary dress sense. Every couple of years I treat myself to something special, partly for work and partly as a reminder to myself that I'm not 'Mr Countryside' just yet. But when even your wife looks at you and says, 'It's a bit Quentin Crisp, isn't it?' you realise that you've reached your peak and you can go no further. I've known Natalie for over twenty years and in that time she has seen me wear some pretty 'special' clothing – there were the Oki-Kutsu two-tone, open-sided crepe-soled sandals, the triumphant shocking pink Sta-Prest trousers, the brief flirtation with the beret while living in Stockwell. This new coat, however, knocked them all into a rakishly tilted, cocked hat. It was magnificent. An oxblood/maroon, faux-mink pea coat with epaulettes and belt that shimmered under the light. It was very fine – very flamboyant – and about as un-rural France as it's possible to be. In fact, I'm not entirely sure where it would fit in, but I loved it.

Even though I hate being recognised in the street as a comedian (it doesn't happen very often but I find it intimidating), I am vain enough to like people staring at me for what I'm wearing. It's called 'peacocking', and I'm good at it. A bleak midwinter's day in the Loire Valley, however, is neither the time nor place for such a display; it doesn't evoke hostility – as far as I can tell the only hostility here is directed at vegetarians – it just evokes total bewilderment.

I was going to be away for ten days and as usual dragging my feet, making me late for my train which meant I had to buy my ticket on board. This is perfectly fine, so long as you approach the guard first, otherwise you get fined.

'*Un aller-simple à Paris, s'il-vous plaît?*' I said to the guard, who was looking me up and down with some astonishment.

'*Paris,*' he nodded, unable to take his eyes off my coat, '*naturellement*', in one word summing up exactly what he thought not only of my coat but of Parisians in general. I then produced my *Familles Nombreuses* railcard which threw him completely; it gives me 30 per cent discount on French trains because I've got three children. The whole coat-railcard-children combination was just too much for him and after that he refused to look me in the eye and kept tutting and mumbling to himself, presumably in response to some internal dialogue about lax modern adoption laws. He walked off to another carriage shaking his head. It is a little-known fact that part of the reason for moving to such a remote, rustic backwater was to begin work as a Mod Missionary and it is a constant battle.

Though secretly quite pleased with the effect my coat had, I don't want to be seen to be belligerent about it. Being eccentric is one thing, but it's best not to go too far. Don't overplay your hand. It was going to be a long winter so I thought I should wear it sparingly when in France; especially if the hunters were out.

WHEN A BUTTERFLY
FLAPS ITS WINGS...

French schoolchildren arrive home every evening with a mountain of homework. For me, it's no wonder they spend a large part of their adult life on strike: by the time they've grown up they're a spent force, exhausted by their admittedly top-notch education. Samuel does more homework in a week than I can remember doing in a whole term, so it's good that while things are still relatively within my academic capabilities I can help him out a bit.

'Can you help me with my science project, Daddy?' he asked, and I was only too happy to oblige. We sat down, he got out his books and then he got out his 'homework'.

'What the sweet bloody hell is that?' I screeched, falling off my chair.

'Frogs' legs,' he replied with a perfect Gallic shrug. 'You've got to help me dissect them.'

I'm all for parental involvement in a child's homework and more than happy to be encouraged by the state in this regard, but this is surely a step too far! Not least because it raises the possibility of a reworking of that old chestnut 'the dog ate my homework.'

'Where's your homework, Samuel?'

'My dad ate it.'

This all felt less like 'Let's get the parents involved' and more like 'Let's wind up the Englishman'. I distinctly remembered parents' evening and there was no mention of frogs' legs; I think I would have remembered that. Parents' evening is quite a different matter to what I remember my parents attending in England. There's no one-to-one unless it's needed; this is more a general overview of school rules and in particular the curriculum for the forthcoming year, explaining what's expected of the pupils and what's expected of the parents. That's quite a good thing you might think, letting the parents know exactly where they stand and what will be covered in the next few months, and in principle it is – but not always.

There were some notable absentees amongst the gathered mums and dads this year, some parents clearly still recovering from last year's debacle in which Samuel's teacher attempted to explain to the gathered crowd the 'new method' for teaching long division. These meetings are supposed to last an hour, but three hours later the place was like a brainstorming session at a failing dotcom company: people had broken up into groups (some might say factions), there were huddles by the blackboard and groups in all four corners of the room; men had loosened their ties, women were telling other women to calm down and nobody, except the incredibly patient teacher, had any idea how the new system worked.

'Why did they change it?' they cried.

'What was wrong with the old system?' they raged, before picking up their pencils again, sticking their tongues out in time-honoured 'I'm concentrating' fashion and 'giving it another go'. I half expected the local farmers to start burning bales of hay in the middle of the classroom, such was the anger and passion in the room, but in the end common sense broke out and someone opened a bottle of wine.

This year's affair was much less controversial; this would be a big year for the children, the teacher said, they go to *college* next year and a stronger work ethic and greater concentration would be required, she thundered, unfortunately just as a llama wandered past the window and everybody's head turned.

The circus had arrived in town the day before, a desultory affair which would clearly struggle to entice even the most entertainment-starved crowds. The posters had been in town for a week – they promised lions, tigers, elephants, a big top, scantily-clad trapeze artists, clowns and all the fun of the fair. The actuality was a few scrawny donkeys, a trapeze artist who would have made Hammersmith Bridge wobble and the clown assassin from *Octopussy*.

But they had cleverly set up on the *champs de foire* opposite the school, automatically pitching themselves at the school audience. They had also set up right on the *boules piste* which had clearly put a few noses out of joint. 'Your llama is in the way of our game!' one irate player shouted at the clown, who leant in close to the complainant and whispered something sinister in his ear, nipping all further complaints in the bud.

How the children were expected to concentrate while even the most pathetic circus you could imagine was setting up around them God only knows, and at this point I really felt for the teacher. Her day must have been hell. Trying to impress upon assorted nine-year-olds the importance of *conjugaison* while a clown (albeit a bad one) was resentfully pulling flowers from his sleeves must have been pretty hard work. And now she had the parents in front of her showing exactly the same lack of fortitude.

Not that 'us' parents were impressed. We just knew that all our children would ask to go to the circus. We were preparing our excuses. I'd already dealt with it the evening before when I'd picked the boys up.

'Daddy, can we go to the circus? Pleeeease?' Maurice had whined, despite seeing the clown cuff one of the circus dogs.

'No,' I said tersely.

'Pleeeease?' he said again.

'Tell him, Samuel,' I said.

Samuel and I had had this conversation dozens of times, he knew my thoughts about circuses, best leave it to him, I thought.

'Maurice,' Samuel began, 'we are not going to the circus. They are bad places. When Daddy was young he went to a circus and there was a lion tamer. And the lion ate the lion tamer. And a clown.'

'What?' I said. 'I never said that. Maurice, the…'

'Yes you did!' Samuel cried, clearly irked that I was questioning his veracity.

'Did I? When?'

He proceeded to tell me exactly when and where and so, I thought, it was time for honesty. I took them around the skeleton of the circus, I pointed out how underfed the animals were, how they were probably mistreated, and that as soon as they could no longer perform their 'role' they'd be kicked out to who knows where. Ethically, I concluded, I cannot take you to a circus like this, it's against my principles.

'OK,' said Samuel, still disappointed I think that the lion story wasn't true.

'Is Mummy going to try and rescue these animals, Daddy?' asked Maurice, always keen for a bit of covert action.

'She would if she could,' I said. 'And I'd help her too,' I added, trying to soften the blow as we walked back to the car.

Maurice's question was a reasonable one given our domestic circumstances, but the answer, only two months after the circus had left town, was no longer as cut and dried as one would have thought. Now that the weather had turned we were all – adults, dogs, kids and cats – shut indoors, trying not to annoy one another, trying not to lose our tempers; it was a permanently fragile atmosphere, like a rough saloon bar in the Gold Rush – one false move and the whole thing could kick off big time.

Natalie had, for some time, felt under pressure from the sheer relentless routine of winter: get up, get Samuel and Maurice to school, feed the cats, get Thérence up, put the dogs out, light a fire, hoover the dog room, feed the cats, make lunch, muck out the horses, feed the cats, put Thérence down, feed the horses, collect the boys from school, feed the dogs, feed the boys, feed the cats. Even in good weather that's a punishing schedule, but when you're effectively snowed in and it's minus whatever it is outside, it is bloody hard work, even when I am there to help.

We were watching the French lunchtime news, which tends to ignore the smaller issues of the day like war, terrorism and financial meltdown and instead concentrates on topics of vital importance like olive harvesting in Corsica, the threat to oysters in the Camargue, the very existence of foie gras. The thinking behind it seems to be 'Hey, it's lunchtime; each news item should be food-related'. If Al Qaeda wants to get noticed in France they'd be advised to bomb a cheese factory somewhere and preferably before noon. After the news there are endless adverts (all for food) which we watch before the post-news, five-minute recipe of the day comes on, which I like watching to see which news items have made it into the recipe. That's when it happened.

There were numerous shots of people filling animal feeding bowls, quickly edited together to suggest that it was an endless routine. 'Ha!' Natalie snorted, 'it's just like here!' I think we'd both assumed that it was an advertisement for cat or dog food or a new animal food dispenser to save owners time. It wasn't. The camera pulled back to reveal a portly man in uniform who began to tell us that at this time of year there were many animals in care, some would never be rehomed but all of them needed feeding, that the system for care was under considerable pressure and could we help? It was a charity appeal that could, albeit on a smaller scale, have been made by Natalie. For Natalie. The look on her face said it all; it wasn't exactly an epiphany, more a confirmation of what she really already knew. Namely, that she was taking on too much.

It's a stressful business being cooped up indoors; it's possible, almost inevitable, that a group will turn on itself, or individuals on one another, and when that group consists of three energy-sapping adolescent cats, a sexually depraved spaniel, the thickest dog in the world, three boys under ten, a Cath Kidston-obsessed cushion-fetishist and an OCD-ridden mod with the temper of a bag of hornets – then something has to give.

When I'm at home I practically live in the kitchen, which is part of a large kitchen/diner/lounge area, and I'm separated from the chaos of the lounge by my 'Maginot Line' of a breakfast bar. Like the real thing, this 'Maginot Line' worked for a while but the cats, no respecters of boundaries, had started to jump on top of it. I'd be in the kitchen preparing lunch or dinner, or boiling the goodness out of fruit for chutney purposes, and they'd take it in turns to leap up on the thing. Cooking times have tripled since the cats came along because I'm constantly batting them off the surface area and wiping the place down again. It's like an arcade game: one of them may jump at first, then another, then two at a time, none for a minute or two, then all three at once. It's exhausting, not to mention the hygiene consequences.

Occasionally we'll act as a family and round the cats and dogs up and put them outside, but that just means that any innocent trip to the garden is fraught with anxiety, in the knowledge that if you open the door even a fraction you'll be floored like a streaker under a gang of stewards at a football match. Seriously, we stopped going outside for a bit, bins stopped being emptied. For the sake of our sanity we just could not carry on as things stood. We were, in modern parlance, going to have to make cutbacks in the cat department.

Natalie had made some tentative moves towards finding good homes for the two male cats; she wanted to keep Vespa, partly because she was the first and partly because Natalie needs more female company around the place. It wasn't going to be easy, though. The boys, Samuel in particular, were obviously going to be very upset – however, we had recently made a point of feeding and housing the cats in one of the barns and they hadn't even noticed their absence! But at some point we had to sit down with the boys and try and explain our decision to them, convince them that it was the right thing to do in the long run for everybody, including the cats. Samuel would be very angry with us for a bit and would have every right to be, but a decision had been made and two of the cats must go.

Natalie had already advertised them – 'free to a good home' – on French eBay and there had been a number of responses, all of them unsettling in one way or another. Most of the enquiries were from people who clearly just hoovered up all the animals on eBay because they didn't think they should be on eBay, a very laudable exercise no doubt, but they tended to be people who already had about forty pets, lived in wigwams in the middle of nowhere and reckoned that they spoke fluent 'cat'. The others appeared to be looking for cheap food. None of which made the task any easier.

'Samuel, we need to talk,' I said, nervously.

'I'm not getting rid of them!' he replied, stroppily.

'What? How did you know?' I was genuinely taken aback. I knew Natalie hadn't spoken to him, so this appeared to be a level of intuition bordering on the Jedi, his *Star Wars* obsession finally reaching its zenith.

'You're always saying that we don't need them anymore and that they're noisy and you're always treading on them...'

'Yes, but...'

'... I like playing with them. All my friends play with them, everybody has at least one at playtime!' He stopped, close to tears.

'Look, I know it's... what? Hang on – what are you talking about?'

'My marbles! I'm not getting rid of them!'

'Ah, right. OK,' I said, cunningly sensing an opportunity to take the upper hand, 'I'll tell you what...'

'We'll sleep on it,' Natalie interrupted wisely, before I committed the kind of parental howler you never really come back from.

Sleep that night was a fitful affair. I didn't feel good about insisting on getting rid of two of the cats; it felt like a mean-spirited thing to do. I remembered one Christmas when I was nine years old. Oswald was a King Charles spaniel I had had from a puppy. He was unruly, disobedient and far too clever for his own good; he was also loyal, affectionate and fun and I loved him. That Christmas Day I woke up, unwrapped my new football kit and went running into the lounge to play the Subbuteo I had just got for my birthday a couple of days before and immediately trod in one of Oswald's finest, squelchiest, smelliest offerings. I howled the place down as my new football socks (not to mention my feet) were caked in dog effluent, the day ruined. Oswald didn't last much longer as my parents took the decision that he was just too much work in such a small house, so he was given away and, I was told, went to live on a farm. 'Never did me any harm,' I muttered to myself unconvincingly and tried to get back to sleep.

I was beginning to have second thoughts anyway, partly because the cats weren't really that bad, and partly because I really couldn't imagine the scenario wherein I told Samuel and Maurice that no matter how much they wailed or sulked the cats were out. I had a dream where the cats were the last three standing in an *X Factor* type vote-off – Louis Walsh had told each of them that they had 'made that "miaow" their own', Cheryl had insisted they had all three 'owned the stage' and so it was left to me, as the Simon Cowell figure, to decide that Vespa was the winner and that the other two were unloved and destined for ever-decreasing guest appearances in dingy, provincial nightclubs. It was a strange dream no doubt, the worst aspect being that I was now feeling so guilty and so evil about the whole cat affair I actually saw myself as Simon Cowell. Again, I woke up in a cold sweat.

I just couldn't do it, I mean really, what kind of person buys a cat on eBay anyway? Natalie couldn't do it either and so we caught each other's eyes one evening as the boys were rolling around in front of the fire wrestling and giggling with the cats. They're staying, we said silently to each other.

'Right, boys!' I said, 'We need some new rules around here…'

I launched into a new constitution, dividing up labour amongst the boys – which cat was to be looked after by which child and the responsibilities involved. But the more I talked, the more Draconian the rules I laid down, the more I noticed their concentration wavering and giggling was setting in. This only made me angrier but no matter what I said, no matter how I ranted, I had lost my audience. They were behaving like the centurions in *Monty Python's Life of Brian* when told of the existence of Biggus Dickus.

'What on earth is going on?' I spluttered.

'Daddy,' replied Maurice, by now practically on the floor, 'you have a butterfly on your willy.'

A couple of weeks earlier Natalie had noticed a chrysalis on the underside of the kitchen windowsill, indoors. Worried about the hygiene implications, my instinct had been to remove it, but of course the Animal Rescue Liberation Front that is my family had practically threatened me and it had been left to develop unhindered. It had now emerged a rather pale-looking, frail creature which would almost certainly not last long as the winter set in, but which had decided that the best chance of survival was to hitch a ride on my privates and therefore putting paid to any serious rule-setting.

The butterfly incident occurred at the end of ten days at home. I had decided to take the first weekend of December off to recharge my batteries and prepare myself for the Christmas gigs onslaught that lay ahead. I had spent the time sitting in darkened rooms, mentally visualising each Christmas gig that lay before me like a comedy ninja preparing his moves for battle. I had been over every possible scenario and revisited every previous Christmas show I had ever done, which is easier to do than it sounds – because they stay with you, like scars.

I always try to be Zen about it and try to put myself in situations which will then form a mental escape route as

I deal with yet another Christmas party audience whose preferred choice, it turns out, isn't stand-up comedy at all but loud singing and arguing with colleagues they don't like. I even cleaned the horse's paddock on Natalie's behalf, the logic being that shovelling horse poo would serve as a reminder while I was being ignored on stage that there were worse things I could be doing. Ultime regarded my efforts to clean the field as something of a joke and kept trying to bite my backside, and although she was being playful I wasn't in the mood, which sent her off on one, charging around the place like a horse possessed and 'buzzing' me increasingly closely while Junior looked on, clearly pleased with the work of his protégé.

Natalie took the side of the horses obviously; my presence and dark, brooding (I like to think 'Heathcliffian') mood were obviously the cause of the problem, she said. She stroked Ultime to calm her down. She'd bitten my arse, but it was my fault.

This triggered a memory in me from a few Christmases ago. I was onstage at Jongleurs Portsmouth: not, it has to be said, a happy hunting ground for any comedian whose shtick involves subtlety, intelligence and the correct use of the English language. The sound system, as usual, was woefully inadequate, geared (at the request of the management) to get people dancing after the show rather than to project comedy in a hangar of a building. I was about eight minutes into a pitiful performance when a Christmas dinner hit me flush in the chest and just kind of hung there. Two women at a table on their own, possibly the result of previous injunctions, had taken umbrage at the fact that, unlike them, I hadn't been drinking since Easter and obviously had some form of stable home life – they had therefore decided that it would be socially acceptable to throw food at me.

I said nothing. I put the microphone back in the stand and left the stage. As I was leaving the building I passed the manageress giving THEM a complimentary bottle of wine to atone for whatever perceived grievance they had. They bit my arse, but it was my fault. Christmas crowds can be like that; any authority or gravitas you normally possess is lost and you can become the wrong kind of 'figure of fun'; ironically, much like a supposedly authoritarian parent trying to read the Riot Act while a confused insect cowers on his wedding tackle.

Eventually of course, the butterfly had to be removed from my crotch and we decided to put the thing outside and hope for the best. I cupped him and placed him gently in a sheltered alcove by the front door. He'd been cocooned in the warm, safe environment of his chrysalis but now he had to go out into the real world, alone, and fight for his survival at this cruel time of year.

Don't we all, I thought, don't we all.

PLANES, TRAINS
AND AUTOMOBILES

If there's anything worse than travelling away from your loved ones to be ignored or abused by Christmas office parties, it's travelling away from your loved ones, getting snowed in and not being able to get to work to be ignored or abused, and therefore not even earn any money. I'd been in Crawley staying with Natalie's parents for ten days, but in the last five I had made it to one gig and had to 'pull' five others. Snow had hit England, it was −4°C and dropping fast, taking my spirits with it.

To be fair, I don't go along with this 'why can't we cope with a bit of snow, they manage in Russia' mantra that gets trotted out every time along with 'Dunkirk spirit', 'mustn't grumble' and nudge-nudge, wink-wink references to 'having six inches in your back garden'. Normally I would; I've travelled all over the world and if there's anything certain about the British transport system it's this: it's bollocks. We have a road system that cannot carry the weight it's put under, the privatised rail network is owned by a different company to those who operate the trains, and the trains themselves are so phenomenally expensive that it's cheaper to hire a car to do most short-notice journeys anyway. It's a scandal that goes pretty much unreported because the politicians who created this mess don't actually have to pay for any tickets themselves. All of their travel is paid for, all of it. Why would they kick up a fuss about a freebie?

The timetables that most rail companies operate are fragile at best, more often than not a triumph of optimism over reality, where the slightest thing will bring the whole system to its knees: leaves on the line, tracks melting in the heat, the wrong kind of snow – farcical examples of a system that's constantly teetering on the brink of chaos. Having said all that, Crawley had been hit by the kind of weather that would have Eskimos rearranging their plans. A foot of snow fell almost overnight, temperatures continued to drop and obviously public and private transport was taking a hammering. To give an indication of just how bad it was in Southern England, some of the shops were shut.

I'm well aware that there is something romantic about being snowed in, making do with what food you have, playing old-fashioned games by candlelight, a warming whisky by the fire and sundry other sepia-tinted winter myths – but I wasn't snowed in, I was snowed out. Natalie was snowed in at home and I was stuck in Crawley unable to travel anywhere. Not only could I not get to any gigs, I couldn't get home either. OK, the upside was that I wasn't being injured by flying marbles, tripped up by Toby, used as a scratching post by the cats, rubbed suggestively by Pierrot or plotted against by the horses. According to Natalie, it was chaos there; everyone shut up indoors with nerves being shredded. 'I don't know,' she mused, 'at times like this I think maybe we have too many animals.'

If I had a lawyer's sharp mind I would have leapt all over that statement and got some kind of promise out of her; but really I knew that that would be a forlorn hope, so why waste my breath? And in any case, chaos or no chaos, I was missing every single one of them. I'd get daily reports from home which only really made things worse. There's no way in the modern age that you can't be in touch. Fixed telephones, mobile telephones, email, Facebook – you can communicate almost constantly, but does it always help? I'm not so sure. Sometimes it's just a constant reminder that you're not actually where you want to be. Natalie would post regularly on Facebook and upload photos from home, and I would look at them late at night after work, if I'd made it there and back, and just end up feeling even more cut off. Even Samuel was emailing on a daily basis, usually just to ask for something or to see if I would contradict whatever edict Natalie had laid down at home.

Maybe it's because of what I do for a living, the fact that I'm usually the centre of attention, that I find it difficult to conceive that life not only does actually go on without me but can actually thrive. Like I say, other people have it worse I know; other people are separated indefinitely, some permanently, I know all that. It doesn't make it easier. Thérence's vocabulary seemed to be improving rapidly which I would only find out second-hand during phone conversations with Natalie, conversations which I actually found harder than not talking to her. My mind usually wandered during these calls, I would feel suddenly even more sorry for myself than usual and angry too: angry at the weather, angry at the distance between me and my family, angry at not being home more often than I was. And Natalie, unaware that my attention would usually have drifted, would still be talking.

'... and so really we're lucky to be alive,' she concluded.

'Sorry?! What?'

Natalie had been woken at five that morning, as one of the big barn shutters that cover the lounge windows had got loose in the wind. The shutters are 12 feet high and very heavy, but she went out to secure the one that had come loose and, thinking that was the extent of the damage, had gone back to bed. What she hadn't seen was that the boys' trampoline had blown away! This isn't a small thing – it is 5 metres in diameter, a heavy metal colossus and the wind (or more likely a whirlwind) had lifted it up and thrown it 30 metres where it had hit the corner of the house and landed on the car, smashing the windscreen and denting the roof.

A couple of years ago there had been massive storms that hit Western France and carried on into the centre where we are. Thirty people had died in those storms as bungalows built precariously on a flood plain were torn apart, flash floods devastated villages and trees had fallen on cars; there were many other casualties too and Natalie and the boys, though unharmed, had been without electricity for three days, frightened and in the dark; I hadn't been there then but had vainly promised that next time I would be. A similar storm had now hit and I hadn't kept my promise.

Natalie had been out in that storm having to muck about with shutters and whatever else had come loose, and if, like me, you'd been on the road for ten days working every night to drunken Christmas audiences and were feeling a bit strung out anyway, your mind runs away with you. What if she'd been hit? What if she'd been picked up by the tornado? At this point I was a gibbering wreck. According to the news the storms in France would blow themselves out by that night but, and this happens at this time every year when fatigue and the weather conspire to make me paranoid, I couldn't think of anything else but getting home.

'Are you OK?' she asked. 'You'll be home soon.'

I didn't need reminding. My remaining gig in Oxford was unlikely to go ahead and even if it did I wasn't prepared to battle my way there and end up not being able to get out again. I told the organisers in Oxford that I wouldn't be able to make it and that I didn't think the other three acts on the bill would make it either. The gig was cancelled and I began to make plans. It wasn't just a case of getting back to France; there was the logistical problem of just getting out of Crawley. As things stood, even trains from Sussex to London were problematic – going further than that looked nigh on impossible. This tends to happen every year. I try and make it back home for 21 December so that I can spend my birthday with Natalie and the boys, but it doesn't always work out like that. I had spent the previous year, my thirty-ninth birthday, sitting in a room at the Radisson Hotel in Stansted Airport and from my vantage point morosely watching heavy snow fall onto the runway, listening to radio reports of 'unprecedented' weather and travel 'chaos'. I was watching this unpleasant wintry scene while sipping from a warm bottle of champagne kindly donated by a comedy club for my birthday and chewing angrily on cheap, shop-bought sandwiches from Spar. I eventually got home on the evening of the twenty-third, but it was a low ebb.

This year I had made contingency plans. I had a flight booked from Stansted to Poitiers, a seat on a Eurostar to Paris and, just in case, a foot passenger ticket from Dover to Calais. The only thing I hadn't done was provisionally hire my own boat. It was the kind of journey that Ranulph Fiennes would write a book about. I got the last train out of Crawley going to London Bridge, then walked across London to King's Cross which was in chaos. The Eurostar trains had been frozen by the 'wrong kind of ice' and no-one could see them moving for a couple of days. I made a decision and managed to get a train from Liverpool Street to Stansted and camped down in the airport hoping that the airline's desire to avoid cancellations and recompense would mean that safety concerns would be loosened and my flight to Poitiers would leave early the following morning. It did, powered not so much by the aircraft's engines but by the sighs of relief from everyone on board. The aircrew, whose main job it seems is to sell stuff on the flight, had a field day on that flight as, despite the early hour, the bar was emptied and weary travellers dared to dream that they might actually make it home for Christmas. The English on board clinked plastic glasses and congratulated each other, while the French on board behaved like it was Liberation Day.

I blame the late French photographer Robert Doisneau for this; he has an awful lot to answer for if you ask me. He's the one who took the famous photo of two lovers kissing on the streets of Paris, and while it would be unfair to lay all embarrassingly public displays of affection at his doorstep, he certainly gave it a veneer of acceptability, especially in France.

I once had a girlfriend who strictly forbade me from kissing her in public – she also strictly forbade me from kissing her in private as well, so it wasn't much of a relationship to be fair. She would never have got on in France. The French are a hot-blooded, emotional race (and they do see themselves as a distinct race) who have no qualms about displaying their feelings in public; on the whole I don't mind it, but the amount of prolonged kissing (older people might remember the word 'snogging') on French railway platforms is frankly beyond a joke. As I almost always travel alone, it is quite awkward to have to stand amongst a group of generally young, good-looking lovers constantly chewing each other's faces off. Other people on these platforms seem to regard this behaviour as entirely reasonable, some taking up positions to get a better view, others just bathing in the warmth of it all like it's one big osmotic love-in, but nobody seemingly prepared to shout, *'Cherchez une chambre!'* for the good of all.

Well, I'd had enough frankly. After thirteen hours of travelling I had made it as far as Saint-Pierre-des-Corps in Tours, just in time to catch the last connecting train home. And then it just seemed that everyone else on the platform began some sort of slow motion dance where they paired up and just started getting off with each other! It was too much for me and that's when I told them in my grammatically unsound French to 'get a room'. Thankfully nobody took any notice of me and my strung out, Anglo-Saxon limitations, except for one old woman who just came and stood in front of me, not in admonishment for my outburst, but clearly expecting to get some 'action' along the lines of what everyone else was up to.

I had effectively been travelling with this woman for the last three hours. We had shared a waiting room at the station in Poitiers, queued alongside each other to get a ticket and, by chance, had seats next to one another on the journey from Poitiers to Saint-Pierre-des-Corps. She had, as the French say, a little too much sugar on her strawberries, which is their way of saying 'mad as a bottle of chips'. For instance, she had complained bitterly about how uncomfortable the seating was on the train until a fellow passenger pointed out that she was in fact sitting in the luggage rack.

She was also carrying a mangy dog in a carrier bag, which she kept calling her *bébé* and which, to its great credit, didn't seem to have much time for her either. At one point she opened a bag of biscuits and instead of offering the animal just one biscuit she shoved the whole thing in its face like it was a nose bag and the dog, clearly not a fan of vanilla wafers, just sneezed into the bag and emerged with its face a wafery mess. The old woman looked at the hapless creature but didn't bother to clean it and offered me the bag of biscuits instead! I declined politely – I'm not a huge fan of vanilla wafers either especially the ones covered in dog snot – and looked at the dog who I swear just rolled his eyes as if to say, 'I know, but what can you do?'

And now here she was in front of me, on a dark, icy railway platform in Central France. We were surrounded by lovers either meeting or parting, and the wind was blowing in along the station, chilling to the bone. She was a batty old dear and her eyes were clearly seeing mistletoe where there was none and her lips seemed puckered up while bits of biscuit clung to the hairs on her chin. I seriously thought of legging it onto the tracks and trying to run home. I looked at the dog, its face so covered in wafer he looked like he had canine psoriasis, its eyes seemed to say, 'Take me with you, please' which instantly shook me from my reverie as for one absurd moment I thought of arriving home and adding another bloody animal to the collection. I plucked up the courage to speak to the woman, but she beat me to it.

'Can I stroke your coat?' she enquired. 'It looks so soft.'

And so I spent the next five minutes waiting for a train while having my coat stroked by an old woman. I had been on the road for ten days, travelling since late the previous evening and was so tired I was actually shaking through fatigue. Tomorrow would be my fortieth birthday – I realised I was just an hour from home; an hour from Natalie and the boys and the dogs, cats and horses; an hour from snowed-in pandemonium, short tempers, noise and marbles. I began to weep silently, exhaustion playing a part obviously but also happiness. I was finally going home and I couldn't have been happier.

EN FAMILLE! EN FAMILLE!

Ah, the traditions of Christmas chez Moore. The *Radio Times* and a highlighter pen, being told to turn off James Brown's *Funky Christmas* CD, the argument over whether the lights go on the tree before or after the decorations, the children deciding a week before Christmas Day that their current interests are old hat, thereby rendering all unopened presents already obsolete and, of course, huge numbers of Natalie's family descending on us for Christmas Eve and Christmas Day.

Growing up, Natalie was always used to big Christmas gatherings hosted by her grandparents, and for the last five years we've carried on that tradition and have twenty or so guests over the two days of Christmas (they don't do Boxing Day here, which is a shame as Boxing Day, once the pressure is off, is the best day of Christmas) and I look forward to it. Christmas Day fare is the usual stuff, turkey and so on, but Christmas Eve has always been my night – a new recipe or a twist on a classic. It's my chance to show off. I love the planning, the preparation, the cooking and, as a stand-up comedian who just needs to be loved, the 'applause'. It's my night and I love it, even the stress. And, as you can imagine, an Englishman cooking for a large number of French people does not come without its pressures.

Last year, in an act of madness I decided to cook a fish curry. The sheer magnitude of it all only dawned on me mid-afternoon when I was preparing the meal. I broke out into a cold sweat as I realised that I was making a meal I had never cooked before for twenty-odd French gourmets (all French people think they are gourmets) and who, for the most part, had never eaten fish curry. Not only did I not know what I was doing, I did not know what I was doing on a massive scale. And it was fish; I might kill someone! Thankfully, the meal was a success, but while every child found it difficult to sleep that night in anticipation of Christmas Day, I didn't sleep either, convinced that I may have started a food poisoning epidemic.

I had planned a safer menu for this year with a selection of English and French sausages; well the sausages were English but the *boudin noir* (black pudding) was French and the *andouillettes* were definitely French. It's difficult to describe *andouillettes*, except to say that they are not for the faint-hearted; they are a local speciality, a large white sausage made up from the parts of animals usually reserved for the strings on tennis rackets or spare patches on a puncture repair kit. Needless to say they are something of an acquired taste and even fans of them very rarely manage a whole one.

All of my planning for this Christmas Eve had been in vain, though; I'd been usurped.

Natalie's grandparents had both died a few years earlier, Papy from a long and inevitably doomed battle with cancer and Mamie a few months later, officially from an embolism but also because maybe she just wanted to. It happens quite a lot I think, when one half dies after a lifetime spent together – in this case fifty-eight years of marriage – the other finds the physical and mental demands of being alone just too much and it takes its toll.

Their house, a massive, almost Gothic monstrosity on the edge of town had been standing empty ever since, partly due to a very depressed local housing market but also because who in their right mind would want it? It's on a busy road, opposite a builders' merchants, next door to a kebab shop, and its rooms are so cavernous that heating alone would cost a fortune. In the meantime, one of Natalie's uncles had moved into the empty house and although it was lovely to have family back on our doorstep, to celebrate his move back home and the fact that his boyfriend had moved in with him, *they* would be doing Christmas Eve. I won't pretend that I wasn't upset, but the decision was taken while I was away, possibly quite rightly, that I was strung out enough as it was without hosting Christmas Eve and Christmas Day.

It was a decision taken as much with my interests at heart as anything, but that had never stopped me from throwing my toys out of the pram before and it didn't this time either.

To me it just represented another chipping away at my life in France, something else I had to give up. It's inevitable of course; one of the many problems of being away so much is that, certainly on a domestic front, jobs that should be mine have to be done by someone else, and so when I do return, I feel a little left out, a bit spare. Obviously there are jobs that could only ever be mine; despite the harrowing journey back the previous week, the first thing I did when I got in was to start rearranging the fridge which was frankly, after so long away, an organisational shambles but also the perfect come down for an OCD-ridden fruitcake high on caffeine supplements. But it's the little things. I no longer prepare Natalie's pre-dinner gin and tonic for instance, that responsibility now lies with Maurice, who clearly has some talent in that area.

The relief for Samuel when I'm home is palpable, though. He's a serious-minded little boy and Natalie thinks that he feels the pressure to be 'man of the house' when I'm away, going so far as to copy my moodiness, speed of temper and 'petty levels of hissy-fitty-ness' (her words, not mine). When I'm back he behaves like a little boy again, plays with his toys more and is clearly much happier. Thérence is like any toddler and wants his mummy to do everything and no substitute will do except, I've noticed, when he's carrying a particularly rancid offering in his nappy and then it's all, 'Daddy do it!', so clearly some coaching has gone on there.

The one small advantage of not 'doing' Christmas Eve was that I had more time for other things. The trampoline that had blown away the previous week needed to be removed from a neighbour's garden across the road, which was quite some task; I was tackling it truculently and wondering how such a heavy, metal structure could possibly just blow away when a passing farmer told me that it was right to get it out of sight, 'otherwise the Roma might have it away.' But by now the thing was useless, so in the end I decided to leave it in full view and hope that the local Romani population would indeed live up to their stereotype and 'have it away', that's not me being lazy you understand, that's just recycling.

My Christmas Eve 'unemployment' also meant that everything was ready. The presents were all bought, wrapped and hidden, though Natalie's was, as ever, a trial as she veered violently between 'I don't want you to buy me anything' and 'I'd love a Pomeranian puppy'. The dogs had had their visit to the Doggy Parlour, a twice-a-year shampoo and set which tends to leave them a bit confused. Natalie had returned from the parlour with horrific tales of what the Spanish do to greyhounds – apparently Sylvie, who owns the parlour, belongs to a rescue charity and greyhound foster home which is good news for greyhounds, but I suspect bad news for me. Thankfully, Natalie hadn't returned with an actual greyhound this time, though I feared a New Year Crusade coming on.

She actually missed an opportunity. I was so pleased to be home, so happy to be back, that she could have turned up with half a dozen and I probably would have just laughed it off; I was full of festive spirit. I love being part of big family Christmases. Christmas is a control freak's time of year: so much to plan, organise and delegate. Orders to be barked, strops to be thrown – I love it. And the boys are obviously excited too. Samuel and I had already done the final big supermarket run.

'Daddy,' he asked as we cut a swathe through Christmas-shopping dawdlers, 'is this shopping list in the same order as the shop layout?'

'Yes,' I replied, a touch defensively, 'otherwise it's just chaos.'

'Good,' he said. 'It's the only way.'

He really was becoming more like me, which while no doubt flattering, isn't necessarily the best way to go for his own sanity. He had even started performing.

The highlight of this particular Christmas Eve was Samuel and Maurice singing 'One More Sleep 'til Christmas' from *The Muppet Christmas Carol*, which is, in my view, the best Christmas film of all time (sometimes I veer towards *It's A Wonderful Life*, but Samuel and Maurice haven't acted out those scenes yet). They had secretly been practising for the previous week with Natalie's dad on guitar and it was tear-jerkingly lovely. It's something of a tradition at French family gatherings, or this French family at least, that people get up and 'do a turn', something which I know to my cost. The first time I met Natalie's extended family (and there are hundreds of them) was at the wedding of an uncle and it was felt that the best way for me to ingratiate myself with the entire clan would be to perform. This wasn't my idea obviously – I would have been happy to write a card of introduction and buy each of them a drink, but that wasn't an option, so I had to sing a song. It was quite, quite terrifying – and long before I'd started stand-up. Even now I feel like I was the victim of some grand practical joke, part of some elaborate initiation test. I performed a drunken, mumbling rendition of Elvis's 'Love Me Tender' and after that, to most people's relief, this tradition seemed to fade away... The fact my eldest children, lovely though their performance was, appeared to be mounting some sort of resurrection of this tradition was a bit worrying and there were some anxious expressions around the table, memories of previous karaoke horrors coming back from the distant past and encouraging some of the more deranged members of the family to insist on doing it every year. Well, you won't catch me warbling away, that's for sure; this Elvis has definitely left the building.

Though I bang on about planning and menus and the like, Christmas Day is actually relatively stress-free. There may be twenty-three people in the lounge, but everybody will have contributed to the meal. Natalie will have prepared the foie gras, someone else will have brought the oysters and someone else the smoked salmon. Natalie's mum might have part-cooked the two turkeys, while I prepared the vegetables. Somebody else will have brought the cheese, another the bread. A fruit salad will be rustled up, other homemade desserts will arrive and someone else will have made a Christmas log. Brian, Natalie's dad, will have baked homemade mince pies and a Christmas cake. Someone will have brought dessert wine (a Jurançon or a Sauternes), someone else the red wine, and there'll always be bottles of the 'family' champagne. Papy once owned some land in the Champagne region, where he was born, and the new owners now provide us with a few cases of the stuff, in what some of the family see as recompense for the underhanded way in which they obtained the land in the first place. Finally, and after having taste-tested various high-class Christmas puddings throughout December, a winner will have been decided upon on and the whole thing will finally be set fire to by someone wobbling after hours of rich food and wine indulgence and wearing a dangerously angled, highly inflammable, paper crown. The children, of course, are spared all this and are excused most of the sitting down; not that they miss any courses.

So everybody does something. It's obviously one of the signature meals of the year and the French want to be part of the preparation not just the execution, a case of too many cooks definitely not spoiling the broth. Having said that, though, Christmas Day didn't start too well for me. Everything was pretty much under control by midday; presents had been opened, wrapping paper folded up and put away for future use (not my OCD this time, but Natalie's), the table was laid, the turkey was on, the vegetables were ready to go, teams of oyster-openers were outside in the watery winter sun and already hitting the wine for their trouble. And then sartorial disaster struck.

I had a chorizo sausage hanging in the larder, drying out for post-Christmas, non-turkey leftover meals; but it was in a precarious position and so really I only had myself to blame. I reached into the larder without concentrating, not looking at what I was doing, until I felt something fall onto my arm. It was the chorizo, as yet undried, and my arm was now covered in its oil. Only it wasn't just my arm, it was my sleeve. My beautiful new jumper, my heavy wool Breton-style sailing jumper which I had got only that morning was soaked in red chorizo juice; I looked like I'd been shot. Of all the potential Christmas calamities that could have befallen me – like undercooking the turkey, dropping the champagne, leaving the cats in charge of the smoked salmon – there is absolutely nothing worse for a mod than gaudy coloured sausage juice on your new sweater.

Now, I like swearing and I think there's an art to it; those who say that it's neither big nor clever or that it shows a lack of vocabulary haven't heard it done properly and are also cutting themselves off from the most vibrant and organic parts of language. Badly timed, unnecessary swearing is crude and jarring, but when your best jumper has just been covered in spicy oil there is an opportunity for some really inventive expletives. I prefer the use of alliterative word plus friendly word juxtapositions and Christmas time offers a whole range of opportunities for the switched-on potty mouth. I was in the larder for a good couple of minutes, giving it the full invective, and eventually emerged to find everybody standing there, open-mouthed, staring at me. The look on their faces was a mixture of shock and awe, like a particularly well-endowed streaker had just skipped through the kitchen. Most of them weren't even aware of what I was saying, but when such venom and poison are spouted, clearly the actual language element is no barrier. So I scurried back to the vegetables and pretended nothing had happened.

Personally my favourite part of Christmas Day has always been the turkey and stuffing sandwiches in the evening but that's not really an option in France, not unless I eat them before we actually finish dinner. The meal lasts all day and it's not difficult to see why: firstly, there are about ten courses, each demanding a different wine, and each course is ambled through – there is no rushing here. Each new plate seems to set off another philosophical debate or moral dilemma which must be debated at full volume. Nothing passes at the Christmas table without comment or counter-comment, nothing. And just when you think things may be flagging another course is introduced (the turkey was the sixth course to arrive) and if conversation gets a little dull, things are always easily livened up with a cracker.

The French, unsurprisingly, don't do crackers; it's a distraction from the important job at hand, which is eating. Most of Natalie's family are aware that Christmas at our house is an Anglo-French affair, the Anglo bits are Stilton, Christmas pudding, crackers and the music, and the French bits are everything else. Watching a novice Frenchman having a cracker explained to him then by another equally sceptical Frenchman is a bit like watching two Americans discuss the rules of cricket.

'We pull these things as we sit down to eat.'

'Why?'

'Er…'

And you know that at this point he wants to say, 'Because it keeps Ian and his kids happy. Just do it, for God's sake, don't set him off.'

'And we have to wear this paper thing?'

'I'm afraid so.'

'Why have I got a luminous paperclip?'

'Ah, foie gras! Thank God.'

I'm not going to defend any of the 'jokes' in the crackers. Most sentient English folk read them, groan and move on. But watching a clutch of French people cope with crackers while already having been through a good portion of champagne, oysters, sweet white wine and a full-bodied Burgundy is funny enough in itself.

'OK, OK, I 'ave one. Oo 'elps a rabbeet get dressed?' one of the throng asked to uninterested silence.

'An idiot!' someone said after a while.

'Rabbeets don't wear the clothes! Is eet a reedle?' another said, a response that set off a flurry of philosophical debate about what constitutes a riddle.

Then came the punch-line: 'An 'are-dresser. Sorry. A hare dresser.' Silence.

'I don't get it,' someone else said, and then came a number of explanations, all of them giving the rather tired pun far more gravitas than it deserved. The French may love their slapstick and puns of their own, but there is simply no room, it seems, for frivolity at the dinner table. The French don't get sillier the more they drink, they get more earnest.

When at last it was explained that it is just a joke, a deliberately poor one as is traditional in crackers, a few of them looked at me, clearly bridging the gap between a joke in a cracker and my job as a stand-up comedian, holding me responsible for this nonsense and wondering just how secure my children's future really is if it's built on this sort of flimsy, substandard punnery.

Eventually, sated enough to render turkey and stuffing sandwiches unnecessary, we all retired to the living room and flaked out like a pride of lions after a particularly good kill. Natalie, having put my injured sweater in to soak earlier, emerged from the bathroom with it miraculously restored to its former glory and I felt magnanimous or festive enough to allow even the cats and dogs in to join us. Immediately Flame jumped on me and settled on to my chest as he usually does, started doing that non-claw pawing that cats do, purring heavily and then – as apparently male cats are wont to do – sprayed the foulest excretion this side of a dirty protest in a Bangkok prison cell all over my bloody jumper!

Like I said, this family likes a performance at a gathering and they got a full five minutes of juicy Anglo-Saxon of the kind that some people would happily pay for. Quite magnificent swearing, to add to the already impressive effort I had made in the larder earlier.

It had been a long day and as Natalie and I put Maurice to bed, the excitement he was still feeling, as children do for the whole of the Christmas period, was still very much there. We talked for a bit about his presents and what, inevitably, he wanted next year and he began to drift off. I got up and went to switch his light off and then he said sleepily, 'Daddy, what's a festive-feline-fuck-knuckle?'

Natalie looked at me aghast. 'Right,' she said, 'there have to be some changes around here.'

AWAY FROM THE NUMBERS

It wasn't just the bad language of course; being at home and enjoying a full family Christmas had underlined just how little time I actually spent there and that had to change. The original plan was that within five years of moving to France I wouldn't be travelling back to the UK nearly as often as I had been. Though the actual 'How are we going to do that?' part of the plan had always been a little vague, and in fact the opposite had occurred. I was away more than ever and sometimes for long stretches.

Over the years we had tried various ways to earn money in France. Natalie had worked as an estate agent, but when her three years' maternity leave was over, which at this point was about five months away, neither of us wanted her to go back to work for Norbert. Also, in the meantime my working week had become more unpredictable, meaning that sometimes Natalie wouldn't be able to work even part-time hours – plus, since Thérence's birth, we had collected more animals, meaning Natalie would find it difficult to do any kind of job that wasn't working from home.

My attempts at earning money in France had thus far been fruitless and physically detrimental. As an English comedian I have worked all over the world – Melbourne, Dubai, Mumbai, Boston, Montreal, Helsinki, Munich, Nice, Hong Kong, Bangkok, Shanghai, Manila, Brussels, Amsterdam, Singapore, Cyprus – basically, wherever there's an expat or at least an English-speaking audience there's a gig. Why not set up my own? In Paris?

People have tried and failed to organise comedy in Paris, but surely I stood a better chance? I had all the contacts, the proximity to Paris itself and the desire to succeed where others had failed. It didn't last long. Finding a venue in Paris was nigh-on impossible; I wanted a nice, small theatre set-up but none of them have bars, meaning that the project would be unviable. I then turned to nightclubs (of which there are many) and had a meeting with a well-known club owner in the Bastille district. She was kind enough to see us but she wasn't convinced – the idea of a stand-up comedy night in France is very new and she just couldn't really grasp the concept. Eventually what we wanted to do sunk in, but, she asked, how would we make money? Well, I said, aside from ticket sales, the bar returns will be massive. There will be 300 Anglophones in your club, all drinking.

'No,' she said, a deadpan look on her face.

'But it works…' and I listed all the places I'd played in where clubs had been going for years.

'This is Paris,' she said, unimpressed. 'People don't drink here.'

I must have looked a little dubious at this statement. I know big-city expats and in my experience they're very rarely ever sober!

'I have an idea, though,' she continued and leaned in conspiratorially. 'We'll secretly film all the comedians and sell the footage to mobile phone companies.'

Illegally filming and selling my colleagues' intellectual property to communications giants was one of the most insane ideas I had ever heard and I gave my thanks for her time and left her to her mad, swivel-eyed view of the world. What about an English 'pub' in Paris, I thought? There are lots of those. One in the Pigalle district gave me the go ahead, but then said if any other client wanted the function room for that night, they could have it and it didn't matter how much notice she gave!

'Let me get this straight,' I said, not quite believing my ears, 'I will have booked three top comedians, brought them to Paris and found them a hotel. Sold potentially 300 tickets and even on the afternoon of the show itself you can cancel me?'

'Yes,' she said. 'Deal?'

Another even less keen on the idea said I could rent his place for €20,000 a night.

'Great!' I said, 'I'll be along with the money just as soon as I find somewhere to land my GOLDEN BLOODY HELICOPTER!'

The Anglo-French Chamber of Commerce gave me a list of people who might be able to help – events managers, PR firms and the like; no psychiatrists, though, which would have been distinctly more useful.

Julia and Pete ran a PR company that had fallen on hard times and they were struggling but thought that stand-up comedy might be their salvation.

'Forget about Paris,' they said, 'there's too many rules there, it's too difficult. Come and try down here.'

'Down here' was the Deux-Sèvres region, but close enough to Cognac and the Dordogne to programme a three-night run there. 'Is there enough of an audience to make it work, do you think?'

'Oh yes,' they said, 'easily.' It was what I wanted to hear frankly and I let that get the better of my, let's be honest, pretty weak business sense.

Maybe expats in France are a different breed. There's always the possibility that they don't crave 'English entertainment' the way expats further afield do and that's to be admired really; they certainly weren't that fussed about stand-up! My role was to help with advertising, book the comedians, their travel and hotels, MC every show, drive everyone around and stump up most of the money. Julia and Pete's job was to make sure the venues were ready and obviously do most of the PR.

'I take it you've spoken to the expat business associations in Dordogne, have you?' I suggested on the phone one day when Julia hinted that ticket sales were a bit sluggish.

'Oh, I hadn't thought of that!' she said enthusiastically. 'I did put a poster up on the side of a fish and chip van today, though.'

It didn't bode well. I booked comedian friends of mine, Paul Thorne and Paul Sinha, who I knew could handle most situations and who would be prepared to give me a little leeway if things were a bit amateurish to start with, but those relationships became definitely strained by the second show when we found ourselves in a massive, 500-seat *salle des fêtes* with no sound system. An emergency system was rented, which we then had to rig up even though none of us had a clue what to do.

'Do you not carry your own microphones around with you usually?' Julia asked, pulling on a cigarette, as we lugged the heavy sound equipment around the venue.

'No, Julia. No we don't.' I looked at Paul Thorne, who was a close friend, and rolled my eyes in a 'what can you do?' way. He looked back at me and mouthed some particularly nasty insult in my direction.

'Don't ever ask me to work for you again,' he added.

In all we did six shows over two months, two runs of three, and a couple of them were very good, enjoyable comedy gigs, but we played to ever-decreasing numbers as Julia and Pete insisted, against my advice, on changing the venues every time.

In the penultimate show somewhere in a tiny village outside of Cognac we had seventeen people in. Of course the show went ahead and I introduced the first act and went outside to lick my wounds. As usual Julia was there, puffing away on yet another fag.

'Why are we in the middle of bloody nowhere, Julia? We've got seventeen people in! Seventeen!'

She looked at me, shocked that I was angry. 'Do you normally get more than that then?'

I had already decided that I was working with idiots, that they were costing me a fortune and putting long-term friendships under considerable strain. The sixth show would be the last, I thought, but decided against telling Julia until the thing was over. Also, it was the effort involved that didn't seem worth it, the organising, the funding, the travelling and the performing was a lot harder than I'd anticipated. It's much easier, I thought, to just walk on stage and tell jokes for half an hour and let somebody else take the strain.

We arrived at the last gig, again at some tiny town in the middle of rural Deux-Sèvres, the venue having been changed from the most successful show we had had on the first run. Again I was with two very good friends, Andy Robinson and Gavin Webster, and I'd already told them that I thought this would be my last; the strain, emotionally, physically and financially was just too much. Andy later described my pre-gig condition as something resembling a stroke. I got out of the car and the entire left side of my body seemed to droop, he said, I then pulled myself up and staggered into the venue and like a man possessed started fiddling about with the sound system. Apparently happy with my work, I then marched out of the back of the hall and promptly collapsed.

'The show must go on!' I kept mumbling like some drunk pantomime dame, as Gavin and Andy tried to persuade me that actually I wasn't in much of a fit state to do anything. The *pompiers* were called and I was rushed to hospital in Ruffeq, travelling in the ambulance with Julia; and that was the last I saw of her as she disappeared when we entered the hospital. Andy and Gavin, to their great credit and despite being obviously quite shaken, went ahead with the show. I still lost money on it, though.

I had been having stomach problems for a couple of years and nobody had diagnosed it properly enough to actually treat it – was it an ulcer, hernia, irritable bowel syndrome, reflux? I had been opened up, had tubes shoved in every orifice and taken more drugs than an East German shot-putter, and still the problem persisted.

'So, Doctor?' Natalie asked nervously on one occasion. 'What do you think?'

The doctor, actually a stomach specialist, looked at me again and shook his head. This doesn't look good, I thought. He took his glasses off, rubbed his eyes, looked at Natalie and sighed. 'You've told me what your husband does for a living, the lifestyle that goes with it and the endless travelling. Of course he's ill.' He looked at me, 'Monsieur, go home.'

In my weakened state I took this to be the rallying cry of a Le Pen follower and told Natalie that I was going to throw him through the window. 'Monsieur Moore!' he said, a bit rattled. 'Please don't misunderstand me.' He went on to explain, very eloquently and very reasonably, exactly what he meant. You cannot keep putting your body under this pressure, he said, nearly a hundred flights a year, the trains, the driving, at least one night's sleep lost a week, eating at odd hours, the drinking etc. etc. It is physically unsustainable, he said, so move back to England. Or get another job.

I thought about this as I lay in that hospital in Ruffeq for three days. I was totally alone. Natalie couldn't leave the boys and drive three hours to come and see me, Andy and Gavin had flown home as planned and Julia had disappeared. Andy had rung Natalie to tell her what had happened and she was in regular contact with the hospital, but I had no working phone, no computer, nothing.

As a child I had read a biography of Peter Sellers and in it there was an incident where he suffered a heart attack on an aeroplane. And while he lay there thinking that this was the end, Sellers says that he had a 'visitation', somebody came to him and said that if he survived he should 'go back to Clouseau'. Sellers had sworn never to play the role again after the first two films, but he survived the heart attack and did indeed 'go back to Clouseau', resurrecting his career.

I'm not comparing myself to the great Peter Sellers, but I had a similar incident. I woke groggily from the anaesthetic, at first not knowing where I was, but there was a voice I recognised and it was my good friend and comedian Mick Ferry, basically telling me that I couldn't change my course, I am who I am, and that I should make a decision early and stick to it. I took this as a reference to my brief, inglorious time as a comedy impresario. The thing is, Mick was talking from the television in the corner of the room – French breakfast television was showing a clip from the film *Looking For Eric* and it just happened to be the bit that Mick was in. It was one of those absurd coincidences that life sometimes throws up and added to the whole surreal nature of the previous twenty-four hours. Though at the time, being alone and not knowing where I was, I found it quite scary!

The diagnosis was actually quite prosaic. The internal scar tissue of my old external appendix wound had wrapped itself around my intestines and finally my body had shut down, unable to cope.

'It's very common,' said the doctor in Ruffeq. A sentiment echoed by our family doctor and the sundry 'medicos' in Natalie's extended family too, 'very common'. For the last two years I'd been poked, prodded, invaded and pumped full of drugs and apparently they'd missed the obvious. Very common indeed! Bloody cheek!

Eventually I got home, a wounded, poorer individual and almost immediately the phone rang. It was Julia.

'I've been thinking,' she mused before I could say anything. 'I think we should do a run of shows over Christmas.' I gave her my reply, going completely against the advice of the doctor who had warned me not to get agitated and to remain calm. I never heard from Julia again.

So we'd tried estate agency and running our own comedy shows; we'd also tried to make a living from *brocantes*, eBay, selling cushions and chutney. Now we needed a radical rethink. 'Why don't you both go away for a couple of days and think about things?' asked Natalie's mum, immediately after Christmas. 'We can take care of the place, can't we, Brian?' Brian looked a little sceptical to be fair, even for a couple of days three young boys and the frantic hubbub of the menagerie wasn't something to be taken on lightly. We didn't give him chance to object.

The city of Tours was once the medieval capital of France and it's one of my favourite places. Less than an hour from where we live, its airport is a very useful Ryanair hub. Every Christmas we go there with the boys to see the Christmas lights and they stuff themselves silly on toffee apples and *barbe à papa* (candyfloss). This time was different though, Natalie and I were on our own for two whole days. Taking advantage of Natalie's parents' generosity, we gave brief instructions of how to feed, clean and care for the horses, dogs, cats and children – and got out of there quick before they changed their minds.

A couple of days to ourselves in Tours was just what we needed. Natalie's life had become a merry-go-round of various kinds of animal droppings and outdoor maintenance, so a chance to go shopping in some of the more up-market French boutiques had her salivating before we'd even got there – and I was eagerly anticipating spending two nights in a hotel and not actually being on my own!

Tours is a cross between the bohemia of Brighton and the academia of Oxford or Cambridge, with the ancient buildings of the medieval capital thrown in. Like any city it has its rough points and its drunks, though even they seem more benign than in other places. It has atmosphere and culture, restaurants, brasseries, *crêperies*, *maisons de thé*, antique shops and chocolatiers galore; it also has a C&A which is 'just great for children's clothes'.

For two days we went seemingly up and down the same road as Natalie shopped the way she always has, the complete antithesis of the impulse buyer. A beige cardigan in Galeries Lafayette would have to be weighed up with a similar cardigan from another shop at the other end of the Rue Nationale, with a multitude of journeys in between and me trailing behind with a dozen shopping bags containing clothes, a very heavy set of antique coat hooks and my ever-failing spirit and good humour. She literally shopped until I dropped.

What we hadn't done much of, however, was talk about what our next step could be, how we would reduce my travelling and still earn money. It's not that we hadn't talked, we'd talked a lot, but like all parents with small children, all we'd talked about when we had the chance to be away from them was the children. So, on the last night we planned to go back to a little restaurant in the beautiful Place Plumereau and chat over a nice glass of wine and some local specialities. My feet, though, simply wouldn't go the extra half mile and could barely scrape their way to the Chinese restaurant across the road from our hotel. We were in one of France's finest old cities, in the gastronomic *Centre*, and we were having a Chinese! In our defence, it was Tours' first ever Chinese restaurant and was established way back in 1977 so, you know, it had history.

What it didn't have were any other customers, so we had ample opportunity to thrash out our 'problem' in public. I got out a pen and paper like a secretary ready to take shorthand – if this discussion needed anything, I thought, it is a list. I wrote a bold number '1' in the top left hand corner and then looked at Natalie who was sipping stiffly on her aperitif. I circled the number and looked at Natalie again. I put a colon just to the right of the circled number and started to underline the whole thing. Natalie grabbed the pen and took it off me.

'Look,' she said, slightly irritated, 'we both agree that we spend too much time apart. It's not good for us and it's not good for the boys. Agreed?'

'Agreed,' I said. 'Can I write that down?'

Possibly for the long-term good of our marriage we were interrupted at that point by the world's oldest waitress, a delightfully smiley Chinese woman who seemed happy to have a bit of company.

'Are you ready to order?' she asked brightly.

Not for the first time on our little break my order was questioned, not because of my bad French accent (which would have been perfectly acceptable), but because I was plainly just ordering the wrong thing.

'Are you sure?' she said, 'You'll never eat all that!'

'Honestly, I've been shopping all day and I am ravenous,' I said and she turned away with a smirk on her face. 'Anyway, agreed. I want to be at home more, that's a given.'

'And I can't easily get a job because when you are working, you could be away at any time and I won't find something that flexible where we are.'

We sat pondering this for a few minutes before the waitress brought us our starters; all freshly cooked, piping hot, wonderfully tasty spring rolls, wontons, soups, toasts, seaweed, the works. Hmm, I thought, I may have a problem here.

'So ideally,' I said, taking a break from the food to get my breath back, 'we need something we can do from home.'

'Like a gîte?' ventured Natalie tentatively, knowing what my reaction would be.

'No way!' I spluttered, 'Come on, we moved here to get away from people! I'm not doing a gîte!'

'It's just an option that's all. If our aim is to work from home and for you to be at home, it ticks all the boxes.'

I sat sulkily back in my chair as the waitress approached to clear our half-empty plates, she tutted at mine. Wherever I go it seems restaurant staff feel they have a right to judge me. One of the first times I went out for a meal in France with Natalie's family I ordered a steak to be 'well done' and the chef came running out of the kitchen, tears in his eyes and told me off. He practically begged me to change my order claiming that he couldn't serve 'leather as food.'

'OK, so not a gîte. Fine. What do you have in mind then?'

We threw ideas around for a while – buy a shop in town, open a dog kennels (not my idea), a *crêperie*, goat farming – each one slightly more bizarre than the one preceding it.

The waitress returned with our main courses which didn't all fit on the table, forcing her to move another table next to us, and as she did so she looked at me as if to say 'I told you so!'

'*Bon appétit!*' she said sceptically.

'Why don't we both do a TEFL course and teach from home?' I suggested. I had actually mooted this idea with my friend Paul one night in London, proposing it as a way forward for Natalie and me. He had laughed himself silly. 'You? A teacher?' And then he was off again.

'You?' said Natalie, barely able to control herself. 'A teacher? You nearly disowned Samuel when you taught him how to ride a bike. No. You haven't got the patience…'

'Oh, that's absolute boll—'

The waitress glided over to us. 'Everything OK?' she said, meaning our food presumably and not our relationship.

'Lovely. Really lovely.' We said together, still piles of the stuff in front of us.

Pleased with the answer she sat on a table behind us and opened a huge box of Ferrero Rocher, which she proceeded to munch through as we continued to eat our meal. It was quite intimidating actually and as we got half way through our main course we simply couldn't eat any more. I got up to go to the toilet and heard her say to Natalie, 'So he doesn't like the wine either, eh?' and pointing at my full glass.

'We could get teachers in!' I said, returning to the table having been inspired in the tiny toilet and still doing up my flies.

'You mean like a writing holiday or a painting holiday, like that?'

'Exactly!' I replied. Natalie looked at me, a glint in her eye.

We thrashed it out over the cooling food for another twenty minutes or so. Convert one of the barns into a classroom, use local hotels and *chambres d'hôtes* to house the students, have the 'teacher' stay with us and we'd provide the meals for everyone. It was using the property to its full potential, we'd be at home together, I would do the cooking and therefore be largely kept away from the 'students' and the local community would gain in tourism. It seemed like the perfect answer, even if it would take time to set up, build and then establish it seemed an ideal solution for us. And I would be at home more.

'Have you finished?' interrupted the waitress from her trough of chocolates.

'Yes, erm... could you box it up for us please? We'll take it with us.'

I hate it when Natalie does this, I find it embarrassing but it seemed to please the old waitress no end, especially when she managed to sell Natalie a bag of Chinese tea as well. And in the spirit of goodwill, and after she'd carefully boxed up the remains of our meal, I even ate a bowl of lychees which I can't stand and she wished us a *Bonne Année* as we walked the 5 metres across the road to our hotel with an almost complete Chinese meal and half a bottle of rosé in our hands.

The lychees had their usual effect on me and I barely slept that night – and just as I was about to, at six in the morning, the fire alarm went off. It was, as always, a false alarm, but it rendered any further sleep utterly impossible and so I spent the early hours sitting in a chair, staring at my laptop and eating cold Chinese food. It was horribly reminiscent of being away at work only this was very different. Natalie was in the bed in the corner of the room, gently breathing and, more importantly, we had a plan. This could be a big year indeed.

AND THEN THERE WERE TWO

For some reason, if you mention French builders to people it seems to strike fear into their hearts. They go pale and start having 'Vietnam Vet-style' flashbacks, recounting their experiences with a due sense of horror and injustice. I think it's unfair. Just marrying the words 'French' and 'builder' seems to have become some sort of comic shorthand for truculence and laziness, but in my experience they are no worse or better than builders anywhere. All builders are tempted by the big jobs and like diva-esque supermodels 'won't get out of bed' for trifling ventures. They'll generally take on too much work and spread themselves thin enough to delay your project while at the same time finding hidden extras that bump up the original quote. This is the same the world over.

We had had a loft converted to a bedroom just after we moved in and invited, as is recommended, three quotes for the work. One of them didn't turn up and one was such a gibbering wreck we felt sorry for him – just not sorry enough to give him the work. The third, Bernard Butard, did turn up and didn't lack confidence. An enormous, jolly-faced man, he had the manner of making us feel like he was doing us a favour with our *combles aménageables* (loft conversion) and that actually he had a number of chateaux on the go but could probably fit this mere *bagatelle* into his hectic schedule. He did, and it was over-budget and overdue, but the finished room was superb. Butard was still the only player in town and so, knowing his lackadaisical approach to deadlines, we had time to play with, time to iron out the details of what we were actually proposing to teach at our 'school'.

However, before the New Year could properly begin we first had to get through 'January the Fourth'. January 4 is a special day in our house; it's the day we moved to France, it's Natalie's birthday and it's Samuel's birthday too. Unbelievably, Samuel was born on Natalie's thirtieth birthday, in the same hospital she was born in and delivered by the same midwife. That one fact goes a long way to explaining my personality traits: I am a control freak because the singular, most important event of my life up to that point – the birth of my first child – felt pre-ordained, an event guided by something else and to which I was essentially an irrelevance. Nonsense I know, but it explains why I've tried to control everything ever since.

The feeling, absurd though it is, that they were born on the same day and therefore carry the whiff of sorcery about them is difficult to suppress. The fact that every year I get congratulated for 'giving my wife a child' on her thirtieth birthday is actually a bit creepy too and makes me feel like a pawn in a wider game. And though I'm aware that most men could shrug off these coincidences with nonchalance; I hear the soundtrack from *The Omen*.

And once again the biblical portents for this year were looming particularly large.

It seemed to have been raining since Boxing Day – not just drizzle but heavy, build-an-ark rain and strong winds. The river Cher, the left tributary of the Loire and at a wide point here, is about 400 metres from the house and its banks had burst. It tends to do this every year anyway, but normally towards the back end of winter when the water table has taken four or five months of deluge, certainly not at the turn of the year. The playground in town, built rather optimistically on the river bank, was almost completely underwater, with just the top of the swings and slide showing; a depressing post-apocalyptic vision, like the Statue of Liberty in *Planet of the Apes*.

Junior of course loves this kind of weather, facing it down like some Nordic god, angrily whinnying at the elements. I can't help laughing at him when he's like this which only makes him angrier. As usual, he came marching up to me at the fence, snorting away like a bluff old colonel, but then for some reason curiously ran out of steam and actually avoided eye-contact with me, which he'd never done before. Maybe I'm finally wearing him down, I thought, and then he snorted in my face like a spitting camel. I don't know what makes him as irritable as he is. A friend of ours suggested that we should give him mint tea, as if that would help. Frankly it sounded about as helpful as trying to massage his chi in the mornings, or rearranging his stable to harness a more positive feng shui.

'Mint tea, you say?' I was unable to disguise my scepticism and caught her boyfriend's equally cynical eye.

'Yes,' she replied without a shred of doubt and held her mug up to his mouth.

The next five minutes was bedlam. He dipped his tongue into the mug and all was peace for a couple of seconds, then his lips curled right back beyond his teeth and he let out a primeval and very unhorse-like howl, stamped his feet, reared up at us as we scattered and fled the paddock and then went galloping off. He hasn't really been the same with me since, clearly holding me responsible for the whole debacle. Whatever properties mint tea actually has, turning a horse into a permanent Mr Hyde is not one of its best.

It's not just Junior, though, who was affected by the weather – we were all going a little stir crazy, even those who were used to it. Jean-Paul owns a farm nearby and he also supplies us with hay for the horses and *pousse d'épine* (a homemade liqueur made from blackthorn shoots) for aperitif. From the start he and his extended family – he is Brigitte the *nourrice*'s father – have made us feel welcome and helped us out when we needed it, but he's knocking on is Jean-Paul, a dead ringer for Albert Steptoe, and his behaviour is sometimes, erm, erratic. As such, it wasn't entirely a surprise when he wandered unannounced into the lounge just after New Year looking for his waders – what was more of a shock was when he asked me to help him put them on.

It took me nearly ten minutes just to get his boots off, but the process of actually getting him into the waders, which clearly weren't his as they were at least five sizes too big for him, was one of the most undignified half-hours of my life. This short, stocky Frenchman barking orders at me to pull harder and do it this way, not like that, like this, hold that, not there! I felt like a serf getting his knight ready for battle and in the end he looked utterly ridiculous; the massive pair of waders made him look like the cruel victim of a shrinking experiment or a small boy in his dad's clothes. I pointed out to him that the waders wouldn't be very effective in water because they weren't the right size, something I immediately regretted saying as I suspected he'd agree and ask me to get him out of them. He looked at me like I was an idiot. 'I'm not going anywhere near water!' he said, rolling his eyes at my obvious stupidity. 'I'm going to kill a rat!'

'Oh,' I said, 'there was a mouse in my car the other day.' Again, he just stared at me. I wasn't making it up, I know it sounds like one of those sentences you say in a foreign language because they are the only words you know like 'the castle is open on Sundays' or 'I have a blue bicycle', but it was true, I had had a mouse in the car the other day. It lives under the bonnet and has eaten through the heat lining and some cables, but I hadn't told Natalie for obvious reasons and Jean-Paul wasn't that interested either.

He leaned closer to me and narrowed his eyes, 'a rat!' he seethed and spread his hands out to show how big it was. He cackled, said a cheery '*Merci*' and waddled off to face what I can only imagine was a quite ferocious rodent and leaving me utterly baffled by the whole episode.

By now, I was ready for a lie down, but there was a lot to do preparing for the next day, what with birthdays and the first day back at school after the Christmas holidays.

'Ian, come and look at this.' My heart sank. It was the way Natalie said it. I knew it wasn't good, it wasn't an 'I've found a four-leafed clover' come and look at this, it was more of a 'there's something amiss here' come and look at this. Had I known then that it was a 'take a look at Junior's dangle' come and look at this, I wouldn't have gone and looked at that at all. 'I think there's something wrong with his willy,' she said.

Firstly, 'willy' seems highly inappropriate to describe a muscle that when fully extended, and it often is, the randy old sod, is actually thicker and longer than my arm. 'Willy' suggests something cute and manageable, not this brute of an appendage. And secondly, Junior tries to attack me when I approach him with food for heaven's sake; the chances of him lying back and thinking of England, or France or Norway for that matter, as I try to get a closer look at his love baguette were pretty slim, so I kept my distance.

'Looks alright,' I said, watching Junior watching me.

'Hmm,' said Natalie, 'looks like it needs cleaning to me. Anyway, look at this as well.' She pointed to Junior's rump where there were a series of cuts on each side, 'Ultime has them too.' My first thought was that we had some kind of horse-arse equivalent of crop circles, something other-worldly and unfathomable, but Natalie knew better having already done some investigating. The horses, clearly feeling that their sex life needed a lift and presumably having watched Pierrot get off by rubbing himself on anything and everything, had taken to doing the same on tree stumps and had cut themselves in the process to such an extent that their wounds needed cleaning and treating.

Natalie stomped off leaving me eye to eye with Junior in the stable. 'Where are you going?' I asked.

'I'm going to Google how to clean these wounds. And cleaning his "thing".' She shouted over her shoulder leaving me and Junior for the first time in our relationship near to some kind of understanding.

'She's going to search the internet for horses' willies,' I said to Junior matter-of-factly.

'Yup,' he seemed to reply.

The rain just wouldn't relent; even the pond in our garden had reached worryingly high levels. In the summer it looks like an asteroid crater with a puddle at the bottom, due to the water table in that part of the garden being quite low, but that didn't stop our predecessors filling the thing with goldfish. Every year they seemed to hibernate in the mud at the bottom, the water being completely frozen, and re-emerge bigger in the summer. That wasn't going to happen this year. The water was high enough to have engulfed the bench that Natalie had erected and a heron had feasted on the entire fish population, no doubt this being the first year he could see the things. Meanwhile the current in the Cher must have been making river fishing more dangerous than usual, even for a water bird.

Natalie was surprisingly indifferent to this massacre; I'd assumed that on hearing the news she'd be straight off to the local Fish Rescue Centre and come back with an angry, maladjusted carp or something, but no. She'd been oddly quiet about animal adoption over Christmas and the New Year, and it left me uneasy, like something was in the offing.

Despite everyone in the family, Natalie's parents included, being aware of my jumpiness around this time of year and the fact that the weather itself was depressing, it was apparently 'no way any excuse' for the quite 'appalling' birthday cards I had bought. And to be fair, they were bloody awful. I'm willing to go out on a limb here: women are good at choosing cards and men aren't, simple as that. In the same way that packing a car boot effectively is purely a male preserve, women have a nose for the right card and also have the common sense to buy blank message cards if, as is normally the case, the printed message is so cloying it makes you feel like you've been licked all over by a slobbery dog.

The French don't really do cards. A neighbour popped round for my birthday just before Christmas and despite being there specifically for my birthday she still asked what all the cards were for.

'Well, they're for Ian's birthday!' Natalie said.

'Oh,' she said, 'why?'

I'm definitely with the French on this one. The proliferation of celebration days just to sell more cards is ridiculous; birthdays are understandable, Father's Day and Mother's Day tolerable, Grandparent's Day laughable and things like Secretary's Day utterly risible. No doubt in the Hallmark head office they're constantly sending each other cards congratulating themselves on such a preposterously successful wheeze. The cards that are on offer in French shops are pretty thin on the ground and pretty ropy too, but we have an English background, so saying to your wife on her birthday that you didn't get her a card because you couldn't find one simply doesn't wash. Believe me, I've tried.

In hindsight, though, I did outdo myself. I spent ages in Super U trying to choose the damn things, but after a while you just become card blind and all judgement (what little I have in these matters) flies out of the window. For instance, Natalie's card appeared to have traffic lights on it, glittery traffic lights, and a picture of the kind of flowers that give flora a bad name – garish, gaudy things like inbred orchids from the wrong side of the tracks; the kind of flowers that would wear a low-cut top while working behind a bar, all wrinkly décolletage.

Samuel's was worse.

He was on the cusp of his early teens, a mature and sensible boy, serious-minded beyond his tender years, but he was on that rickety bridge between being a little boy and thinking he's an adult. As a result, choosing his card was always going to be a thorny issue. I didn't want to patronise him with pictures of clowns and balloons but neither did I want to weigh him down with images of champagne flutes and ties. I thought I'd chosen well; he'd recently developed serious computer skills, making his own films and uploading them to YouTube and so on, so I thought a laptop-themed card was ideal. It was only when I got it home that I realised that a picture of an early, massive laptop with an obviously adult hand hovering over the keyboard actually suggested a 'Beware of Predatory Grown-Ups on the Internet' campaign rather than being a 'Hey! It's Your Birthday!' effort.

In the end though, none of it really mattered.

As usual, I had 4 January all planned: Samuel and Maurice would be at school until late afternoon and Natalie and I were to have lunch and spend the day with Thérence trawling various garden centres. I was in the kitchen that morning and I heard Natalie screaming down to me that Toby was barking. I didn't think anything of it as Toby, when not being constantly surprised by his own tail, barks a lot – I just assumed it was the postman arriving. I went out to find Toby in something of a state and Natalie shouting from a first-floor window that one of the cats had been hit by a car, but that she didn't know which one or where it was. I found the poor cat by our own car near the gate and it had clearly been hit so hard that it had been thrown almost back to the house. I could see no obvious signs of injury, though, and the poor thing was still breathing so I ran off to get its bed to rush it to the vet. By the time I got back it was dead and Natalie was holding it in her arms sobbing.

We live in a very rural area, but almost because of that the road is *more* dangerous because there are fewer traffic police around; the traffic might be less frequent but, certain in the knowledge that they won't be caught speeding, cars drive at ridiculous speeds. But worse, worst of all, it was Fox that had died, and Fox was Samuel's cat.

Telling your son on his birthday that his beloved cat has been run over and killed is a truly gut-wrenching thing to have to do. We toyed briefly with the idea of not telling him until the day after, but that would never have worked as he would have asked where Fox was. We were all there, Natalie and me and her parents too. He was distraught. He's since said that he just wanted his birthday to end there and then, that he'll never forget Fox and that he will always think of him on that day. Like I say, he's a serious-minded boy, mature beyond his years and I believe him. How could you not now associate your birthday with this event? For the rest of his life a little part of him will always be sad on his birthday, and on that day he will always remember Fox.

Maybe I was projecting too many of my own feelings on to Samuel, in my mind saddling him with a never-ending grief that would resurface every year. Taking my anger and bitterness at the injustice of life and the world and passing it on to my first born. Maybe. But it was so difficult to watch my beloved son, so young, hurting so much and on his special day. And like his dad, he's not one to let things go.

In many ways he actually dealt with the aftermath better than I did, trying to be positive and remember the good times with Fox rather than the end, though he did take to wearing Fox's collar which was a bit of a concern. He looked a bit like a trainee emo, wearing a sullen expression and a collar, though it was on his wrist, and it was luminous with a bell. All the cats have bells on their collars to give the local bird population a fighting chance. With Samuel having taken to wearing the now sadly unemployed collar, it was difficult to tell whether the remaining cats were upstairs wrestling somewhere or if Samuel was just energetically venting his anger and frustration on the Wii. Wearing the collar seemed to give him some kind of catharsis – he took it off after a week or two – and maybe Fox's death actually affected me more in the long run.

The winters seemed to be getting longer and harder with every year. I was leaving home early, and in the dark, to arrive somewhere else in the dark to stay in bland hotels and make other people laugh. I left home for work on more than one occasion in tears, wrenching myself away from my loved ones and every time with dark thoughts in my head, ridiculously, about whether I'd ever even see them again. A cat had died, but for a time (as the constant merry-go-round of travel took its toll) I built it into so much more as Fox's death left its mental mark on all of us. It also left its physical scars too. You try digging a grave in frozen ground when it's −10°C.

THE NAPOLEONIC CODE-BREAKER

Keen as we were to begin work on the 'school', Fox's death brought with it more pressing matters. Natalie decided that the cats now had to become house cats, whether they liked it or not, a situation which they obviously found quite confusing since they were born feral, brought inside, sent outside when they became too boisterous and were now inside again. The ruthless weather meant that they weren't too fussed about being indoors, though, and even if they had been I'm not sure I'd have been able to tell the difference. All cats it seems have the demeanour of truculent teenagers and a permanent look of 'yeah, like whatevah'. They certainly don't give much away; they would be good at poker would cats.

The other change was to have the surviving cats neutered, which had always been on the cards anyway with the appointment booked for the following week. And we still wanted to go ahead with that. We'd been told that it would calm them down a bit and mean that

Flame especially wouldn't be tempted to spray. Spraying being a cat's calling card as it were, containing all the details another cat may need to know, like your age, sex etc. and presumably that you have a nasty habit of making furniture smell like acid wee. It's a filthy business and my wardrobe, following 'Spraygate' on Christmas Day, was demanding action.

The French have a strange attitude to neutering that hovers between ambivalence and outright hostility. For the most part those who have animals around us here have working animals, hunting dogs for instance, but there is a definite reluctance to have male animals castrated. The French do not want the 'maleness' removed from their male animals, even if that means dealing with the inevitable consequences further down the line. It is considered an affront to all males, animal or human.

I had some experience of this, as in the previous year I'd had a vasectomy. There, I said it out loud. Ever since I'd had 'le snip' I kept it as something of a secret because of the taboo nature of the subject in France. We'd even kept it a secret from the boys in case they said something about it at school; it really is that sensitive a subject. The reasons for having a vasectomy may, on the face of it, have been 'new man' altruism, 'long term the pill can't be that good for you, love', 'let me take the burden of contraception' etc. etc. but it was actually selfishness. I have three lovely children, I love them dearly – but three is enough, I've done my bit and it's time to let somebody else fight the good fight. And if I hadn't taken the decision to have a vasectomy there would still be that possibility...

And I couldn't allow that to happen.

Here are some facts. According to the World Health Organisation and their 'official' figures there are no vasectomies in France at all. None. Officially it doesn't happen. Vasectomies only became legal in France in 2001, as up until then it was considered to be self-harm and therefore against the Napoleonic Code. My arguments against this are numerous. Firstly, it's not 'self-harm' – quite the opposite, this is 'self-preservation', particularly in respect of my sanity. Also, what do you mean by 'self-harm'? Am I doing the operation myself? And anyway, the Napoleonic Code was established in 1804 as a central codifying of numerous local, sometimes, conflicting by-laws, so it's time to move on, right? Time to look at old laws through modern eyes, after all this is the twenty-first century, we can move on, can't we? Our local doctor, it turns out, is a big fan of the Napoleonic Code.

'Never,' he said, genuinely astonished and quite flustered, 'never, in over forty years as a doctor has a man, a REAL man, asked for this!' We tried to put our case to him but he was having none of it and he leaned forward conspiratorially. 'You,' he pointed at me, 'you could still have children, for years to come.' He leaned back again. 'Your wife, no.'

I was stunned. Not only had he said this to me but he had said it in front of Natalie, who was sitting next to me – and via Natalie, as she was translating! There is no pun intended when I say that one almost has to admire the balls of the man, but there's also a certain irony in that I had to restrain Natalie from performing exactly the kind of operation on him that he was so dead against.

Reluctantly, and with a look on his face that suggested that this was indeed the 'end of days', he referred us to a specialist; in fact, he was so upset that for the first time ever we left his surgery without a prescription for something, though if he could have had had me incarcerated I'm sure he would have done so. The specialist was equally zealous about vasectomies. We knew something was wrong when we were kept waiting an hour beyond our appointment time in the gloomy, 1960s clinic waiting room. French doctors tend to play a bit fast and loose with punctuality at the best of times, but the previous 'patient' had left earlier and no-one else had gone in. The harassed-looking specialist, however, kept emerging from his office and welcoming in some sharp-suited individuals. We couldn't work out what was going on but it was all quite comical, and he reminded me a bit of Peter Falk in *Columbo*. The delay, it turned out, was because he needed to clarify his legal position. 'Legally,' he began, quite flustered, avoiding my eye and constantly referring to a tall man next to him who was clearly a lawyer of some kind, 'legally, I don't have to perform this operation.' I stared at him and couldn't help laughing which only made him more distressed. 'And ethically, it's against everything I stand for!' He said with a flourish and opened his office door to indicate that the interview was at an end.

'This is ridiculous!' Natalie said to him, also trying to suppress a laugh. 'We told your secretary over the phone why we wanted to see you, why didn't she tell us then that you don't perform vasectomies?'

Even the word seemed to wound him and he visibly winced. 'She doesn't need to know about my affairs!' he replied huffily.

Has any man ever tried so hard to have a vasectomy? It wasn't, believe me, a masochistic pursuit to have my giblets mucked about with; it became more a quest to see just how wound up some French people could get. Granted, I could have chosen other ways to annoy the natives – walking into a restaurant and declaring oneself a teetotal vegetarian would have had much the same effect and would hurt the French psyche just as easily.

It was another three months before we finally found a surgeon prepared to perform the operation and who, surprisingly, after all we'd been through so far, wasn't a back-street practitioner reeking of gin, but a modern doctor who claimed that many of his colleagues were living in the past. It's a simple procedure, he purred, you'll be in and out in a day, up and about in another two days and within a week you'll be back to normal. This matched all the (very) extensive research I'd done: a simple procedure, a bit of discomfort for a couple of days and no complications. Well, almost no complications. A tiny percentage. You'd be very unlucky to be in that tiny minority. Really. It never happens. Well, it hardly ever happens.

A week after the operation I was back in hospital with the doctor shaking his head, muttering something about this never having happened to him before, like he was the one in pain. I had developed a blood clot in my testicles and it stayed for a further month, time, apparently being the only healer. I don't want to linger on the details of this, but let me put it this way, you only really get an idea of how limited the legroom is on an aeroplane when your genitals are the size and colour of an aubergine. I'll leave it at that.

My point in all this is that the French are not only reluctant to neuter man or beast; they don't seem to be very good at it either. And does it really have the desired effect anyway? Junior is a gelding and about as wild and boisterous as any 'fully-equipped' horse; Toby is neutered and hasn't calmed down at all, I have been emasculated but I was pretty docile beforehand and not given to spraying unless there was an overwhelming need to do so. The more I think about it, the more convinced I am that poor Fox saw the writing on the wall and just took the easier way out. And if you think that all the rigmarole is probably designed to put you off having the operation in the first place then the post-operative care is there to remind you that nobody, nobody likes the decision you made.

A few months after the operation, and once the aubergine had withered to prune-like proportions, I was sent an appointment card to have tests to see if the vasectomy had worked or not. Following the initial conversation with our local doctor I was surprised that these tests didn't involve shacking me up with an aggressively fertile young woman to see if I made her pregnant or not; no, I had to visit a *laboratoire d'analyses*. Not my local *laboratoire d'analyses* but one a half-hour drive away, presumably to protect me from local gossips identifying the nature of my visit.

So I headed off with my dictionary, which unsurprisingly was pretty low on masturbation vocabulary. I obviously knew what would be involved in the test, namely that I'd have to produce a sperm sample, I just didn't think I'd feel quite so seedy, no pun intended. I was greeted coldly by the stern receptionist who told me to wait; I was the only one there, adding to the sense that I was some kind of pariah. The wait was mercifully short and the smiling, quite slick-looking doctor showed me into a small room directly opposite the receptionist. Sit down, he said, relax. I just need to ask a few simple questions: 'What's your full name?' he said. 'Your date of birth? When did you last ejaculate?' Simple, straightforward questions, the kind that always crop up between men.

Then he got down to the nitty-gritty. 'This is what you do,' he said. 'Wash your hands,' and he pointed to a tiny corner sink, 'rub this solution on your "gland",' pointing to what looked like a hand-soap dispenser and then my 'gland', 'and then masturbate into this *flacon*,' again needlessly pointing at the thing. 'Close the *flacon*,' he continued, 'place it on the counter and leave.' He didn't say 'quietly and with your head hanging low' but he may as well have. 'Oh, and by the way', he added, almost as an afterthought as he was about to leave and opening the bottom drawer of the desk, 'here is some *matériel suggestif. Au revoir.*' And he was gone.

The whole thing just felt so dirty. The *matériel suggestif* was all American for some reason; the French clearly feeling that their own pornography was too good for vasectomy-requesting milksops like me. But these *Playboy* and *Penthouse* magazines, with their ridiculous-looking, oiled-up mannequins with fake breasts and no pubic hair felt so out of place here in rural France and the fact that this plastic, generic vision of woman was all that was on offer to me just added to my sense of complete displacement. Here I was, in a sterile cupboard in the Loire Valley being told to 'fiddle the flesh flute' into a cup and then to leave without fuss. It all felt so grubby and undignified, like I was the victim of some particularly sordid hidden-camera TV show. I have never felt less aroused or more embarrassed; I have also, inexplicably, never felt more English or more foreign.

I can't remember how long I was in there and I think I spent more time washing my hands than anything else which, as any man will tell you, is a fatal thing in a tiny wash-hand basin: as I was preparing to leave I noticed the water had splashed all over the front of my beige trousers. Bearing in mind what I was in this room to do, this was the final ignominy and certainly not a good look.

I unlocked the door and was confronted by the receptionist, still on her own, but thankfully, given my appearance, refusing to look up from her notes.

'*Au revoir, Monsieur,*' she said coldly.

'*C'est tout?*' I asked and for the life of me I don't know why.

'*Oui,*' she replied, looking up and at the same time seeing the 'mess' I was in. Her lip curled in total disgust, '*Au revoir, Monsieur.*'

I scuttled shamefacedly out of the building, embarrassed at my own embarrassment and although that town isn't very far from us, with a nice little chateau and a welcoming brasserie, I have never been back there and never will.

In short, although I'm sure that Flame and Vespa are incapable of feeling the kind of shame that I felt, the whole issue was more sensitive than it had previously been and I felt for them as I dropped them off at the vet's to be physically butchered and mentally scarred by the French and their old-fashioned attitude to manliness and reproduction.

'You know what? I think there's a touch of early spring in the air,' I said, trying to lighten the mood when I returned from the vet's that evening with two shocked and sleepy cats. I looked around at Natalie and the boys but saw nothing that qualified as a response. 'Don't you think? Definitely spring-like.' Still nothing. 'No? Just a little bit?'

Maurice sneezed so hard his face nearly fell off and it served as a collective response; I was definitely the only one feeling 'springish'.

In hindsight it may have been some sort of tiredness-induced mirage that had taken over my senses. I had been in London at the Comedy Store the previous weekend and had yet to acclimatise to life on the road again after the festive break. I had wrapped up the late show at about half-two on Sunday morning, finally fallen asleep at five, was up at seven for the Eurostar and had arrived at Vierzon station on Sunday afternoon to be met by Natalie and the boys and their attendant germ cloud. Natalie was clearly suffering from a heavy cold as was Maurice, though neither of them was letting it get to them unduly; Natalie, believing that all forms of illness are a sign of weakness, and Maurice not interested in anything that may slow him down. Thérence was fast asleep in his car seat, though by the look of his cheeks was teething again and Samuel was glowering out of the window clearly resentful of the fact that he was feeling perfectly fine and so would definitely be going to school the next day. Though obviously pleased to see me after a few days away, they weren't a happy bunch.

I wasn't feeling too great either. One of the many fallouts from my vasectomy was that I had started to put on weight and I had chosen this week to start a diet and exercise regime, though to be honest 'chosen' here is a euphemism for 'badgered into'. A few years in France had taken their toll, and actually my lifestyle on the road doesn't help either, with irregular meals, little exercise and late-night drinking; but add to that years of freshly baked baguette, heavy cheese consumption and playing a leading role in increasing the local wine sales had left me teetering on the cusp of the social oxymoron that is 'Fat Mod'. There seems to be a perception of France that everybody is chic and sleek, but away from the Boulevard Haussmann it's largely a myth. There was a book out a few years ago seeking to explain how French women stay so slim, when the answer is that actually they don't, certainly no more than any other Western nation. Even the book concluded that it had a lot to do with wearing tight underwear. And if you pretty much restrict your research to a certain class of women who pick at their lunch in the finest Parisian brasseries then obviously you'll conclude it's a nation of Carla Brunis with nary an Ann Widdecombe in sight. French society is really no different from any other developed nation – it is putting on weight at an alarming rate. And whereas once obesity may have been frowned upon, or mocked, it is becoming increasingly the norm.

It became clear by the Tuesday morning, however, that item one on my exercise timetable – 9 a.m. Remove Clothes from Exercise Bike – was going to have to wait. Natalie had, despite my entreaties to 'man up', succumbed to gastric flu and was, against her will, bedridden, leaving me to deal with the boys and the animals.

Samuel and Maurice need to be up at seven, so that they have time to get ready and breakfast properly in time for school. I got them up at half past, thinking that they might operate better under pressure, but as it turned out Maurice was quite clearly too ill to go anywhere, despite his protestations. Samuel treats mornings with the disdain they deserve and needs to be cajoled constantly as he has a habit of falling back to sleep while getting dressed, but he made the bus, just.

I put the dogs outside so that I could feed the cats whose litter tray looked and smelt like an open sewer, but which would have to wait until I had the fortitude to deal with it. Next, I went out and got the logs and kindling for the fire and returned to find Maurice on the sofa, half dressed, nose and eyes streaming. Then Thérence started giving off, so I got him up, gave him his milk and got him dressed. He was still teething and his nappy contained what appeared to be the results of a chemical-warfare cowpat experiment. I decided to skip breakfast.

The temperature outside was −3°C so I let the dogs back in, which was a mistake. At first I thought the post-op drowsy cats and Thérence had got together to form a dirty protest somewhere, the stench was so numbing, but it was actually Pierrot's breath! He has a tendency to eat any carrion he finds, no matter what state it's in, and it was taking its toll. Put together with his offputting sexual habits the old boy was something of a disgrace, a bit like Regency period aristocracy – he looks nice from a distance but you wouldn't want to get too close. I put Maurice back to bed and decided to take Thérence and the dogs for a walk to get some fresh air.

'Don't forget to take the cats,' Natalie called croakily from her bed.

In my absence Natalie had bought the remaining cats leads. A nice idea in theory and one I hope she'll enjoy the benefit of, but I was still at the very limit of acceptable eccentricity in the opinion of the locals, so I would not be walking the cats. Our neighbours are all hunters – they own firearms – the temptation would be simply too great. Besides which, the cats were still too 'ginger' to be going out and needed a couple more days of rest to recover from their travails.

Going out had an immediately soothing effect. It was a sunny day, cold but invigorating, and Thérence and I watched some deer running and jumping in the next field. Deer are naturally skittish creatures but clearly something had startled them, Pierrot's breath perhaps; I couldn't see any hunters out. Then I realised I'd lost Toby. Sure enough, there he was at the back of the deer herd, barking maniacally at his inability to catch them up, and I could still hear him long after they'd all disappeared from view. I didn't see him again until dinner time.

On our return I hoovered up, made lunch and gave everyone their medicines. I fed the horses, which I'm pleased to say Ultime appreciated, though Junior, in a show of petulance that was needless even by his standards, tried to take a chunk out of my arm. I gave Thérence his milk and put him back to bed. I picked Samuel up, helped him with his homework, made him and Maurice an afternoon snack, got Thérence up, fed the cats and the dogs, made dinner, played with the boys, sprayed breath-freshener in Pierrot's face, washed Toby down on his return, bathed the boys, got them ready for bed, read them stories and opened a crate of beer fully intending to down the whole lot. The diet, I reasoned, could wait – I had too much to do.

The previous weekend I had done a day's filming – seven live shows in five days, a radio show and two showbiz parties – and considered myself to be on the brink of exhaustion. But it was nothing compared to just one day filling in for Natalie and her routine with the kids and animals. She joined me downstairs briefly to stock up on Advil. 'Don't forget tomorrow morning,' she said, 'Monsieur Butard is coming to give us a quote about the building.'

'Oh yes,' I replied, 'I'd forgotten.'

'And,' Natalie continued, wearily reaching the top of the stairs where she paused to get her breath back, 'we need to decide where to put the hens.' And with that she was gone.

This wasn't something I'd forgotten. This was news.

A BIRD IN THE HAND

It was clear that a decision on hens had been taken with me *in absentia*, and that any opinions I might have on the subject, like whether I felt we had enough livestock to be getting on with, were now an irrelevance. The most I could hope for was to put it off for a while, call for the family equivalent of a public inquiry and just delay things until spring at least. The early year weather was atrocious and, I argued, we should wait until we were outdoors more so that we could make the hens feel at home. It would also give us more time to research exactly what looking after hens entailed.

Subterfuge and chicanery are the only ways to operate sometimes. My family did it with me to get what they wanted and Natalie and I were doing it with Monsieur Butard in order to chivvy him along with a building quote.

'What sort of thing are you looking for?' he asked over the phone, already weighing up whether it was worth coming out to give us a quote or not, or whether to just amble by over the next few weeks, if he had the time.

'Total renovation of the *dépendances*,' Natalie said, 'to create a classroom, an office, a kitchen area and four or five en-suite bedrooms.'

'I'll be there after lunch,' Butard said, excitedly.

In truth, we did want a quote for all of that, but we knew that for now it was beyond our means and that a classroom/office would be the first stage. Butard arrived shortly after lunch, wheezing heavily, not because he'd rushed round but because since we'd seen him last he had ballooned in size. He was still the only serious builder in town but the suspicion was that he may have spent the last three or four years literally devouring the opposition.

He tapped walls, needlessly measured windows that would have to come out, shook his head, sucked his teeth and all the while took extensive notes on the 'project'. It would be two phases, we said, first the classroom/office and then once that was done we could set a timetable for the rest of the work. Butard looked at us both over his glasses; he wasn't fooled at all but there was the prospect that further on down the line he may hit the jackpot with us so he was happy to play along. He would have a quote for us in a week, he said, which meant three if we chased him up, and that his 'Phase one could start just after Easter and would be finished by June' – also optimistic. It was his turn to play games and we all knew that while June was technically possible, it was also unlikely in the extreme.

We had a sense that we had finally started on something and as we watched Butard wander slowly off to his van, totally unfazed by the howling gale that was buffeting the rest of us, Natalie and I looked at each other, pleased to be making progress, however slow that might be.

'Right, I'm going to make a dash for it,' I said, intending to go back to the warm indoors.

'I'll be along later,' Natalie said, tightening up her scarf and summoning up her outdoorsy courage.

Despite her flu Natalie alone was venturing outside in the bad weather, arguing reasonably that 'poo won't clear itself' and feeling that the horses could do with the company. The rest of us, though sheepishly in admiration of her fortitude, were staying indoors doing indoor things like guessing which cat had made that awful stench, running a book on which piece of furniture Pierrot would sexually assault next, moving Natalie's cushions about to see if she noticed and buying stuff we used to own anyway off eBay. We were bored and running out of patience, family goodwill and firewood, with winter showing little sign of clearing off just yet.

There was one faint sign of a slight thaw but it was an unwelcome one: the moles were back.

The mole, Latin name *Talpa europaea*, known colloquially as 'total and utter bastard', has had a pretty soft ride of it if you ask me. There's the sweet and cuddly mole from *The Wind in the Willows*, the sweet and cuddly Morocco Mole from *Secret Squirrel* and, er, the sweet and cuddly mole from *Secret Squirrel*; only recently, thanks to *South Park*, *G-Force* and *The Incredibles*, is the whole 'moles are

OK' fallacy being readdressed. And it's about time too. We have one sizeable piece of lawn that isn't given over to the horses and, because the ground had thawed enough for the moles to do their thing, it was beginning to look like it had been attacked by drunken *Time Team* researchers.

I despise moles.

Since we'd been here I had tried a variety of ways to get rid of them, ranging from the highly ineffectual to the 'box said it was poison, but it's clearly an aphrodisiac' variety. As far as removing the pests from the property went, I had run the full gamut of failure. They mock me with their tunnelling, sticking two fingers up to the purity of the Englishman and his lawn; and here they were, back again, and having a bloody Mardi Gras at my expense.

We've sought advice about them, but apparently they're the 'yeast infection' of the animal world, only ever temporarily removed. There is a local artisan whose entire business is devoted to mole extermination, which gives you some idea of the scale of the problem; he's a haunted individual, a sallow, sunken-eyed chain smoker who clearly started out with high ideals of laying the mole to waste, but who has been beaten down to a mere shell of a man by their sheer relentlessness. 'I could get rid of them,' he said, surveying the wasteland that was my lawn, 'but they'll be back.' He turned to me, tears in his eyes. 'They'll always be back.'

Another expert suggested explosives, at which point you are probably thinking to yourselves that that sounds a bit drastic, which it is. But who hasn't wanted to play with explosives at some point? I for one couldn't wait. Obviously, there are certain safety measures that have to be observed, but none of them really ruin the fun; keep the kids indoors, animals on leads, don't get blottoed on local wine before you rig it all up etc. I've found that it all adds to the excitement of the exercise really.

I unearthed a tunnel, placed the explosive at the mouth of it, primed it like David Niven in *Guns of Navarone*, and from the safety of the lounge and with binoculars at the ready, waited. Boom! A small discharge of soil went flying into the air! 'Haha!' I shouted. 'Death to moles! Victory is mine!' and then I saw a tunnel being made in double quick time away from the supposed death charge, the mole playing Roadrunner to my bested Wile E. Coyote. I laid another, and then another – all with the same ineffectual result. Six bloody charges I laid in one afternoon and the mole was still there at the end of the day, burrowing away just below the surface, unharmed, unfazed and utterly superior. Between us we had completely destroyed the garden; it looked like a World War One battlefield. It is the same dance every year and it doesn't matter what I try, my defeat is inevitable.

We got off on the wrong foot you see.

Before we had the horses, we just had a great expanse of land that constantly needed mowing and that meant the dreaded *tondeuse*, the sit-down mower from hell. The final indignity occurred one spring when I was once again reluctantly mowing the field. As I went under a fruit tree one of the front wheels went down a mole tunnel and bounced back up throwing me into the air. My head hit a branch whereupon my headphones got tangled up and trapped, I was yanked from the mower onto the ground, one half of my headphones still on my head, the other half dangling mockingly from the tree. The mower continued on its merry way, clearly better at the job unencumbered by me. I chased after it, turned it off and never got on the bloody thing again. Maybe I was a bit concussed but I swear I could hear moles laughing.

I can't even argue that the moles could make the horses lame with their indiscriminate burrowing because, and I just cannot fathom this out, they don't go in the horses' field! Whether they have come to some kind of arrangement I don't know, but the moles stick to the lawn and Junior and Ultime have no fear of injury.

The moles also had allies in their campaign of terrorism – the cats. I don't know what I expected from cats, but outright disobedience is something I just cannot tolerate. I don't put up with it in audiences, children, mechanical objects or cravats, but I was finding that cats operate on a whole other level of nihilism and we were beginning to clash. The idea of turning Flame and Vespa into house cats had presented its own problems. Firstly they liked going out and secondly they were acting like they owned the bloody place whenever they were inside. I had set up a nice quiet little corner for myself, built a desk, bought a pen tidy, etc. but the place was now virtually unusable as Vespa insisted on ambushing me from the adjacent banister every time I sat down to work. At one point I was woken up in the middle of the night by Vespa, who was perched on my bedside table slurping noisily from my glass of water. 'You shouldn't have left it there,' Natalie said and went back to sleep. Their worst crime by far, however, one that was simply unacceptable, was that they were still jumping up on to the kitchen surfaces. To give you an insight as to how this was making me feel, imagine Al Pacino saying 'On to the kitchen surfaces!' the same way he said 'In my home, Rocco!' in *The Godfather Part II*. It made me very angry indeed. Natalie said it was my fault for leaving food out. It's a bloody kitchen! Where the hell else was I supposed to leave it, the bathroom?

I'd tried water pistols, rolled-up newspaper and simply batting them back down with my hand the second they landed, but nothing, nothing seemed to work. Are cats even trainable? Does anyone know? Has anyone ever got a cat to do anything against its will? (And I mean house-cats not lions and the like, they're pussies.) As far as I'm concerned domestic cats seem to just slink their way through life putting two fingers up to authority and offering a big 'yah boo sucks' to any sense of order and propriety whatsoever. Dogs can be trained – dogs want to please their master, the important word being 'master' as dogs are very aware of hierarchy and their position within it. If cats are aware of hierarchy at all it's simply that every other creature is beneath them. Cats are French.

I've had success training dogs, the only failure being Volcan. He was quite wild when we first got him and a local Brittany spaniel 'expert' suggested we try an electronic collar to train him properly – the idea being that whenever the dog is disobedient you press a button on your remote control pad and the collar gives the dog a short, sharp shock. It's as Draconian as it sounds and we weren't very keen from the start, preferring instead to offer treats for obedience rather than pain for the opposite. Also, every time we pressed the button, the television would turn off and the car boot would open. We tried it on a walk once and felt very uncomfortable about the whole thing, and after a good long chat when we got back we decided that we wouldn't pursue it. Unfortunately what we hadn't realised was that a then two-year-old Maurice had wandered off with the remote while we were in earnest debate and was subjecting the poor beast, quite unknowingly, to an absolute barrage of electric shocks to the extent that by the time we found the beleaguered creature cowering in the hay barn he looked less like a proud Brittany spaniel and more like Britney Spears after a rough night out. Our relationship never really recovered from that, though he would always do what Maurice told him to do.

We had started putting the cats outside more and more, much to Samuel's quite understandable horror, but they just couldn't stand being cooped up all day and I couldn't stand being cooped up with them all day; and they also seemed to have a decidedly laissez-faire attitude to what

I thought would be their main occupation, namely rat destruction. Don't get me wrong, it was a big rat and it scared the life out of me when I found it nibbling on my winter quince stock, but I reckon that if the cats had got together and worked as a team they could have brought it down. As it was, they just watched it at work, all cat-rodent harmony like a bloody Disney film or something. Unfortunately for them though this big love-in was short-lived; the weasel arrived.

I was genuinely excited by the weasel. He was, and let me make this quite clear, a nasty little bleeder. Venture out at night and the screams from various creatures being attacked and, as is the weasel's wont, decapitated were really quite horrific coming at you out of the chilly, misty night air. I imagine it was like Victorian London when the Ripper was on the prowl. But to give him his due, since his arrival there had been no sign of the rat. Now whether the weasel had given him a right good seeing to and the rat was no more, or whether the rat had taken one look at the weasel, who was about a quarter of the rat's size and thought, 'sod this for a game of soldiers, I'm off' is unclear as I didn't find any rat remains, but I wasn't quibbling.

What was clear, however, was that our set up – animals, fruit, warmth and so on – was attracting the hunters of the animal world. As winter continued to bite and natural prey was thin on the ground we were offering relatively rich pickings to the suffering local carnivores; pretty soon we would be literally chasing the wolves from the door.

I hadn't seen or even heard a fox since we had moved in; I'd come to believe that like coffee shops, immaculately kept 4x4s and socialism, foxes had become an entirely urban phenomenon. They are here though, just a little less brash than their town-dwelling cousins, and the big freeze was bringing them out of their shells. Toby heard it first and possibly even saw it through the door as it set off the night-time security lights, so as I came rushing downstairs to see what the fuss was all about and let Toby out into the cold night, the fox may already have scarpered. We heard it, though, a few minutes later – that arresting fox screech that sounds like a teething baby – but it was clearly moving further away, with Toby now patrolling the garden and making enough of a racket to act as deterrent.

It was a rare foray near to humans for a local fox, but needs must and he wasn't the only one who was suffering. Most of the bird population around here was too. The ponds and lakes were frozen over, the river running a fearfully dangerous current and the ground was, more often than not, covered in snow. We were trying to feed them but what with the cats jumping onto the bird table and Toby also trying to eat the bread we were leaving out, their rewards were marginal.

And for some it seems, it was all getting a little too much. Apparently some birds cannot make the distinction between what is genuine countryside and what, sadly, is a reflection. Either that or they had just had enough of the cold weather and, kamikaze style, were flying into the large lounge windows on a regular basis. There would be a resounding thud, then echoes through the house as the poor creature bounced back off, dazed and confused. Some of the smaller ones even died. The bigger ones eventually picked themselves up, shook themselves off and tottered away like a happy drunk at the end of the evening, but some needed extra help.

I was sitting with my back to the barn doors reading when a thud hit the window so hard I almost felt it. I immediately hit the ground, for some reason thinking we were under attack, and it took a few moments for me to realise what had happened. An adult kingfisher had hit the window with such force that it had knocked itself out, but as it lay there, its beautiful blue-orangey coat shimmering, I could see that its tiny chest was still moving. I don't know what I thought I could do, but I certainly couldn't leave it where it was so I went outside and picked the poor thing up.

It was definitely still breathing, and quickly too which I considered, based on no kingfisher-related medical knowledge whatsoever, to be a good sign. I decided to take it down to the pond and just sat there with it in my hand for a while. I didn't like the angle its neck was at, it looked like it may be broken, and I knew sooner or later I would have to make a decision: leave it to itself, put it out of its misery or, at the risk of being laughed at in a harsh countryside community, take it to the vet.

Then, slowly, it opened its eyes. For another five minutes it just lay there like it was coming out of a coma and didn't want to rush things, its breathing became less hurried which I now decided was better than the other way around and then very slowly, very gingerly it began to move its head as though testing each part of its battered body. It seemed to be flexing its little feet too. It obviously felt safe with me – it didn't panic or try and rush its recovery, it was like you or me waking up with a biting hangover, every movement was done slowly, methodically and then repeated to make sure its senses weren't playing tricks on it.

After a further ten minutes it stood up on my, by now, completely frozen hand, but still it didn't fly away. It was one of the most privileged moments of my life; this small, beautiful creature trusted me so much that it just sat there with me, on me even, while it got its breath back. And then it turned to look at me, chirruped a little bit and flew away, doing a few circles of the pond, flying quite close to me on each circuit and then went, gliding away into the darkening afternoon sky.

I stayed at the edge of the pond for a while longer, taking in what had just happened. The serenity of the moment was breathtaking, the silence of the frozen countryside adding an eerie atmosphere to the scene. It was taking me a long time to get used to country living – I am a city boy and was still happily surrounded by concrete and carbon monoxide every weekend at work – but this one moment was so affecting, so out of keeping with my work life, my image and my usually frenetic sense of order and angst, that it felt like a turning point. I was rescuing our injured feathered friends and harnessing the wild instincts of weasels; I was turning into (a better-dressed) Grizzly Adams or Dr Doolittle.

I felt something rub against my leg and looked down to see Pierrot 'enjoying' himself on my slippers. 'Oh, Pierrot,' I said, the moment with the kingfisher partly sullied, 'you really are a disgusting old man!' Dr Doolittle never had to say that.

THE OUT-OF-TOWNERS

'So you must know your wine, then?'

It's a question I'm often asked when people learn that I live in France, along with 'You must be fluent by now?', 'Why?' and 'What are the French like with you, because they hate us, don't they?' To which the answers in order are, don't be silly, don't be silly and don't be silly.

The answer to the wine question though is 'No', I do not 'know my wine'. I like wine and certainly since moving to the Touraine I have developed a taste for crisp, dry white wine to go with my only other previous wine preference of the catch-all 'a heavy Bordeaux'. I know nothing of grape, vintage, nose or assemblage. I am a happily ignorant amateur who occasionally stumbles upon a good wine (you know it's good because other people tell you it is) and has no idea how.

There is the myth of course that to find a good French wine you merely need to hang around the wine section of the supermarket long enough to see what the locals are buying, the logic being that they're French, they know what they're doing. It's a remarkable generalisation, a bit like saying that if you're not sure which firearm to purchase hang around the streets of Nottingham for a bit, or if you're unsure what shade of fake tan works best for the 'orange' look, visit Liverpool for the weekend. Not everybody in France knows about wine and loitering around the shop isn't always recommended anyway.

Natalie and the boys may get their fix from rescuing various animals and living the countryside to its flying, buzzing, itching extreme, but for me it's supermarkets. I have a weakness for French supermarkets, growing up they seemed incredibly exotic and offered far more in those days than their UK counterparts and though that is now the opposite (because you know, the English must have their kumquats in January) the love affair persists. Most of their products are now as ubiquitous in the UK as they are over here, for instance the local, world-famous goats' cheeses, the AOC Selles-sur-Cher and the AOC Valençay, are both readily available in most out-of-town supermarkets in England these days, though obviously at four times the price. Also, the loyalty schemes offered in French supermarkets are largely derisory affairs and customer service begrudging at best, but maybe that's another reason why I like them.

I asked an assistant in our local Super U if they had any more gin, as there was none on the shelf. He looked at the shelf perplexed and then wandered off, I thought to see if there was any in the warehouse, but he never came back. I quite admire that attitude. As someone who was sacked from Tesco three times, the second time for guessing the prices (a pre-barcode world, kids!), I have an affinity for low-level supermarket employee truculence.

Up to a point, that is. Things have changed in our local Super U, 'progress' has reared its ugly head and it just doesn't feel right. The self-service till has become something of a comedy cliché in a very short space of time, with most comedians having their own variant on the 'unexpected item in the bagging area' line. I know. I'm one of them. But while the self-service till has become ubiquitous in UK shops it is a rare thing indeed in France, especially in rural backwaters like ours. Until recently, that is. My own view is that they are actually not providing the speed of service that they are supposed to and are just another way for people to avoid any sort of human interaction with each other. Granted, checkout tills are operated either by the very young, who grunt at you and avoid eye contact fearing that they will be aged immediately just by looking at you, or the retired who, in my experience, only work on supermarket tills so that they can be judgemental about your purchases and mutter about the modern world going 'to hell in a handcart'.

But I prefer both of those options to the smooth-voiced female bullying you to get on a self-service till, and if the argument is to cut down on the number of staff needed then that palpably doesn't work either. On the face of it, self-service tills are giving the customer a level of autonomy, we are being trusted – well, if that's the case why are there so many customer service agents hanging around like guard dogs in a junk yard looking at you suspiciously, ready to pounce? The supermarkets don't trust their own staff on the tills and they don't trust us on them either.

The thing about the UK though is that we put up with these things; comedians will make sarcastic remarks about them, columnists will write visceral caustic pieces too and people will by and large agree, but that's it. It's why we've never had a revolution.

The French on the other hand...

The proliferation of speed cameras in France, while acknowledged generally as a good thing because they may save lives, is also seen as an invasion of privacy; a sneaky, cowardly attempt at law enforcement, where the police state spies on the ordinary working man through remote technology, unfair and un-French. As a result, the roadside cameras around us are constantly having to be replaced following acts of vandalism by people who presumably still hanker for the old-fashioned gendarme jumping out of a bush at you, telling you to slow down, lay off the Cognac at lunchtime and that'll be €30, *s'il vous plaît*.

And these people, in all probability, are the ones who even now are gathering in the fresh produce section of the local supermarket muttering darkly about slippery slopes and thin ends of wedges.

And then it happened. The place shut on a Sunday lunchtime and reopened on the Monday morning with a row of three shiny new self-service tills, only no-one went near them. It was a standoff. Despite being very busy, and only four tills being open, even customers with only one item preferred to wait behind other customers in the queue doing their weekly shop. Assistants were sent to speak to these people, to invite them to try out the new system and cajole them into breaking rank.

One old man reacted angrily by pointing out that he wasn't being paid to work on the till so why should he do all the work. The lady on the till was being paid, he said, gathering support for his cause, and he would not sentence her to unemployment by using 'your robots'. Other customers around him angrily voiced their support and clapped him on the shoulder, 'Bravo!' said one getting over-excited by the prospect of a bit of civil unrest.

In the first few days of their existence I didn't see anyone use them. Their shininess went unsullied and bagging areas were left without unidentified items as a war of attrition began to break out between old values and new ways. Slowly, though, as the supermarket realised that providing only one manned till at peak shopping times would do the trick, people began reluctantly to try the alternative. It was painful to watch. Previously proud and determined people started using the things sheepishly, avoiding eye contact with their comrades still queuing on the manned tills. The queues began to build on the new tills as friendships became strained in the community; one Parisian started berating the locals for taking too long on the self-service tills. 'This would never happen in Paris!' she said huffily, endearing herself to no-one. 'Go and do your shopping there then!' was the riposte.

In their first few weeks I saw one farmer punch a machine, people swear at the till's inability to realise that not everyone wants to put something in the bagging area and others just walk through without bothering to scan anything at all. They had to employ a security guard to stand with an assistant and install electronic gates that another assistant would release assuming the till had finished bullying you.

My guess is that these machines will go the same way as the local speed traps; some latter day Luddite will sneak up on one from behind, throw a bag over its head and beat it brutally with a big stick. The machine will fall, like a soured symbol of modernity and whine dolefully, 'Did you use your own bag?'

Anyway, it hasn't put me off. I am still in the supermarket a lot, partly because I like it and partly because having three growing boys at home is like catering for a plague of locusts, not to mention the dog food, cat food, horse food and wine stocks. As a result I'm there pretty much all the time and clearly therefore, not to be trusted. The fact that I'm there nearly every day and that I'm a man has apparently set some alarm bells ringing. Quite a lot of men actually stay in their cars and let their wives do the shopping, only emerging from the car in a cloud of Gauloises smoke to pack the boot and get their trolley euro back, they certainly don't do all the shopping themselves and dress as a 1960s English dandy. As a result, everybody who works in the supermarket thinks I'm up to no good.

It all stemmed from an incident a couple of years ago. I had picked up a television guide, moved on to the beer section and then placed a crate of beer on top of the magazine. At the till I then ripped off the beer crate barcode and handed it to the lady at the checkout forgetting all about the TV guide underneath. While unpacking the trolley into the car I noticed my mistake but probably wouldn't have done anything about it had Samuel not been with me. Some children are like the good angels that sit on the shoulder in *Tom and Jerry* cartoons and rather than explain to my son that taking the magazine was actually a small victory and that Daddy was 'sticking it to da man', it seemed easier and good parenting to go back, explain the error and pay for the thing.

It wasn't.

'So, you stole the magazine and you've come back to tell me?' The assistant said, looking over her glasses at me in time-honoured 'I'm going to condescend the hell out of you' fashion. This wasn't going to plan. I explained again what had happened but through a combination of poor French and her staggering disbelief that anyone would bother to own up to such a thing, she simply wasn't having any of it. Even Samuel explained, in obviously better French than mine, but it didn't change a thing; in fact, it just made things worse as she now regarded me as some sort of Fagin figure, using small children as a cover for my grand larceny.

Eventually she let us go, though without the magazine, clearly feeling that flicking wildly through TV channels without printed guidance was fair penance for our crime. It means that I'm a marked man. Every time I go there now I am asked to open my empty shopping bags at the till and to lift the beer crates to make sure that I'm not hiding anything underneath. They say that it's now store policy and that they're not singling me out, but I'm not convinced. Even new checkout assistants seem to know my reputation, it must be part of their training: they get tested on various apple varieties, how to swipe the barcode on a bag of pasta and oh, if you see this man, whereupon they'll be shown a grainy CCTV image of a mod, frisk him. Frisk him good.

Just before Christmas last year they employed someone to dress up as *le Père Noël* and wander around the shop with a microphone, asking customers a question which, if they got it right, earned them a free gift. It was actually quite intimidating to some people who clearly didn't want the fuss and he was given short shrift on a number of occasions. I found the whole thing quite amusing, an old-fashioned approach that was doomed to failure as you simply do not disturb the French when they're eating food or even, in this case, choosing it.

I didn't expect him to pick on me, but I was wrong. He cornered me near the tills one quiet afternoon when I had popped in just to get a few things that I'd forgotten the day before.

'*Bonne fête!*' he cried, a little too close for comfort and putting his hand on my trolley, a definite no-no in my opinion. '*Monsieur, une petite question...*'

I couldn't believe what he asked me: 'Who won the football World Cup in 1966?'

'*Angleterre,*' I replied suspiciously.

'*Oui, oui! Vous-avez gagné!*' he cried, and on this note of frenzy placed a child's stationery set in my trolley! It's a set-up, I thought, they're actually planting evidence on me now! I looked around nervously, waiting to see if *les flics* (the cops) were hiding behind the piled-up Christmas *bûches de Noël* and seasonal tins of *marrons*. They weren't, but still I felt uneasy going through the till, even though I explained with the help of Father Christmas why I wasn't paying for the stationery set.

It's all conspired to make me rather nervous about the place, and certainly if my intention one day was just to observe people and their purchases in the wine section I really think they'd ask me to leave. And really, is that the best way to buy wine? Just because a Frenchman likes it? They're French, they will, all of them, give the impression that they know their stuff; it's ingrained in the national character and good for them. I have never, in the years I've lived here, heard a French person admit to lacking in knowledge about wine and they are also fiercely patriotic about it too. Our local supermarket has until recently only stocked French wine choosing to ignore that there may even be others; it has now begrudgingly started stocking Lambrini as if to say, 'Look, this is the muck the others are making. Plebs.'

Following a local around the wine department presupposes that that person has good taste and not everybody has, and they are also sold on this myth themselves. I was in the supermarket one quiet Monday lunchtime, and as usual dressed more for a late-night Central London mod 'all-nighter' than shopping with farmers, and I noticed that I was being followed. Now obviously this isn't entirely unusual in the supermarket as they have it in their heads that I am a rampant shoplifter, but this wasn't an employee, this was a local and I could tell that she was checking out what wines I was looking at and then picking up the same ones. I played up to it for a while (and I hope she liked her selection) but really she would have been very disappointed by my wine-choice criteria.

I was looking for wines with rude names.

Look, what else have I got to go on? Like I said, I don't know about grapes or what was a good year; rude names are a starting point, that's all. I found a beauty, a red from the Languedoc-Roussillon region called Seigneur d'Arse, literally the Lord of Arse. I bought a couple of bottles, thinking that any more would open me up to claims of immaturity, fully intending to go back for a couple of cases later. Unfortunately, even later that day, they'd sold out, clearly to some other expat using the same childish wine selection technique as me.

I gave a bottle of Seigneur d'Arse to my friend and fellow comedian Paul Thorne, who is not only as puerile as I am but also considers himself to be something of a wine aficionado. Again, I haven't the knowledge to contradict him on this, but it seems his expertise manifests itself by asking 'What shiraz do you have?' then swilling the stuff around his mouth and declaring it to be 'metallic'.

Paul came out to stay while Natalie and the boys were away in England and the idea was to do a fair bit of wine-tasting – unfortunately things didn't quite go to plan. Like the rest of France I was under the weather as, according to the newspapers, we were in the grip of a gastric flu epidemic; Paul was walking into a germ factory and it didn't take long for the symptoms to make themselves abundantly clear. Both Paul and I have worked in India a lot, after the London Comedy Store opened a franchise there, and the anti-diarrhoea drug of choice is Smecta, a vile clay powder-like substance that as far I can tell simply builds a wall inside you and stops anything from coming out. It's effective if you take it regularly, but hardly conducive to a wine-tasting road trip and we decided to limit ourselves as sensibly as we could.

Sancerre is about an hour and a half away from home and seemed a 'reasonable' distance to travel bearing physical frailties in mind, Pouilly-sur-Loire would be an extra twenty minutes or so but worth it to go to the renowned

Chateau de Tracy and sample their Pouilly Fumé. So, though neither of us felt particularly well, we Smecta-d ourselves up and hit the road. It was a glorious crisp late winter's day and the countryside around Sancerre was simply stunning, it's much hillier than where we are, the green and brown forests on the hillside were breathtaking and occasionally the turrets of small chateaux would poke through the budding, very early spring colours, giving a hint at their hidden grandeur.

We reached the Chateau de Tracy just as they opened for the afternoon. We hadn't risked much of a lunch and though both of us were keen to taste the wine, we were feeling pretty rough by the time we arrived. We waited in the cellar to be served, both our stomachs gurgling mercilessly and the sound echoing off the chilled underground walls.

'You do the talking,' Paul said.

'Why? You know wine! All you need is the word *metallique*.'

'Because you're "fluent",' he said, sarcastically. Our stomachs gave a big heave-ho in unison just as a small woman approached.

'*Messieurs, bonjour, vous-connaissez notre vin?*'

'*Er, non.*' I replied, hoping I'd heard her correctly over the gastric cacophony.

'See? Fluent,' Paul said, smirking.

Despite not being in the best shape for a wine-tasting, what followed was sublime. Let me repeat that I know nothing about wine or viticulture, but the four wines we tasted were magnificent, each very different and each going up in price but, and I've never felt this way about wine before, the price was immaterial. The wines were superb and we bought bottles of each, not wanting to leave any behind. I've been wine-tasting before with Paul and he's convinced that we were robbed last time and that the wine we'd sampled wasn't the wine we were given to take away, but even his suspicious nature was quelled by what we had just tasted and although we had intended to try other *vignerons*, both of us felt that anywhere else would have been a step down that afternoon and we raced home before the Smecta ran out.

We sat in the kitchen later that evening feeling pretty pleased with ourselves, that despite our gastric handicap we'd ventured out and had a really good day. I swilled my glass around, sniffed the contents and swallowed some of the liquid.

'It's got a chalky, clay-like taste,' I said, 'and there is actually a hint of metal in there.' Paul nodded and we downed our Smecta-filled wine glasses in one.

'Natalie and the boys are trying to persuade me to get hens,' I said casually trying to make small talk over the sounds made by our moaning stomachs.

'Great,' Paul replied sarcastically. 'Next time I come, I'll get bird flu!'

LIGHT AT THE END OF THE TUNNEL

I don't hold much store by countryside predictions; by that I mean those grizzled old folk who appear on local news at the fag-end of winter, point a gnarled stick at a copse 'on yonder' and declare that because there are twenty-six rooks present, the summer will indeed be glorious. Well, you have a 50 per cent chance of being right, but save it for the tourists please. Madame Girresse, a farmer's wife and neighbour (in as much as someone who lives 3 kilometres away can be a neighbour) always seems to make accurate weather forecasts – is it because of bird movements, cloud formations, soil density? No, she says, she watches the weather forecasts after the lunchtime news. According to various local predictions, which as far as I could see were based on nothing more than optimism and wishful thinking, the coming summer would be a good one. But just so long as it's on time that's all anybody really wants after such a long while without seemingly any sun at all. There had been the odd, rare hopeful sign of spring but it was quickly crushed by stubborn clouds and chilling winds. The winter had been like Mother Nature's version of prog-rock, repetitive, dull and seemingly endless. The awful weather was also delaying the building work, which we were desperate to see make some progress.

Winter had clearly taken its toll on Natalie who, while bombarding me with email links to various far-flung dog rescue centres and pictures of Jack Russell puppies in the hope of tempting me to further chaos, had now declared her intention to own a peacock. A small chateau nearby had a dozen or so which roamed freely and often onto the road.

'They wouldn't miss one,' Natalie said as we drove past.

'No!' I said, putting my foot down metaphorically and literally, only narrowly avoiding a big feathery roadkill.

We hadn't been to the local zoo for months, much to the chagrin of the boys, but there was a definite fear that she'd try and smuggle out one of the more accessible penguins.

Even the cats were bored, just lying around languidly, stirring only to annoy me if I was in the kitchen; the dogs were asleep all day, waking only to annoy me when they wanted a meal and Samuel and Maurice were doing their best to annoy each other, which really annoyed me. Pierrot remained unaffected by the weather, largely because deafness and blindness can do that to you but also because if he can't eat it, rub himself against it or urinate on it, he's just not that interested. One of the cats, Vespa, fell asleep in Pierrot's bed and he just got in and lay on top of her; he really couldn't care less for niceties and the rules of polite society. Vespa on the other hand was most put out and slunk off to my office/cubby hole where I found her later watching the photos on my laptop screensaver, a judgemental look on her face like Brian Sewell in a provincial art gallery.

It was all too calm and as a family, we just seemed to be waiting for something to wake us up. Obviously I'd come to France in search of peace and this inactivity and all-round somnolence should have suited me down to the ground – but it didn't feel like peace at all, more like an uneasy truce, the calm before the storm. It felt like the end of a siege and we were all getting a little stir crazy.

Even my weasel seemed to have upped sticks and left, staying only briefly to rid us of the rat, he had now gone, his mission complete; an itinerant dispenser of justice, The Weasel With No Name. At least the horses were showing signs of spring in that they were moulting; every few metres there were big piles of hair in their paddock as though there had been a hairdressing competition and nobody had bothered to sweep up. You'd think of course that this might put Junior in a friendlier mood, but no. Manuel and Natalie had been building a new fence in preparation for the building work (the builders quite rightly having refused to work until we could guarantee that Junior wasn't going to take a lump out of them) and so now he had taken to just standing there most of the day angrily staring at the new, unbreachable wooden fence and snorting the French/ Horse equivalent of 'You Bastards'.

His mood isn't helped by Natalie frequently standing behind him with an empty wheelbarrow hoping to break the world record for 'World's Fastest Manure Delivery'. It's an arresting sight and clearly confuses the poor animal who although he dotes on Natalie, obviously feels that the whole wheelbarrow thing is a bit of an imposition.

'Why don't you just tie a bag to his arse?' I said, venturing outside briefly in the hope of annoying someone.

'Don't be silly,' she replied, by now impervious to my winter-induced 'looking for a fight' mood. 'A little bit to the right,' she continued cajoling the horse to greater accuracy.

Despite almost terminal boredom, job creation isn't in my nature, especially if it involves eccentric methods of animal-dropping entrapment. Natalie, however, is an artist at work all year round. There is to my mind absolutely bugger all to do outside on days like these. They are cold, frequently wet and the sky is usually dirty and grey, like an old smoker's beard, but she'll be out there all afternoon until it gets dark, humming away to herself, talking to the horses and wandering around the place planning for spring when there will be genuine work to be done. In winter, she's like a horticultural snooker player, planning in advance the next colour and where exactly it will go, only breaking from her reverie to peer in the window and tut at me for my continuing inactivity.

Even when it's dark she will still be working on the garden; at one point just as it seemed winter would never actually end she came in and started cutting out pictures of roses and sticking them on to cardboard, completely in her own world. I watched her for a while, not sure if I should interrupt, in the way that you shouldn't interrupt a sleepwalker. I was full of admiration, she had turned a huge, plain garden into something interesting and beautiful, but I was also bored and had nothing of my own to do.

'What are you doing?' I asked, deciding against all reason to provoke her.

'I'm going to stick these on the roses,' she replied, like it was the most natural thing in the world.

'Really? Won't people be able to tell that they're not real, though?' I said sarcastically in what I hoped would be the conversational equivalent of knocking over a big bloke's pint.

'I'm making identity cards for the roses in the garden, so that I can identify them properly.' She said this very slowly and as if to an idiot. The big bloke had just looked at me and told me to run along.

There had been no talk of chickens for a while, but the lacklustre effect of winter finally seemed to have made everyone aware that we really had enough to be getting on with and that chickens would only add to the list of outdoor chores that nobody, Natalie apart, really cared for. I was wrong. As the seemingly interminable winter finally started packing its bags I emerged one morning, blinking into watery sunlight to find Natalie attempting to bottle feed two newborn baby mice that she'd found struggling across the lawn first thing. They were tiny, hairless creatures whose eyes hadn't yet opened to the world and if they had would have seen two lascivious-looking cats eyeing them up, though only as a pre-meal snack as they were that small.

'What shall we keep them in?' Natalie had asked. My response being that they would struggle to get out of a dessert spoon.

I didn't mind Natalie feeling like she had to rescue every creature that she comes across in distress, it's just that I felt she should pick her battles. These minute creatures couldn't possibly survive, could they?

She had hesitated as to whether or not to bother – even Maurice's opinion was sought on the matter, though swiftly ignored as it boiled down to Maurice giving her a strange look and just saying, 'Why?' After about twenty minutes she'd made her mind up and Operation Baby Mouse was under way. Initially there were four of them, one had already perished, two of them she had and so, while she set about making some tiny rodent hospital I was detailed to find the fourth. It had crawled under an ornamental barrel by the pool and it meant sticking my arm under the barrel and just blindly groping for anything that moved. I was doing this while complaining loudly and in no uncertain terms just how absurd this whole thing was.

'You're very brave, Daddy!' Maurice said, by now completely immune to my default setting of 'irate'.

'Really?' I replied, partly proud but also fearful as to what exactly it was that I was displaying such bravery in front of.

'Well, there are probably snakes under there.'

I scrambled back up off the ground, probably quicker than if I had actually been bitten, and sat a few metres away breathing heavily. In my desire to show some level of support for one of Natalie's insane rescue missions I had come this close to death. This close I tell you.

'Couldn't find the other one,' I said breathlessly to Natalie a few minutes later, 'I reckon the snakes got it. I could have died.'

She looked at me, trying and failing to make sense of what I'd just said. 'Can you put the kettle on, please?' she said eventually. 'And fill up a hot-water bottle.'

The emergency ward was already taking shape: an old shoebox had been converted and one of Thérence's jumpers had been commandeered and cut up into smaller bits for them to sleep on. Already Natalie was cleaning out the small bottles used to feed the cats when they were first found. I blame the internet for all this. It's all very laudable to go about thinking you can rescue these creatures, and sometimes it's done successfully, but posting your results smugly on the World Wide Web only encourages others to think they can do the same, Natalie in particular. I didn't fancy their chances, and what if they did survive and they were male and female? We'd be overrun! This really was madness in the extreme – part of me wanted the poor things to pull through and reward Natalie for her efforts and part of me wanted them not to, so as not to encourage this madness any further.

And what if they were both male? I have some experience of warring rodent brothers and it's not pretty. When we were younger my sister and I had two gerbils, Sammy and Lee (Sammy Lee was my dad's favourite footballer at the time); Lee, my sister's gerbil, was a large albino and Sammy, mine, was clearly the runt of the litter and born without back feet. Yup, sometimes you're dealt a rough hand – or not, as the case may be. Anyway, seemingly everything was going fine for a couple of months until one morning we came down and found Lee nonchalantly eating Sammy for breakfast. It was a rude awakening to the rodent world.

One of Natalie's mice didn't last the night. It couldn't take any of the milk Natalie had paid a fortune at the vet's for. She had also asked the vet if she had any mice as clients.

'No…' said the vet, racking her brains, 'only the ones used to feed pet snakes.' Seriously, what kind of bedside manner is that?

After the demise of mouse number one (thankfully no names had been given yet), Natalie's steely determination to succeed with number two took over. Every hour, on the hour the thing was bottle fed and steadily, and quite obviously, was getting stronger. The hot-water bottle, kept under the shoe box, was warmed repeatedly to keep a constant temperature; Natalie even managed to make the thing do a poo by rubbing a warm cotton bud on its tummy, an event that elicited a quite ridiculous level of celebration. Hopes were high.

By morning, however, the thing was dead and a sense of gloom pervaded the house. I don't know why I said it, I just wanted to cheer everyone up I suppose; I wanted to lighten the mood.

'Why don't we look into getting some chickens?' I said, hoping to sound vague.

Within seconds Natalie had produced her 'Hen File', which I didn't even know existed, and made it clear that the subject had already been 'looked into' and in some detail. The coop, left by the previous owners, needed disinfecting and thoroughly cleaning out (my job), some kind of outdoor run needed building and securing (my job) and a perch, step and shelf needed constructing in the coop (my job).

I pointed out that I seemed to be copping most of the workload here.

'Ian,' Natalie said, talking to me like a child, 'if you want hens, you have to look after them.'

Un-bloody-believable!

'Hang on! You lot have been banging on about chickens...'

'They're called hens, Daddy. Hens lay eggs,' Samuel said, a touch patronisingly.

'Hens, then. You lot have been asking for hens for, for, for...' I stopped and looked from face to face, each one a picture of innocence. I'm not saying it was planned, but somehow in the blinking of an eye I had gone from being the one stumbling block in the whole chicken ownership saga to being not only the catalyst but owner with chief responsibility for the damn things.

Which is why, if you'd happened to be in the Loire Valley late one Thursday night you'd have seen an impeccably dressed mod being given the run around by two hens who had escaped their run on the way to the coop. You would also have seen Natalie and the boys laughing uncontrollably as I chased the hens with the swimming pool net one way and then was chased back again by the hens who were being chased by Pierrot and Junior. An hour it took me to get the birds back in their coop, an hour; you can see why free range chickens are bigger – it's their bloody leg muscles.

ON THE MARCHÉ

Our town, while being surrounded on all sides by more famous towns and chateaux, is renowned locally as having the best market in the area. In the UK it would be called a farmer's market so that prices could be upped accordingly, but here it's just a market. Farmers, or at least artisans and *producteurs*, faithfully turn up every Thursday morning and take over the not-inconsiderable town square while people are bussed in from miles around for their weekly shop and social.

   And it is very much a social. As we headed into town in search of hens the sun shone brightly and seemed more permanent than it had for months, less watery and with no chill in the air. Instead there was a comfortable warmth and spring, which had clearly been hitting its own snooze button and just rolling over for the last few weeks, was now up, yawning, stretching and scratching its bits maybe, but it was up nonetheless and the local community was waking up with it. The hardy souls who had braved the market throughout the winter were still there but greeting each other anew, as if it were for the first time in months; their numbers were swollen by the holiday-home weekenders from Paris and the first wave of Loire tourists. The shops, which had stoically remained in business throughout the lean, almost deserted months, at last had customers again – although one or two had fallen by the wayside simply unable to remain viable with so little custom. The old man who ran the *alimentation* had finally given up the ghost as had the *boucherie*, though there were rumours that a new one would open soon.

I love the individuality of the small town French high street. There are few big chains dominating and there seems to be a desire to protect the tradition of high street shopping. I had recently bought a Kindle and I was still having problems with the whole e-reader thing. I'd been backed into buying one by the increasing vigilance of Ryanair and their refusal to allow a gram over their paltry 10 kilograms and that the bag must conform to a certain size and shape. Really, they should take over WeightWatchers. I like proper books and proper book shops and feel guilty about owning a Kindle because it's another, possibly last, nail in the coffin of the UK high street where I had always bought my books.

The traditional UK high street has taken a battering. There are very few butchers left, virtually no ironmongers, Greggs counts barely as food let alone as a bakery and Waterstones, the last bookshop, is hanging on by its fingernails. It's depressing. The British high street has been left with estate agents, Wetherspoon's pubs, clothes shops all selling the same designs and McDonald's. Any individuality or small-scale entrepreneurship has been all but destroyed, trampled underfoot either by the internet, out-of-town shopping behemoths or ridiculous car parking charges.

As yet, in France, certainly rural France, this hasn't happened. The big supermarkets are there obviously, but internet shopping is still largely distrusted and small towns just don't charge for parking. In our town alone there are two *charcuteries*, four *boulangeries*, no candlestick makers, but a *quincaillerie* (ironmongers), two florists and three independent chemists; all serving a population of about 4,000. But that's not to say that the French should be complacent about hanging on to these things, the high streets of France have their own problems. The exodus from small, rural towns to bigger conurbations continues as people quite rightly migrate in search of work, leaving villages and the like facing a tough future. There are other problems too. Whereas in England you might feel harassed on the streets by clusters of dayglow-vested charity muggers with their drama school enthusiasm ('Hi, you look great, thought about Third World Prostates?'), or intimidated by groups of school kids thinking that they're the first generation to try and wear the school tie in a rebellious fashion, France has a far more sinister group of street botherers: the old woman.

They gather in groups, usually outside the chemist, and no-one is safe from their unsolicited 'advice'. So far, in the time I've lived here, I've been 'advised' on what my child should/should not be wearing, my parking, the wisdom of sitting outside a bar when surely rain is imminent, food purchases, wine purchases (all purchases, in fact), the speed I walk, smoking/not smoking and the value of a solid forward defensive stroke. OK, I made the last one up – but on one occasion when I pointed out to a group of old ladies that the child, my child (Thérence to be exact), who they were declaring to be a 'pretty girl' was in fact a boy, they all paused for a second and then shook their heads in unison: 'No', they said, 'definitely a girl.' They are a menace, like I say, and the one thing they haven't yet pulled me up on is what I'm wearing. They've obviously never seen a full-on mod before. They fall silent and begin crossing their chests.

Another issue I have with the French high street is piped music, which is pumped into the streets almost daily through strategically placed speakers but with no apparent thought whatsoever as to playlist. I don't mind the idea of it – as someone who wanders through life constantly with some soundtrack running though his head, I'd go as far as to say it's actually quite a nice idea. But if you're in rural France think about what you're playing! This is the Loire Valley, so some classical Baroque would be appropriate, the theme tune to *Jean de Florette* would work well in Provence, *musette* would set a scene all over the country;

you get the idea. What I don't want to hear as I stroll through a sleepy town is how some sociopath, who hasn't yet managed to work out that jeans stay up with belts, wants to 'gun his hoes down' or do this, that or the other to his 'bitch'. Rap music may have done a brilliant job of highlighting racial tensions and domestic hardships in the bigger cities, but frankly there are few styles of music less appropriate to French village life – except for maybe Death-Slash-Metal or whatever it's called, which shouldn't be allowed anywhere, Scandinavia included.

For once, though, the music seemed appropriate and the busiest market day in months was bustling about its business to the silky sounds of Tino Rossi and Charles Trenet. There was a happy hum in the air as people wandered slowly through the lanes between stalls and refrigeration vans. In the winter, market shopping is more like a raid as you know exactly what you're after and are unlikely to hang around to browse. The numerous *boucherie* and *charcuterie* vans had long queues, the cheese and *saucisson* stalls were all doing a roaring trade – each having their loyal and distinct followers – the vast and buxomly stocked fresh fish counters were gleaming and the individual *vignerons* were giving away more freebies than they'd possibly have liked but were happy to have the attention.

This year there were new sellers around too: a fresh pasta seller, a stuffed olives stall and a ground spice man, and though always welcome I feared they won't last the course.

The market is a conservative place where traditional wares can thrive and have done for generations, but unlikely to support exotic interlopers in a sleepy, rural backwater like this. Though, having said that, some of the most unlikely stalls return every spring and for the life of me I can't see how they survive. There's the African/West Indian stall selling Bob Marley towels and dubious-looking 'cigarette' paraphernalia, like this is Camden on a Sunday morning; there are the 'clothing' stalls which are ideal if you want your young daughter to dress like a streetwalker or your son to look like he still hankers for that East 17 or New Kids on the Block look; and there are the shifty-looking watch sellers who constantly scour the crowds hoping that whoever bought a cheap timepiece the week before won't be back looking for a refund.

The same faces are there year in, year out, a comforting presence for the regulars. There's Ali, the gruff Moroccan fruit seller, who towards the end of the morning will start begrudgingly giving away rotten fruit and then moaning that we are 'taking money from the grandmother he has to support.' Jean-Jacques, the ribald *charcutier*, whose risqué jokes nearly always have a variant of *pain au chocolat* as the punchline; there's the depressed fisherman; the man who sells vegetable plants and if he doesn't have what you want he'll 'go and dig some up'; there are successive generations of Romani selling baskets; salesmen who in the winter sell *chauffage* (central heating) and in the summer it's air-conditioning; and there's the woman who

233

owns a lingerie stall but who, in a tragic example of bad marketing, spends the entire morning adjusting her own obviously ill-fitting bra.

And so into this veritable hotbed of rural Frenchness we strode. A family with a mission: hen hunting. It's true that all of our animals were rescued in one form or another, and although we were paying for these hens there was a feeling that we were rescuing them too. There was one stall selling hens, cocks, geese, guinea fowl and ducks and, even though it was outdoors, it reeked. Somehow I was the only one who seemed to care enough to put his cravat over his nose. The woman in front of us wanted to choose three *poules* for Sunday dinner as she had the whole family coming over, which is why we felt we were rescuing 'our' birds, but she thankfully refrained from actually wringing their necks in front of us. She most certainly hadn't, unlike us, given them names.

The stallholder roughly picked up Tallulah and Lola, hens chosen by Samuel and Maurice, and shoved them in a cardboard box without ceremony, the poor, obviously startled birds hardly making a sound as they seemed resigned to their fate. Little did they know that after a short drive they were about to reach animal paradise, where their every whim and foible would be catered for to the detriment of co-habiting human life. I had been resigned for some time to the extra responsibility, but had decided on a change of tack. If Natalie and the boys really were determined to build their own ark then I had to somehow try to control its growth. Simply putting up objections hadn't worked at all – far from it, like prohibition it had merely sent the whole farce underground where it seemingly thrived.

Take, for example, the issue of our recently acquired rabbit. I should have seen the signs when Maurice had asked blithely at lunch a couple of weeks earlier, just after I had returned from a long trip abroad, 'What shall we call the rabbit?' It never occurred to me that we had, while my back was turned, actually gained a rabbit.

When Maurice, who is innocent enough to be incapable of keeping a secret, asked about the potential naming of 'the rabbit', it just didn't register with me. I didn't notice the holding-the-breath silence or Maurice reacting to being kicked under the table. I had prepared a sleeping draught in water the night before, but had miraculously fallen asleep before I could drink it. Unfortunately, when I woke up thirsty the next morning, it was the first thing I saw and I downed it and spent the rest of the day in something of a fuzz. They could have had the rabbit on the dining table and I'm still not sure that I'd have noticed.

I was in a vulnerable state, something which Junior took full advantage of. I had been despatched to get the garden furniture from the loft above the stables, which meant shooing Junior and Ultime out of their stable and setting up a ladder to get to the loft. For once I was able to move Junior relatively easily and I locked him out, erected the ladder and climbed into the loft. I went searching in the dim roof light for the hammock and the deckchairs and returned to the top of the ladder to find Junior at the foot of it. I clearly had not locked the stable door. Junior looked up at me and, I swear, smiled as he sent the ladder crashing to the floor. I was stranded in the loft – it was too high to jump down and anyway Junior was in the way if I tried. So, for twenty-five minutes I was calling out for rescue, which eventually came with lots of sympathy and concern. Not for me you understand, but for Junior in case he had been startled by the crash of the ladder; the poor dear.

'He pushed it deliberately!' I whined when I got down. 'He bloody hates me that horse does!'

'Go and have a lie down,' they all said, guiding me back to the house. 'Have a rest.'

'He did, though. Deliberately!'

'Shush-shush-shush now. Go and have a nap.' I should have known they were up to something.

When I came back outside about an hour later, still a bit groggy but with more faculties than at any other time that day, I couldn't find anyone. I thought at first that they may have gone for a walk, but I could hear muffled voices coming from the wood store. Well, actually not muffled but muted, whispered, conspiratorial. Toby, who seemed to be standing guard, saw me and slinked off. I sneaked up to the door to try and hear what was going on, but couldn't quite make it out. Whatever it was I was obviously to be kept out of it.

'What's going on?' I demanded as I swung the door open. And there they were, the traitors, all four of them bending over a cage, shocked by my entrance and quickly shuffling into a line to block my view of whatever it was they were hiding. 'What is it?' I asked, 'What have you got now?' I wasn't angry, more resigned.

Between the four of them – Thérence punctuated their explanation with the word 'tractor' – I got a picture of what had happened. They had found three baby rabbits, but unfortunately Vespa and Flame had found them at the same time and now there was only one left.

'We're trying to save it, Daddy,' Samuel said. 'It's all on its own now.'

'Yes, well I know how it feels,' I responded a touch dramatically. 'So, let me get this straight. We are now rescuing animals from the clutches of the animals we've previously rescued, is that right?'

They all looked at the floor like naughty schoolchildren, except for Thérence who said 'tractor'.

'We're going to release it back into the wild...' Natalie began, before I interrupted.

'What? Like the cats?' A killer blow to any logical person or argument and therefore utterly useless in the face of these miscreants.

I'm all for rescuing animals, it's a 'good thing to do' but when you start effectively building your own domestic food chain there is bound to be trouble. Toby, who is actually scared of the cats, has become a disappointment in his own right. He has an excess of growth hormone and has high cholesterol. He's like the Orson Welles of

Guard Dogging, a career that started off so promisingly has descended into mediocrity and obesity. The horses hate me. Pierrot disgusts everyone, and the cats are silent killers without remorse. Now we have a rabbit presumably introduced just to destroy my vegetable patch. With all the secrecy I felt it was one concession too many, and I was determined to be strong and draw a line somewhere and this, without doubt, was it.

As I was about to make this clear, Vespa sauntered into the wood store and dropped her latest victim. A lizard's tail; just the tail. And it was angry. Lizards' tails, like headless chickens, can carry on for quite some time after being separated from the body, but this one was practically jumping! It was like the Black Knight in *Monty Python and the Holy Grail*, seemingly saying to Vespa, 'Come on then! Is that all you've got?' Vespa, bored, left the tail to it which appeared to make it even more livid. We all just stared at this astonishing performance, unable to tear our eyes from the seething reptile body part.

'Aww,' said Maurice eventually, 'can we keep it?'

I realised there and then that resistance was utterly futile.

The rabbit, to no-one's particular surprise, stayed. I always knew it wouldn't be released back into the wild anyway; I could never imagine a moment where Natalie would be able to let it go. The thing was tiny and the reason why rabbits have such a well-earned reputation for levels of procreation is that they're just not very good at staying alive in the first place. This rabbit in particular seemed especially under pressure, what with both cats sitting on top of its makeshift cage most of the day, oh, and because it only had three feet. It seemed strange that none of us had spotted this flaw for the first four days that we had it, very strange indeed, especially Natalie who had held it quite often. Like I say, strange.

As it was staying, the thing needed accessories like a hutch and a run. Natalie, taking my resignation as enthusiasm, had set about finding every bit of spare wood and chicken wire in the place, dumping them by the hammock in which I was dozing and telling me to 'get on with it'. My history in the woodwork department is brief and inglorious; I once made an egg rack but made the holes so big that it could only hold ostrich eggs; my attempts at shelving are notorious for their quirky angles and brief staying power. In short, I am not a handyman. Necessity has meant that I've improved a little bit over the years, but I enter into these things begrudgingly, short-tempered and foul-mouthed.

Perhaps because I was embarking on some misguided, badly planned Heath Robinsonesque rabbit run, the tension between Natalie and I had mounted; especially when I insisted that it shouldn't be called a 'run' but a 'limp'. All couples argue, or at least they should otherwise it's unnatural – the important thing is to keep those arguments private, not just away from the children but away from old friends. And their children. Who may have popped over to France for the Easter weekend.

We've known John and Rebecca for a long time, they are good friends, but it's fair to say that they had never seen Natalie and me when she is in full treating-me-like-staff mode and I'm stroppily arguing with her, with the wood, with drills, screws, limb-challenged bunny rabbits and every bloody thing in the world. It must have been an uncomfortable few hours for them, not knowing whether to referee, disappear for a bit or just get back in the car and drive home. It was brutal, but by dinner time I had magically made a run that was solid and unlikely to collapse in a light breeze. It was safe for the rabbit to lollop about in and also secure enough to keep the cats and other sundry predators out. I was, to be honest, quite proud of it; Natalie was very grateful, and John and Rebecca just relieved that Natalie and I hadn't actually killed each other. It was, though I say it myself, a thing of beauty.

So you can imagine my annoyance the following morning to find that the rabbit had only gone and bloody died! The ungrateful little bastard! Most of Easter Saturday I'd spent building the sodding thing, I had cuts and bruises from the effort, I'd put friendships at risk, sworn at inanimate objects and the thing had just upped and died. I was furious and no amount of children's tears were going to change my mind that this ex-rabbit had done this deliberately just to annoy the hell out of me.

'Never again!' I said. 'That's the last one. That run is bloody brilliant and it got twenty minutes of use! What a waste!'

There was an uncomfortable silence as three adults and five children tried their best not to anger me further.

'Perhaps you could use it for hens?' said Rebecca, which cheered Natalie and the boys up, got a look of 'What are you doing?' from John and stony silence from me.

She was right, though, and as Tallulah and Lola nervously scraped around their run and pecked at the ground it really did seem ideal. The dogs were hovering a bit close and the cats were sat on top of it obviously weighing up the whole thing, but the new arrivals didn't seem unduly stressed. Maybe they realised that it was definitely better than a tight squeeze in a Le Creuset casserole dish. Finally, I thought, stress-free animals and ones that may actually pay their way.

'Right then,' I said, clapping my hands together, 'who wants eggs for breakfast tomorrow?'

TREADING ON EGGSHELLS

Perhaps I was naive in thinking that eggs would be that immediate. It's possible that despite being a comedian who rails against the modern world and the tyranny of the next-day delivery, I've actually become the kind of person who must have everything NOW! But three weeks into our hen ownership and there wasn't a dicky-bird, nothing. I was beginning to think we'd been sold duds. Natalie's theory for this was that they were bored, but as her theory for Junior's sadism was loneliness, and company certainly hadn't changed his maniacal attitude towards me, I was taking it with a pinch of salt frankly. Can hens be bored? Really? They're hens for God's sake! Do they need to be stretched intellectually before they produce any eggs? What am I supposed to do, read them Chomsky?

She had also suggested that we let them out of their run, but I had dug my heels in on this – no way – at least not until they had settled in and were used to us. I still hadn't recovered from trying to round them up the day we got them. Having finally cornered Tallulah I dived on her, sliding through a pile of Junior's finest, and grabbed her successfully. Rather than take the long way round to her coop I decided to try and climb through the wooden paddock fence, but I hadn't considered firstly that the gap isn't as wide as I thought and secondly, that a winter spent moodily downing wine and cheese while watching bad weather meant that I wasn't at my slimmest. I got stuck. Natalie and the boys couldn't contain themselves as I lay, horizontally trapped in the fence, covered in horse manure, still holding a frightened hen who was pecking at my hands while I pitifully asked for help. 'If you choose to let them out,' I said to Natalie, 'you can bloody well round them up.'

'When are they going to lay eggs?' Maurice asked angrily one day, clearly running out of patience and feeding off the angry images of rioting and looting on the television news. Realising that he was feeling the same way about the hens as I was – namely, that we'd been duped – I felt for him, but despite my own hypocritical feelings on the matter it seemed like the ideal opportunity for a bit of textbook parenting.

'You have to be patient,' I said, 'you can't just have what you want, when you want it. Sometimes you have to wait.' To be honest he looked a little confused by my portentous tone. 'Look at those kids,' I said pointing to the telly, 'just taking what they want, with no consideration for others. It's wrong.'

'What's going on?' Samuel said, walking into the lounge.

'Daddy says we can't smash open the hens to get their eggs,' Maurice replied.

'No,' I said, feeling defeat coming on swiftly. 'No. Look at Toby,' I pointed out into the garden, without actually looking it has to be said. 'All day he's just been sitting there by the chicken run, staring at a piece of old baguette.' He had too; he'd maintained a kind of concentrated vigil, like the fabled dogs who wait for their masters to return from war. 'He hasn't moved, but he's been very patient, he's been very good.'

Just then Toby came bounding up to the large window, his muzzle covered in mud, the longed for bread hanging out of his mouth and followed nervously by the newly freed hens.

Natalie's second argument was that actually their run and dislocated coop wasn't ideal for creating the sense of tranquillity and stability that they needed. It was difficult to disagree with this. Every morning one of us would take them from their coop, which actually was more like the cooler from *The Bridge on the River Kwai*, and carry them in the box they had arrived in to their run, where they were gawped at all day by either the cats or the dogs. Like hopeful parents-to-be being told the best conditions in which to conceive, we were obviously going to have to get this right or forever have barren hens.

As usual Natalie was on the case. 'I've found the ideal coop!' she said triumphantly. 'It's three hundred euros and...'

'Three hundred bloody euros! How many eggs do they have to lay before we make that money back?' This seemed to be the case with all the animals. I'm given a load of hogwash about them really not costing much and before you know it I'm mucking out a stable with a golden shovel.

'It's too much,' I said, 'we'll just have eggless hens. Or take them back, get ones that work.'

'Finished?' Natalie asked, used to having to let my initial outburst subside. 'Right,' she continued. 'The same coop is less than half the price in England and you are picking up the new car next week. You can bring it back then. OK?'

Seriously, why she can't just give me all of the relevant information from the start rather than letting me go off half-cocked every time is utterly beyond me.

We had bought a car – a Citroen C4 Grand Picasso seven-seater people carrier. Not exactly the car of my dreams. The mistake, though we didn't know it yet, was buying it in England and importing it back to France; not that we wanted to, we wanted to buy from our local garage, but it was £5,000 more expensive to do so. We went to see our local *garagiste* and I showed him a price list from the UK and he nearly burst into tears reading it, and yet a few months later we were the ones at a low emotional ebb; we should have just stumped up the extra five grand.

Even if you have never had to deal with 'French Bureaucracy' just the term will probably strike fear into your heart, as it seems to have become synonymous with a lot of the antipathy that some English reserve for the

French. But bureaucracy is a blight everywhere, this isn't an anti-French thing. Let me try and get a few things straight. In my opinion, the French can be divided into three groups: there are the Parisians, who look down on the rest of the population; there's the rest of the population, who don't consider Parisians to be proper French; and there's *Les Fonctionnaires*, the civil servants who are feared and despised by both Parisians and the 'proper' French.

Very few will have a bad word to say about *Les Fonctionnaires* in public – they are like the old East German STASI, nobody wants to upset them and nobody really wants to talk about them either or your file might disappear. There is this notion that should *Les Fonctionnaires* go on strike then the country would be strangled, everything would stop; what it seems to me hasn't been considered is that their grip on everything and their vicious use of duplicate, triplicate, multi-departmental (accent on the 'mental'), labyrinthine, make-it-up-as-you-go-as-long-as-it-causes-confusion modus operandi means that the country is already being strangled – it is already practically at a standstill.

When we first moved to France we brought our existing car over and the process of having it locally registered was painful, elongated and merciless, but in the intervening five years the process had been changed. It was now much, much worse. Firstly, you needed to get a *carte grise* (proof of French ownership) but our garage, despite importing cars regularly, wasn't sure how to go about doing this. They weren't the only ones.

The garage suggested we should go through the DRIRE (Direction Régionale de l'Industrie, de la Recherche et de l'Environnement), while on the other hand the Mairie (town hall) told us to ring the Trésorie in Chateauroux. They moved us on to the Centre des Impôts, which we visited, got something stamped and were then told to go to the Préfecture, which was shut because it was a Monday. In the meantime, the DREAL (I'm still not sure who or what they do) got involved and informed us that we couldn't get a *carte grise* without a *contrôle technique* (MOT). The *contrôle technique* people wouldn't perform an MOT without a *carte grise*. Don't worry, said the DREAL, we'll send them a letter (meanwhile retaining all our original documents). We then went back to the MOT people with the letter, that's fine they said, but we still can't do a *contrôle technique* because you don't have a *certificat de conformité*. Apparently, you can't get a *certificat de conformité* without a *contrôle technique* or the original documents, which were still at the DRIRE. The garage rang the DRIRE who insisted that a *contrôle technique* had to be carried out and so it was. The garage then realised that a *contrôle technique* was unnecessary as the car was less than four years old; it had taken a month to get this far and the DRIRE or DREAL (frankly I'd lost the will to live by now) admitted their mistake. But, hey, what are you gonna do, they're *fonctionnaires*? In reparation the lady at the DRIRE promised to send us the *certificat de conformité*. Isn't that just doing your job we asked?

Yes. The *certificat de conformité* arrived, though it is now called an *attéstation d'identité*.

By this time the image of the admin branch of the Keystone Cops was running around my head, I was seeing stars and we still hadn't got the *carte grise* – plus, we still had to visit the Préfecture. We decided to take a break from the whole thing, a week or so just to lick our wounds and take stock. If we needed to go back to the Préfecture then we needed to make sure that we had everything necessary or it would be a bloodbath. Our first stop however was the Mairie to get an *attéstation d'immatriculation* (*carte grise* application form) and *une liste des pieces à joindre* (a list of accompanying documents). Apart from having a rank inability to say *attéstation d'immatriculation*, even without a boozy lunch, I managed to complete this task and the list of accompanying documents was a bonus too and so we set off for the Sous-Préfecture, if not exactly optimistically, then at least with closure in mind.

We arrived at the Préfecture's office, laden with files of documents, took our ticket from the machine and waited to be called. The waiting room was a desultory place, full of people who had lost all hope as they – French people who had bought French cars in France – are forced to go through the same hoops of fire that we are. French Bureaucracy isn't singling us out because we're foreigners or trying to do something unusual, it does this to EVERYONE. It isn't discriminating, it hates EVERYONE.

We were called in to the office where there were two *fonctionnaires* waiting behind desks; one, the man, was insulting the 'customer' who had just left. They were angry people, one could sense it, and obviously the more cases they can dismiss without success the more satisfaction they got out of their job. We were lambs to the slaughter. The first ten minutes was spent trying to explain that we lived in France and that we weren't actually here just to get the UK address switched to a French one, because you know, that would be fun wouldn't it? We'd all do that for kicks and giggles right? Once that was established, and they had been incredibly rude during what was their error, we worked through our list of supporting documents and then the alarms went off, the portcullis came down and the smiles, thin, wan cold smiles, spread across their faces.

'You don't have an electricity bill here?' the *fonctionnaire* said, for the first time catching our eye.

'No,' Natalie said, trying to keep her temper, 'the list here says a water bill will do.' He picked up the list, took a red pen, put a line through the bit saying water bill and handed back the list.

'Electricity bill,' he said menacingly.

'Next!' shouted his colleague.

'You know what you're doing wrong?' said Serge, a French friend from Natalie's *agence immobilière* over lunch that day. 'You are being too French. You speak the language and so they can talk to you how they want.' We all nodded sagely. 'What you need to do is play the dumb foreigner, not speak the language, make them do the work; cause them problems they are not used to.'

I continued to nod sagely and only then did I notice that Natalie and Serge were both looking at me, the dumb foreigner. Normally I spend my time wishing the weekends away, but the one between me and my showdown with the 'Axis of Evil Twins' on my return, was welcome to stay awhile.

I sat in the ante-room in the Sous-Préfecture sweating profusely, not because of the spring heat, but because of the atmosphere in the room, the impending meeting and nerves. It was busy, people obviously preferring to get their bureaucratic dealings out of the way first thing so that they could either spend the rest of the day getting on with their lives or, more likely, drowning their sorrows.

An elderly man walked in and offered his greetings. '*Messieurs et Dames*' he said, without hope or genuine geniality, took a ticket from the machine and stood in the corner as there were no seats left. Immediately the man sitting next to me shot up cursing and went to retrieve a ticket for himself, clearly having forgotten to do so initially. Heaven knows how long he'd been there, certainly longer than me and I'd been waiting twenty minutes already. I was beginning to have doubts about this whole situation – the idea that I could finally put an end to this bureaucratic nightmare by playing the dumb foreigner was all well and good until at some point the authorities realised that I wasn't playing at anything, I really am that dumb foreigner.

I reflected on what we'd had to go through to get this far just to get the car registered, it really was Dante's Nine Circles of Hell; seven of them had been the various agencies and departments we'd shuffled between, all of them contradicting each other, none of them giving a damn about it; the eighth was the permanent state of limbo and the ninth would presumably be the driving of the car itself. For years the French have been pilloried for their driving but now I see that it's a product of the licensing system; like a mistreated Rottweiler puppy they've come through a desensitising process and so, once behind the wheel, drivers are prone to unpredictable, sometimes violent, behaviour. The authorities have recognised this and a few years ago apparently introduced a 'courtesy' module into French driving lessons – and I think it's fair to say that it hasn't yet caught on.

Driving in the UK is almost a team sport, in France it's an individual pursuit. I've sat at junctions here trying desperately to wave someone out – not because I'm inordinately polite, but because it would make it easier for me to turn – and they sit there staring at you like you're insane! They have a look on their face like, 'What do you mean you're letting me out? Why? What do you want?' Eventually, when you've lost patience and start to turn anyway, they'll pull out and then start waving their arms about, incensed at your obvious idiocy.

The melancholy silence was broken violently as a woman stormed out of the office, clearly upset, while one of the 'public servants' shouted after her, 'I told you! Electricity bill!' The glass doors shut quietly behind her and we all sat and watched the impassive expressions on the two Valhallan Ice Warriors left within; there was no triumphalism but nor was there any contempt, in fact there was no emotion at all. They were deadpan automatons serving the bureaucratic machine, doing it by the book, albeit one they seemed to make up as they went along; a truly fearful pair who knew the power they possessed because the Civil Service are the clerks and pencil-pushers that won the French Revolution, nobody now dares to cross them for fear that if you brought one down three would replace them, like a bureaucratic Hydra.

Another unfortunate left the office, but clearly nearing the end of the process he'd emerged just to write a cheque, he hadn't reckoned on a time limit.

'Monsieur, I'm waiting!' one of the gargoyles shouted.

'Yes, I'm just writing the...' he stammered in response.

'Monsieur, now!' And he rushed back in or at least would have rushed back in had they actually pressed the door release button for him, which they didn't, preferring to let him stand for a few seconds in penance.

A younger man in the waiting room giggled at this, but was immediately tutted at by an old woman as if to say, 'Don't antagonise them young man or you'll pay', and getting the message he shut up quickly. You never know, I thought, she might have spent most of her life in there.

Despite having no-one to complain to, we had come up with the idea that I should try and record this meeting, but as my number was called and I pressed record on my phone I felt like an ill-prepared Donnie Brasco. What would happen if they cottoned on to what I was doing? I'd never get the car registered then, I'd probably be 'disappeared' – in fact, I'd become convinced that the large boards on the walls of all government buildings apparently listing the names of the millions who had died in the two World Wars were actually just a cover and were really a list of people who'd never made it back from the local government labyrinth.

I began slowly and tried not to look like I was speaking into a discrete microphone. '*Bonjour,* I was here last week with my wife...' I didn't finish the sentence as his slate grey eyes held mine while at the same time he picked up my documents and turned his back on me.

'*Quatre-vingt-quatre!*' shouted his vicious female colleague, and then in an instant, '*Non? Quatre-vingt-cinq!*'

A timid woman crept in; almost hidden by the enormous file she was carrying. 'Ha! Is your car in that file?' the *fonctionnaire* said mirthlessly, humour not being her thing. Seriously, what event in her life had led her to this level of toxicity? What kind of upbringing had this woman had? If she'd played with Barbies as a child, she'd definitely had the Klaus variety. I tried not to attract her attention and returned to staring at the back of her colleague as he slowly typed my details into his computer; one finger typing, angrily punching the keyboard and then, as he was copying from another document, he would move his ruler one line further down the paper. It was painful to watch.

The man turned his attention back to me and asked me to check that he'd copied my details correctly. He had. And at that, it was over. The car was now, at last, licensed. I slumped back into the chair and breathed out heavily – his demeanour didn't change one bit.

'Two hundred euros,' he said, flatly.

I hadn't been expecting this, €200? What for? Local taxes! Are you serious? I had already paid the taxes on the thing! Are you lining your pockets? Eh? Planning on running off with Medusa over there and setting up some kind of Stalin theme park? It's disgusting...

'*Merci*,' I said, and gave him €200. If someone had told me that morning that I could just pay money and this nightmare would be finished I'd have taken it. I was just grateful that the whole thing was finally over, but I didn't saunter out, or skip; I didn't want to rub it in the faces of those still waiting. I wished them luck – '*Bon courage*' – and as I was leaving I noticed for the first time that this office wasn't just for car registration but for gun licensing too – and I'll bet they were getting better treatment.

Natalie texted me as I made my way home exhausted by the stress of it all, but also quite jubilant.

'Can you get some eggs for lunch?'

Bloody hens.

Eggless hens or not, I was still determined to enjoy my triumph and as I stepped out of the car brandishing official documentation like it was a Bill of Rights to be greeted by a happy, smiling family, I felt like a returning hero.

'Well done!' Natalie said and then she paused. 'What do you think of Irish setters?'

Clearly she'd thought that this was the perfect time to broach the subject of further animal adoption; that my defences would be rendered so low by the monumental effort that she could just sneak this one in. Luckily for me there was still some of my natural defence system that hadn't been eroded by the *fonctionnaires*.

'Are you mental?' I raged. 'We already have...'

'Her name's Lulu, she's eighteen months old and...'

'What the f—'

'Just think about it that's all. She looks lovely. I've got some pictures of her. Let's have some lunch, we can talk about it later.'

There was, of course, no chance I could concentrate on anything else now. Another dog? What's the matter with her, does she not have enough poo to pick up? I started to pace up and down, the stress of the morning finally getting to me and bringing on the full Basil Fawlty mode. I wasn't angry, just really disturbed, eyes darting all over the place – 'gloriously discombobulated' as a friend once described me. Natalie, however, knew how to distract me, take my mind off the upset and set it a new challenge.

'Maurice can't find his Nintendo,' she said, like it was a pre-arranged buzz word to snap me out of hypnosis.

And that was it. I didn't sleep, I didn't even rest and all thoughts of Irish setters with the names of strippers left my head as my OCD kicked in and I couldn't do anything else until the Nintendo was found and all would be at peace. It was two in the morning when I found it, put it in Maurice's room and finally hauled my empty husk of a body into bed.

'You're so easy to distract,' Natalie said dreamily as she rolled over, 'it's like throwing a ball for a dog.'

Honestly, the woman's obsessed.

TAKING THE PEACE

Not having grown up in the countryside I had always harboured certain misgivings about the great wide open and that generally it was a place best avoided, what with its flying-buzzing-stinging things, its reactionary politics, its seemingly lackadaisical attitude to inbreeding and its fresh air. As a townie born and bred, it wasn't for me. I can see now that these opinions, though largely correct, weren't insurmountable and that if I were to achieve my goal of moving my family and me as far away from civilisation as reasonably possible, I just had to put up with certain things and accept the rough with the smooth. I have even grown quite fond of fresh air.

There are certain things, however – things that are peculiar to a country life – that I simply will not tolerate: the lack of appreciation for a sharp suit, for instance, early mornings, muck and the like. But by far the worst is 'facial mushrooms'. Yes, you read that correctly, 'facial mushrooms'. For some weeks Thérence had had a rash on his face which the doctor insisted was eczema, and so prescribed a cortisone cream to deal with it. The rash continued to spread like a bushfire, however, and by this time was covering most of his face. It was an alarming sight; fiercely red, it looked like second degree burns and had spread into his ears and around his eyes.

Natalie had already made an appointment with the dermatologist, but it wasn't going to be for another three weeks, so we went back to the doctor who, realising he'd made an error, changed Thérence's prescription. By now, however, our confidence in him was pretty low and we thought a second opinion was needed. The simplest way to get a second opinion on child healthcare issues in France is simply just to walk your child down any given street at any time of the day and just wait for old women to spring from the recesses and offer their unsolicited advice on matters of health, clothing, haircuts etc. The French still have a very strong sense of family – but not just their own, everybody else's too. There is also the opinion that if you are a man alone with your child or children you are probably quite inept and therefore would appreciate a bit of advice. Which we do – no, really, we love it; me especially. There's nothing I like better than to be stopped in the street by a bearded old woman and be told that my son isn't dressed warmly enough and then have my hand slapped away while the old crone tightens the coat up herself! This kind of thing really happens. I was in the supermarket once and when I returned to my trolley I was given a lecture on not leaving my child unattended while looking for groceries, not by one woman alone but by a group of women, a coven, who then decided to follow me around the shop just in case of further parental lapses.

Fortunately we were spared the amateur medical opinion in this instance when the dermatologist rang back with an immediate appointment, which I think was down to the doctor who had probably rung her and explained how bad the situation had become. It was, she said, a very bad case of *champignon* – a skin fungus basically – but was certainly treatable and shouldn't leave any scarring. The question is, she mused, how did he get it? Do we have any animals?

It is fair to say that Thérence is quite feral; the way he insists on playing with the cats and dogs, climbing into their beds, even eating their food when our backs are turned makes him seem more Mowgli than the Mod-Padawan I had him marked down as – he loves his pets. But as we listed the volume of animals that we have the dermatologist's face went ashen, not because it's particularly unusual in the countryside but because we had to try and narrow down which animal, if any, was carrying the fungus. My chief suspect was Pierrot – whose insatiable appetite for pleasing himself on furniture was surely just asking for bacterial trouble. Then there's Vespa who briefly had ringworm; Toby takes himself off to places of an afternoon, so who knows what he's up to; Flame of course; the horses shedding their winter coats as they had been, that can't be healthy... it could have been any one of them.

Or, because it's the countryside it could have been none of them, just something poor Thérence had picked up in the air, like germ warfare. We arranged for the vet to come out the following week and begin an investigation, but in the meantime Thérence had some scrapings taken from his cheeks to see if they could determine the cause. Apparently they do this by seeing what cultures grow from the scrapings, in other words what vegetation can be cultivated from my lad's face! As Marlon Brando said in *The Godfather*, 'Look what they did to my beautiful boy.'

The course of treatment he was prescribed was also quite harsh. Firstly tablets, which are 250 milligrams but of which he can only take 200 milligrams, which meant us crushing the tablets in a pestle and mortar and then in rather dubious fashion, chopping the powder into lines and placing it in wraps. He was also given some cream which was so strong he wasn't to be allowed out into the sunlight! For two months! A situation which got Natalie especially quite angry about the whole misdiagnosis thing, but what do you do? This is a very small, rural community and the doctor is a very powerful figure here, it's not a case of simply changing your doctor; that would be a very public insult and a decision not to be taken lightly. It's not wise to upset local bigwigs; I've seen *Jean de Florette*.

Despite her frustration with the doctor and the logistical difficulty in keeping an adventurous toddler locked indoors on a sunny day, Natalie's mood is always lifted in the spring and at last it was here in all its glory. Like the popular bloke who turns up deliberately late at a party, spring had sneaked in, been forgiven for its tardiness and was being worshipped by all. Immediately the mood changed at home, rather than coming downstairs in the morning and being greeted with leaden skies, spring brings a freshness to the day; there is hope, there is potential.

'Spring is my favourite time of the year,' Natalie said for the fourth time that evening, as she concentrated hard on her garden design drawings and her notebooks. I had had the rare pleasure of being at home for a week but had barely seen her in that time, though in truth I hadn't really expected to. When spring arrives she is outside from sunrise to sunset and if we could rig up powerful arc lights for the night she would be outside then too.

My outdoor roles are, by choice, fairly limited but I am occasionally called upon to perform some menial task and one of those is 'small animal rescue', which hitherto has consisted of only two actual rescues. The first was the kingfisher that flew into the lounge windows and knocked itself out, and the other rescue was when a small rabbit, which must have been dropped by a clumsy buzzard, landed on Eddie's head. That all changed with the advent of the cats. I was now constantly on call, like a lifeguard, always ready to rescue small animals of differing varieties from the clutches of the evil cats. Mice, shrews, birds, lizards – their cruelty is indiscriminate while they just toy with the small beasts. They had actually taken to dragging whatever creature they'd caught to the front of the house where they knew we'd watching, because they knew what would happen next. Natalie would stop humming and shout, 'Ian! Vespa's caught something!' The boys would come running and generally get there before me, the cats would have a crowd and then I would turn up like a wheezing David Hasselhoff and the chase would begin.

The cat would pick the thing up in its mouth and make a dart for the open field, I'd go after it, rugby tackle the cat, whereupon the other cat would pick up the ball/mouse and run with it. I'd go after that one too. This would go on for as long as they want it to and is quite simply exhausting, rendering me a sweaty mess in whatever area of the garden we would finish in, unable to walk anymore, triumphant in my rescue of whatever creature I might have saved that day, but physically spent. This is where Natalie's shrewd garden design would come into its own, as fortunately there are plenty of places for me to just sit down and have a rest; she certainly never uses them, especially in spring.

One of Natalie's most endearing qualities has always been her quite monumental determination – her utter refusal to yield to the inevitable, despite overwhelming evidence that she is fighting a losing battle, is almost superhuman. I don't mean that in an unflattering way either, the reason we are able to have what we have despite me hardly being around is because of her strength and resolve. But when she first insisted on keeping the cats I did point out, with a certain degree of 'I don't know why I'm even bothering to say this but...', that they would kill everything in sight. The small rodents that scurry across the patio, the lizards that bask on the walls, the fish in the pond and the myriad of birds that nest in the garden; all of that, I said, you are putting at risk. Are you really sure that that's what you want?

'Don't worry,' she replied, 'I'll teach them not to kill.' And in one fell swoop went from endearingly stubborn and resolute to downright deluded.

The kittens were, by now, eight months old and it was carnage. Now obviously the countryside is a brutal place and as a lifelong 'townie' it takes some getting used to, but the sheer level of slaughter was frightening. I honestly didn't realise how much wildlife we had at the place until it started turning up in piles on the doorstep, and it was relentless. All day, every day, without rest or pause. If they hid what they killed, had any shame whatsoever it might have been more bearable; and if Natalie and the boys also didn't feel the need to have a state funeral every time another poor creature fell prey to the murderous felines that may have helped too. It was getting like Wootton Bassett at home, another senseless death, another outpouring of emotion, another burial. There was so much butchery at one point that even Natalie had to start using a mass grave instead of the individual plots she'd been regularly preparing and it also created a level of desensitisation with the boys. When the rabbit died, Samuel was in tears for hours afterwards but now neither he nor Maurice felt able to raise their heads from their Nintendos, a certain level of ennui having set in despite the heavy death toll.

For any sentient human being this presents a stark choice, either accept what is going on or get rid of the cats, but seeing as neither of these seemed to actually be an option for Natalie she moved onto a third alternative, which I nicknamed Operation King Canute and was, I fear, always doomed to failure. The plan was this: acknowledge that cats have, over millions of years, evolved into brutal and efficient hunters and that they have their rights, but then teach them new skills while still having all the temptations around them. I admire Natalie's tenacity, I really do, but it was a bit like watching Tim Henman at Wimbledon, noble and backed up with fanatical support maybe, but ultimately doomed to failure.

The cats of course were completely bemused by the whole project, when Flame was forcibly removed from a large mouse and picked up by the scruff of his neck one day and told he was being 'very naughty', he had a look of utter bewilderment on his face. I pointed out to Natalie that he wasn't being naughty at all but doing only what comes naturally to him.

'You used to wake up every morning and light up a cigarette!' she shot back. 'But you changed!'

'Fair enough. I'll just nip down the vets and get some 'Instinct Patches' then, shall I?' I said and scurried away before she picked me up by my neck too.

'Cat Bibs' were the answer apparently. Having trawled the internet for potential solutions, of which there are unsurprisingly very few, it seemed like Cat Bibs would do the trick. And they definitely work, according to the makers of Cat Bibs. The Cat Bib is exactly what it sounds like, it's a brightly coloured bib, made of rubber and foam and attaches to the cat's collar. I did some research of my own on this and not only did I not find a great deal of evidence to suggest that they do work, but even the people who say that they work aren't really sure why. To my mind the cat looks ready to eat which is hardly an impediment and surely will only muddy the waters further. It's suggested that the bibs either work because the prey can see the predator coming (eyewitness testimony), they act as a barrier to a successful leap (manufacturer's explanation), or the cat feels like such a berk having a bib-shaped computer mouse mat hanging from its neck that it's shamed into staying indoors (my theory).

None of which matters, as they didn't work at all. Oh, they were slightly off-putting for the first couple of days but that was only while the cats got used to carrying the things around their necks. But it didn't take long for them to actually be a positive spur to hunting! The cats found a way of swinging the bibs around so, rather than look like a bib hanging from the neck and ready to be splashed with food, they were now hanging from the back of the neck and looked like small capes, giving the cats a new-found confidence as they leapt on anything that moved in the misguided assumption that they were now SuperCats!

I fear that this dealt something of a blow to Natalie's confidence as once again the bodies mounted up. An air of resignation set in, mass graves were left open waiting for the next inevitable victim, even the bibs were put on forlornly and with no real expectation of success. Experience told me that this was the time to lay low, don't gloat, don't draw attention to yourself. While Natalie ruminated on the inevitable failure to turn back millennia of feline instinct she would have to turn her attention to softer targets so it was best to just stay out of her way, which was easier said than done.

We have a big house, a lot of land and a lot of outbuildings, and yet there is nowhere I can go that will offer any respite whatsoever, there is nowhere to hide, no oasis of calm. You're probably thinking that this is a ridiculous complaint and you'd be right – I spend an awful lot of my time moaning about being away from my family and then when I do get home I'm moaning about that as well. In my defence, I could argue that I am an 'artiste' and therefore need my creative space, but actually I'm just a moody git who needs five minutes to himself occasionally for his own good and for the good of those around him.

It was easier when I was a smoker; I used to wait until everyone else was in bed and disappear to my makeshift office in one of the *dépendances* and 'write' until the early hours of the morning. In reality all I did was smoke, sample too much of the local wine and pointlessly practise cricket shots until the early hours of the morning. I gave up smoking and moved my office into the spare room in the main house, a naive move, frankly, that lasted about as long as it took to turn on the computer as my desk rapidly became the go-to place for ironing and toys that 'Daddy would mend'. So I moved my 'office' next to a wardrobe at the top of the stairs, where it couldn't have been more open plan if it was in the local town square, and besides which I couldn't use my chair as 'that's where the cats sleep'.

I thought I'd found my oasis one afternoon. Samuel and Maurice were at school, Thérence was in bed and Natalie was occupying herself in the garden, so I vainly planned on setting up my laptop in the workshop and doing some 'work'. What I soon realised was that a family of swallows had built a nest in the workshop and now regarded the place as their own, angry little so-and-sos they were too. They quite clearly regarded my presence as an invasion of their privacy and sat angrily on the shelf above me telling me in no uncertain terms to 'bugger off'. I don't know if you've ever had a row with a pair of breeding swallows, but it's a pretty unedifying affair – the more they chirruped swallow obscenities at me the more I threw back exactly the same at them.

'What is going on?' Natalie shouted as she rushed into the workshop. 'Who are you swearing at?'

'The damn swallows!' I said, a tad embarrassed. 'The little sods won't leave me alone.'

Natalie then spent the next five minutes telling me that this was their territory now and that I shouldn't be disturbing them while they lay eggs and no wonder they were angry – wouldn't I be if my territory was invaded? I tried to point out that technically and legally I was within my rights to stay and that it was my territory that had been invaded, but she'd already gone. I shut my laptop and left as well, but not before I'd given the cantankerous pair a right mouthful which they duly gave back. I moved into another room next door and the same thing happened, only this pair weren't content with verbal assaults and felt that swooping low over my head in an aggressive fashion would get me away from their nest. They were right too.

Besides which, my grumpy animal rescue skills were apparently needed again. I could hear Maurice, just back from school, calling me.

'Daddy, it's a snake! A big snake,' he shouted excitedly. Bloody hell, I thought, that's really not my department at all. I hate snakes.

The three of them proceeded to describe the snake. It was big, smallish, greeny, beige with a square, triangular head and 'tractor', which was Thérence's contribution. It was like trying to get some sense out of a family of rednecks convinced that they'd been abducted by aliens. It's well known, apparently, that hens kill snakes but Tallulah and Lola didn't seem even remotely interested preferring instead to dig up Natalie's roses, much to her annoyance. Snakes can be a problem around here; years ago they released more snakes into the area to control a growing rodent population, so now people have hens to control the snakes. Presumably once the hens are out of control they'll release foxes and then when they're running wild they'll release a load of red-jacketed hunters 'tally-ho-ing' all over the shop.

I looked for the snake, a bit gingerly to be honest and rather hoping that I wouldn't come across it, but I couldn't find the thing and assumed that Maurice had been mistaken or that it might just be a harmless grass snake. Then the next day the evidence arrived. A rat, a huge rat at that, had been killed just where they'd seen the serpent. There were no visible signs of attack on the thing and it was so big that I doubt even the cats could have got it, had they been inclined. It was a monster and Natalie took me to one side.

'You have to find this thing,' she said simply. 'Somewhere it has found a place to hide, where it isn't disturbed by the cats or dogs and where the children haven't stumbled on it.'

'You're right,' I replied with determination. 'Don't worry, I'll find it and when I do I'll ask him to budge up a bit.'

I never did find the snake and no more evidence turned up suggesting that it had set up permanently somewhere on the property; my guess was that there was too much activity going on, too much noise and that he felt threatened by all the activity and just cleared off looking for a bit of peace and quiet. I had every sympathy with him too.

SELF-INSUFFICIENCY

Spring was now in full effect and although there was lots to do in the garden, in the house, with the animals and the children, I couldn't have been happier. Finally, the renovation work was due to start on the 'classroom' for our school. The idea, we had decided, would be to set up 'Writing Holidays' where we would hire an author for a week and they would teach the students how to write in a particular genre. One of the most important points of selling this idea to potential students was that we could offer total peace, a bucolic haven which would provide a distraction-free environment for aspiring authors. Yes, well, good luck with that I thought. The place was feeling about as distraction-free as Piccadilly Circus.

'I think we should build into the loft,' I ventured tentatively to Natalie, 'the loft above the classroom.'

'What for?' she replied, really knowing the answer all along.

'I just need a bit of space to work in. Rather than combine the office and classroom, we could separate the two. I could take all my stuff out there.' I added quickly knowing that would clinch it. I had chairs, dressers, shelf units you name it that simply didn't fit the farmhouse look that Natalie was aiming for in the house; they stood out like modernist warts against her shabby chic background.

'Will you take those awful, metal bar stools out there?'

'Definitely,' I said, and went out to check on the hens.

It had taken a while, but Tallulah and Lola were finally 'with egg'. One small one each at first, but they grew in size and then it became a daily ritual to go to their coop, say good morning to 'my ladies', and return with the spoils. It became the first thing we did in the morning and made me, and everyone else inordinately happy – Thérence, by now released from the tyranny of his fungal condition, especially, as it became 'his' job. A lovely way to start the day.

Their new coop, which I had ferried from England, had done the trick. Logistically it had proved something of a problem – it barely fitted (flat-packed obviously) into the car, but having squeezed it in I had difficulty getting it out again. This thing was going to be huge, I thought. It wasn't. In fact, it was disappointingly small after I'd eventually put it all together, a triumph of illusionary packaging. My ladies didn't seem to mind, though, as I tempted them into their new home. They scratched about a bit, went up the ramp to their beds, sat on their perches, ate from the trough, drank from their 'well' and generally nosed about the place like a particularly judgemental pair of old spinsters on *Location, Location, Location*. But I could tell they liked it – they clucked contentedly, a surprisingly heart-melting sound, and settled down for bed. It made me feel ineffably proud to watch them, like an expectant father and I left them to it.

Within a couple of days the coop had made them contented enough to start laying and I returned home one Sunday to find Maurice coyly hiding his hands behind his back.

'Guess what I've got, Daddy?' he chuckled, and before I could answer (the lad just cannot keep a secret), 'EGGS!'

He showed me one, which surprisingly had a supermarket 'Best Before' date stamped on it. 'Oh poo!' he said, 'I've picked up the wrong one!' And off he went to find a 'home-grown' example. Having access to one's own eggs may be small beer in the grand scheme of things, man cannot live on eggs alone, but it never fails to put a smile on my face. It's just one of those things that you just can't be cynical about or bored by. And it made us all feel more a part of the countryside we were surrounded by; we could look our farmer neighbours full in the eye from now on.

If only everything else was as rewarding as my ladies. I am constantly amazed how many times people compare my life with *The Good Life* – I mean, it's a 'good life' don't get me wrong, but *The Good Life* was a sitcom about a married couple who drop out of the rat race and live off their own land in suburban Surrey. Tom, the male character, was a relentlessly chirpy, optimistic individual. He wore jumpers with holes in them. I am not Tom.

Of course, that doesn't mean that I don't knuckle down and work the land when I have to, I do, though not optimistically or cheerfully and definitely not in shabby knitwear. The combination of spring heat and regular moisture meant that the garden was running wild, which also meant that Natalie had to call me in to lend a hand. I was hoping it would be more moral support than physical, but after the damage left by the receding winter's scorched earth policy and the now violently rampant spring, I didn't have high hopes. Manuel was also roped in to tame the spring garden and while he worked like an old-fashioned African explorer machete-ing his way through the jungle, it meant that I was awarded the trickier tasks like writing labels and mending the gate for what had become known as 'my' allotment.

Lots of people have allotments, or potagers, these days as they tick all the right boxes – healthy, organic foodstuffs, a sense of community, local produce, exercise, etc. – but does anyone really know what they're doing? It strikes me that people talk an awful lot of guff about loam quality and shade while secretly crossing their fingers behind their backs. I'll admit I'm not particularly green-fingered, but so far my allotment results have been repeatedly on the disappointing side and so when spring rolls around and once again I have to dig the thing over, I do so with a sense of impending disappointment, knowing that the whole exercise while on the one hand being worthy, will only bring forth a crushing sense of boredom and disillusion, like a Coldplay album or non-alcoholic lager.

I can grow beetroot. Believe me, if we wake up tomorrow in some post-apocalyptic wasteland I'm your go-to guy for beetroot. Even I can't kill that stuff, which leads me to suspect that beetroot is so easy to grow you could actually just throw a few seeds at a multi-storey car park and still get a decent harvest a few months later. I'm also a dab hand at tomato growing, which is something of an irony as I'm allergic to the things. I was once stung by a jelly fish in Tunisia where the local remedy for such an incident is either to rub a tomato into the sting or urinate on it. They are lovely, warm people the Tunisians but even their generosity can be stretched if you lie on their beaches and demand that innocent passersby wee on you.

I'm also a success with Swiss chard, again a seemingly indestructible vegetable that survives rain, sleet, direct sunlight and routine indifference. It never stops growing! My children are good eaters and will try anything, but offer up Swiss chard ten days in a row and the novelty wears off, I can tell you. I know lots of parents find it difficult to get their offspring to eat their greens, but how many are greeted at the dinner table with 'Oh, Daddy, Swiss chard again? Really?' I tried growing spinach as an alternative, actually a 'cut and come again' spinach which was just awful and relentless; even Popeye would have baulked at this bitter, stringy variant. Samuel quite reasonably asked one day if we couldn't 'just put it out of its misery.'

Some things you plant on advice, 'This will keep you going all summer' they say in spring, only to follow it up in early autumn with 'Well, it worked for me.' Carrots, for instance. Carrots should be simple, surely? It's a carrot, they're everywhere – who can't grow a carrot? I can't, that's who. I did exactly as the seed packet suggested, the correct depth, the right level of watering, I 'thinned' the seedlings when required, I nurtured the little sods through all the elements and how did they repay me? By being so measly, so pitifully small and thin, you'd have been forgiven for thinking I'd invented the 'Pre-Julienned Carrot'. Broad beans were the same, three months I waited for those things and in the end had barely enough to sprinkle on an omelette for one.

I think I'm much better suited to orchard husbandry – there's no digging involved there, just a bit of judicious pruning over the winter months and then harvesting when ripe. It's lazy farming and suits me down to the ground; the orchard also acts as a surrogate office for me too. One of the reasons why the Loire Valley is supposedly a haven for peace is that mobile phone signals are something of a lottery and for some reason at times the best signal can only be found standing next to the plum tree in the orchard.

Generally though, I try not to take advantage of this as the orchard is a calming place, disturbed only by the bees going about their business, but I needed to take an important call and that was the only place (in between a plum tree and the fence to the paddock) that I could guarantee the necessary signal. It was during this call that Junior, never a horse to miss an opportunity to be a complete bastard, decided to stand just the other side of the fence and urinate so loudly and for such a long period of time that by the end we were both standing in a huge puddle of horse wee. Obviously under normal circumstances I would have moved but I was in the middle of this call and worried about losing the signal, despite it being pretty obvious to the person on the other end that something was amiss as I was trying to shoo Junior away under my breath and gagging from the stench rising from the puddle.

'Is everything OK?' the caller asked. 'Is it raining there?'

'No, no,' I replied as I flicked Junior the V-sign, 'Everything's fine. I'm standing next to a waterfall.'

All of us, at some time or another, have been victims of crime. The violation one feels afterwards can linger and promote a kind of debilitating paranoia until the transgression, no matter how trivial, gets blown out of all proportion. Serious crime is worse; it feels like a personal attack and recovery, if it happens at all, can take years without ever being fully completed. The doubts always remain. The thing is I didn't expect this particularly drowsy corner of the Loire to throw up this kind of problem but it did, and my bucolic paradise had become, albeit temporarily, somewhat tarnished. In short, we had been 'scrumped'.

Now some of you may be thinking that apart from the victims of queue jumping this is pretty much as trivial as crime gets and that it would take an incredibly petty and small-minded individual to make much of an issue out of it. You'd be right of course, but in my role as pin-up boy for the 'Petty, Small Mindedness' minority, I did make an issue out of it. I was bloody annoyed.

Someone was stealing my cherries.

Natalie, of course with her sunny disposition and belief in the basic goodness of humanity was convinced that it was the birds that were doing it, but the evidence definitely suggested otherwise.

'If it's the birds,' I said, scratching my chin and giving it the full Poirot, 'why are there no cherry stones at the base of the tree, eh? Answer me that!'

'They take them away?' she replied, a touch patronisingly.

'OK, but point two: why are they only taking cherries that are at arm's reach? Hmm? The top of the tree still has loads of cherries on it.'

Incontrovertible evidence, in my book, that it was a human behind this travesty and, unable to argue against it, she stomped off muttering something about mental illness.

The problem I now had was to try and stop the remaining cherries from falling into enemy hands. I couldn't climb the tree because the fruit was right at the top and the branches wouldn't take my weight; Natalie forbade me to send one of the boys up there as it was pretty high and possibly a bit dangerous and the third option had disaster written all over it: me, on a very rickety old wooden ladder standing precariously on uneven ground while I stretched myself up to pick the fruit. Natalie did offer up a fourth option which was to leave the fruit where it was, stop arsing about and stop obsessing about things.

'Hmm,' I said, 'have we not met?'

I placed the ladders in what I thought was their safest position, but even then they were decidedly wobbly – frankly, a mild gust of wind and they'd be over. I walked round the tree a few times and weighed it all up. If I fell down I would either land on hard ground some 3 metres below or, and this was definitely the worst possibility, I would fall into the tree, not only breaking a lot of branches but quite possibly becoming impaled on the thing like some low-rent Aztec Fruit God. Neither option was particularly appealing and it was with some relief that Natalie reminded me that we had been invited to one of the local farmer's places for a pre-lunch aperitif and to sample some of their homemade *pousse d'épine*.

Like all good homemade hooch, *pousse d'épine* lulls you into a false sense of security making you think that really it isn't that strong actually and yes, I'd love another. Well it *is* that strong and I did have another, and a few more too. We returned home about an hour or so later and I was literally fortified by the stuff and determined to tackle the cherry tree. It was not one of my finest ideas.

Now fully briefed with our plans and at last showing some appetite for the job, the builders had begun work in earnest. They couldn't, however, avoid regarding me with some suspicion. They weren't particularly keen on the way I dress for starters, and I'm pretty sure they were bemused by the fact that it was Natalie mowing the lawns, moving benches, sawing wood, etc. while I flitted about wearing my kitchen apron and sweeping the terrace. But they were friendly enough, when eventually they turned up, and I admired the way that they would bring their own barbeque for lunch and ask us to keep their meat refrigerated and their wine chilled. They were enjoying their lunch when we returned.

'*Bon appétit!*' I cried, brimming with confidence as I made my way unsteadily back to my ladders. '*Il fait beau, eh?*' They all nodded slowly, noticing not only that I was a little more garrulous than usual, but also that I was about to stand on top of wobbly old ladders while under the influence of moonshine and try and pick fruit. They turned their deckchairs to face the orchard and sat down slowly.

I think for the first ten minutes or so I handled things pretty well. I concentrated hard and, much to the disappointment of the gnarled onlookers harvested a fair few cherries without it ever looking like disaster might strike. Yet... I hadn't reckoned on Junior. That he is a fractious, nasty piece of work is a given but he is also possessed of whatever the equine equivalent is of Machiavellian cunning. So while I was concentrating hard on my harvesting and trying not to look a complete berk in front of the locals, I hadn't noticed that Junior had become agitated and was building up a head of steam charging about in his paddock. There was just one bunch of cherries I had to get and as I reached out for them, Junior hurtled past and kicked out his back legs as he did so. Whether it was the ground that shook under his movement or I just lost concentration I can't say (though I do know he was trying deliberately to knock me down) – anyway, I fell, not into the tree thankfully but heavily to the ground, squashing most of my harvest.

I lay there for a few moments, dazed, but alert enough to see the builders unhurriedly get out of their chairs and shake their heads mournfully. To them it must have looked like a crushing defeat but I'd stripped the tree bare of cherries and though they were now largely unusable, at least no other bugger could have them.

I wasn't the only one having crop issues though, everybody was. There was a drought in the Loire Valley, a serious drought, and the farmers were not only obeying laws, they were wandering mournfully around their arid fields, pursing their lips and letting handfuls of soil sift through their fingers in time-honoured 'Look, it's a drought' fashion. There's not an awful lot of sympathy for French farmers, they have become a potent symbol of everything people believe is wrong with the European Union. Fair enough. What shouldn't be forgotten though is that where the UK goes wrong in 'Europe' is that we moan about certain laws and directives, but do as we are told anyway. The French, and their farmers in particular, take a more pragmatic approach: they do what the bloody hell they want and Europe can go hang.

The river Cher, no more than 200 metres from our house and therefore right next to farmland was dangerously low for the time of year and the industrial-sized irrigation system, as well as the more prosaic hosepipe use, had been outlawed in the area. The farmers, knowing there was little point in disobeying this order, were powerless and were just standing by watching their infant crops withering. All of which had a knock-on effect for us. For one, we had got used to having the massive sprinkler systems shooting over the hedge and watering the garden and allotment; Natalie had even started parking the car strategically to get a free carwash. Hay was the main problem for us. There is perennially already a massive shortage of hay in Western Europe (what do you mean you didn't know?) thanks to previous springs being too wet, and now with this spring being too dry the shortage was to get even worse. Apparently, the horses had been eating straw for the last month. I'm not entirely sure that I know the difference between hay and straw but apparently it's akin to the difference between an own-brand shepherd's pie and a super-deluxe alternative. Needless to say, it had passed me by.

'But haven't you noticed that Junior has been moodier recently?' Natalie asked earnestly.

'No,' I replied, and honestly, as far as I can tell the straw diet hasn't hampered his capacity for violent equine love-making so it can't be that bad. 'He's always like that.'

On the plus side, I managed to get the swimming pool filled before the water ban came in, though that is something of a mixed blessing. The pool, for somebody with OCD, requires constant attention. What temperature is it? Is the water at the right level? Do I need to clean the filter? Add chemicals? What pH is it? But by far the most time-consuming element is the bugs: the flies, the bees, the ladybirds, hornets, mayflies, anything that lands on the surface and hasn't the wit to get off again and therefore blemishes what should be clear water. I know it's a level of madness that I seem to have created for myself, but I don't even go in the pool these days, I just stand at the side with the pool skimmer net fishing bugs off the surface, like a demented butterfly catcher, constantly tutting and swearing at the insects for their stupidity and impertinence.

'Why don't you come in, Daddy?' Maurice would ask.

'I'll just get this last fly,' I'd answer, but there'll always be another one.

Also, it's bloody freezing. Electricity is four times more expensive in France than in the UK, largely due to the fact that the one state monopoly supplier, Electricité de France, would rather pay the EU fines than open up the market competitively (see what I mean about 'Europe'?), which means that I'm far too tight to put the heater on. Ironically, Electricité de France own a fair amount of the UK electricity franchises, where they charge a great deal less! Maurice decided to brave the temperatures, and to herald the start of summer rather boldly took a flying leap into the crystal, temporarily bug-free waters. He practically bounced straight back out again as he realised that, although the thermometer read 22 degrees, that was actually only the surface temperature and bore little relation to the temperature further below. He was still shivering a couple of hours later.

The flies were everywhere too. I tried, sometimes overzealously, to keep the doors and windows shut but the little sods still got in. When I wasn't batting them away from the pool I was indoors with a fly swat in each hand like some Jedi fly catcher, manically bounding about the house going 'There's one!' and bringing the swat down, usually a fraction too late. I asked Natalie, as I was angrily attacking the flies in the lounge, whether if we got rid of the horses we would have fewer flies and she didn't even bother to answer.

It was *monstres* week again, so as well as the flies there was the possibility of us gaining even more old furniture and random knick-knacks. Once again Natalie had insisted on driving me around the streets of local villages picking up other people's bits of discarded furniture and general household flim-flammery. However, in thanks for forcing me to endure yet another *monstres* run Natalie bought me a present: a magnificent battery-operated fly swat. Shaped like a tennis racket, it has a wide head housing a metal grid which stuns the fly like a taser. It is a splendid instrument and meant that I could swat flies with an overhead smash or a stinging backhand down the line. It was more fun than the Wii and actually meant that I was getting some physical exercise into the bargain which, seeing as I was unlikely to be able to get into the pool because of bugs, was about the only exercise I was likely to get – that and laying traps for fruit thieves.

DIFFERENT STROKES

Of course, guarding the house and gardens shouldn't have been up to me at all, this is very much Toby's department and to his credit most of the time he does a decent job. He has a deep, angry bark which tends to unnerve anyone who approaches the main gate, but once inside he reverts to type, rolls over on his back and sticks his legs in the air. Bless him, he's just desperate to be loved. His guard-dog duties, however, had been made more difficult than usual by the dreadful late spring weather. There were no drought fears anymore – the heavens opened and stayed that way. Not only was he cooped up inside for most of the time but there was very little fruit to defend. The awful weather meant that most of the orchard was actually fruitless – no plums, peaches or apples to be had – putting my chutney production into severe difficulty. A corporate booking agency that I work with a lot had even asked if I could supply fifty jars of chutney to add to the Christmas hampers which they gave to their clients; I'd blithely committed myself to this just expecting the fruit to be there and it wasn't.

Toby was also preoccupied with Pierrot, as we all were now as his health suddenly began to deteriorate. It didn't help that everything about Pierrot's history was shrouded in mystery. We assumed that his previous owner was an old lady who spoilt him rotten and who had just died, leaving him homeless. We didn't know his breed for certain, though he seemed to be a cross between a King Charles spaniel and a dachshund, his age was unclear, and even his name, Pierrot, isn't his name. His owner left no papers, or if she did they were never found, so the rescue centre had given him the name Pierrot. Though it wasn't entirely chosen at random.

Having guessed that Pierrot was about nine years old, the rescue centre put his birth year as 2000 and the corresponding letter was P. The only problem with this is that he's clearly not Pierrot and at the grand old age of nine he wasn't going to start answering to a different name. We've tried calling him all the names beginning with P, but pet naming is a personal thing and there's no guarantee that his P is any kind of recognised and traditional name anyway; and believe me when you've got three boys who like nothing better than to giggle at rude words there have been some pretty salty suggestions. And all of that is on the assumption that he was even born in 2000, he might be a year either side, an O or an R. Yes, even the French didn't insist on 2001 being the year Q.

He simply didn't respond to anything, and OK that may be largely because he was actually quite deaf by this time, but it all served to make him quite impenetrable. In the past month he had become incontinent and despite running a battery of tests there seemed to be nothing physically wrong with him other than the ravages of old age. The vet had prescribed some eye drops to fix the problem, which sounds bizarre but apparently, according to the chemist, the old folk around here swear by the stuff. They didn't work, however, which meant we had to move his bed into a large cage at night so that we didn't wake up to his mess everywhere in the morning. It seemed a little cruel and undignified, but as he was also by now practically blind as well he wasn't really aware of that either.

His loss of senses (other than the one that told him it's feeding time) meant that he was relying more heavily on Toby, and that surely must have been the final indignity. Toby's judgement at the best of times would compare unfavourably with that of a drunk twelve-year-old boy in possession of a chainsaw, so to watch poor old Pierrot hanging by his side, like Donald Pleasance did with James Garner in *The Great Escape*, was pitiful. And Toby is no James Garner – he specialises more in hapless, clueless and world-class stupidity (occasionally barking at passing clouds) and even Pierrot, laid low as he was, recognised the absurdity of that.

Despite Toby's noble efforts, however, Pierrot was getting worse. I had been in England for only a couple of days when Natalie phoned to tell me that Pierrot had suffered a series of strokes that left him briefly paralysed and completely disorientated. He had even sought comfort with Natalie and the boys, something he hadn't done with any of us since he arrived. I made a decision to cancel the rest of my trip. There are many advantages to operating below the 'showbiz' radar, but one of the best is that a replacement can easily be found at short notice and very few people mind. And I definitely wanted to go home. I will never forget Eddie's last night; I stayed up with her all the way through it as slowly each of her organs failed, but she battled on to the morning when I was able to take her to the vet's for the last time. Pierrot isn't Eddie and it was naive of me to think he could be and an unfair pressure to put on him, but he's family and the old pervert deserved the best.

I decided to run the gauntlet of the London to Paris bus, partly because it was by far the cheaper mode of transport at such short notice but also it meant that I could definitely be home for late morning. It was, however, the most uncomfortable option especially as a couple of young, aggressive-looking North Africans were trying to intimidate and threaten some of the other passengers. The Spanish driver, who spoke neither English nor French, steadfastly refused to get involved so by the time they decided to pick on me they felt pretty much invincible. I had been sitting behind them the whole journey yet it was only now, with an hour or so to go, that they thought my attire was worthy of comment. I wasn't in the mood for it. I am not a hard man, far from it, but I refuse to be bullied and just laughed at their rather childish attempts to intimidate me, which only made them angrier. 'Wait until we get to Paris...' they said darkly, to which I just laughed again and they settled down to bide their time.

We arrived in Paris around dawn and descended from the bus, bleary eyed. I kept the two aggressors in sight, watching them as they got their belongings together, though I wasn't really wary of them as I was just too tired to be on guard. I then watched them with utter incredulity as they ran off! They just scarpered! What a waste of effort. They had spent almost the entire journey on some pointless crusade to intimidate and then they just disappeared for some reason. Maybe on arrival they thought that a man who was prepared to wear a cravat on an overnight bus journey wasn't actually someone you'd trifle with unnecessarily. Either way, it was a surreal journey.

Even travelling on the Paris Metro was harder than usual as I got unwittingly caught up in an accordion-busker turf war. I don't know whether it's the law, and it wouldn't surprise me if it is, but buskers in Paris only ever play the accordion and apparently only have a repertoire of about five songs. Normally I don't mind that. Accordion music is so much a part of the Parisian stereotype that it feels comforting to have it wheezily bleating away in the background; I know where I am and it makes a change from London buskers and their increasingly bizarre 'interpretations' of Simon and Garfunkel. The other difference with Parisian buskers is that they are on the train with you; again that's not too much of a problem if the Metro is quiet or if they're at the other end of the carriage.

This guy, though, was in my face. Literally in my face. Every time he pushed and pulled on his accordion there would be accompanying percussion as the metal buttons on my coat got caught up in his squeeze box; something he resented enormously, clearly regarding passengers on the Metro as a hindrance to his performance. There was nowhere to go, though, the tube was jam-packed, but rather than get off and wait for a quieter train he just ploughed on regardless, breathing God knows what kind of fiery liquor right at me.

Just before the stop at Jacques Bonsergent he appeared to accept defeat and just stopped his version of 'La Mer' mid-beat, but as he did so another accordion started up at the other end of the carriage clearly causing massive effrontery to 'my' man who immediately dived into a stirring, if slightly tuneless rendition of 'La Marseillaise'. This upped the ante from the interloper who, like a DJ mixing tunes at a deck, seamlessly switched from 'Coeur Vagabond' to 'Sous le Ciel de Paris', barely missing a beat. This toing and froing continued for another few minutes, each round played more aggressively than the last and sounding like a sweary row between two drunken dolphins, until from the other end of the carriage came the killer blow: 'Je Ne Regrette Rien' played, it has to be said, with some skill –

but not only that, the other guy was singing too! My God it was awful, but as with most Edith Piaf songs, tune isn't the point, it's the passion that counts and this bloke was giving it both barrels.

There could be only one winner and my man stopped playing, looked up into my eyes and shrugged in acknowledgement of his defeat. As he did so his accordion got trapped on one of my buttons, so not only did he lose in the duelling accordions battle, he had to suffer the ignominy of detaching an angry mod from his instrument. One can only hope that his day improved after that but he looked very forlorn as he got off at the next stop.

Pierrot seemed in decent spirits when I eventually got home. His strokes, though apparently less frequent, were horrible to witness. He would screech loudly, clearly in distress, and seek comfort from us when they occurred, but in between times he actually seemed more active than usual. It was difficult to know what to do for the best. The vet prescribed some more drugs for him and maybe they helped a little, but while he was obviously in some physical pain it was only brief and in between these bouts of torment he was actually more lively than he had been for months. He was eating well, that was never an issue, and was even dry at night, so we decided just to see how things panned out for a bit. Maybe the strokes would stop and he would be fine or maybe we were just putting off the inevitable, but Toby wasn't leaving his side for now so we agreed to just wait and see what happened next.

Despite worries over Pierrot, I was actually enjoying some unexpected time off at home and intended to put this windfall to good use. Officially the reasons why we chose to move to the Loire Valley are that Natalie had family here, the bucolic pace of life suits us and that it was cheap. Also, and this wasn't necessarily uppermost in Natalie's thoughts at the time, the Loire Valley represents the limit of what could be deemed acceptable Radio 4 Long Wave reception; it's about as far down as you can go in France and still listen to *Test Match Special* on a crackly old portable radio.

I love cricket and if there is a downside to having relocated here it's that my children won't get to play the game. There is a cricket club just a couple of hours from here in Saumur, which counts occasional local resident Mick Jagger (yes, that one) among its membership, but we didn't move here to join an expat community and actually the boys show very little inclination to play the game, cricket having become synonymous with me lying in bed all day moaning and being sick. The reason for this connection is that whenever I go to watch a Test Match live I, er, over-indulge somewhat and spend the next day curled up in a foetal position, whimpering like a puppy and occasionally asking death to 'Take me now'. Any debilitating illness therefore, in which I am bedridden or obviously nauseous is greeted with the expression, 'Daddy's been to cricket again.' I am not then selling them the game's finer points.

Cricket is such an iconic symbol of Englishness that it crops up regularly in the English-language media over here, seemingly just to remind people of their roots. There was a report in the English-language *Connexion* newspaper that cricket was to be 'taught' in 'some' primary schools in France, which I'm not for at all. While I deplore the popularity of basketball here (to my mind it's a sport that, more than any other, rewards physical freakery), trying to introduce cricket into the French education syllabus is the kind of expat delusion that leads to people exploring the possibility of opening a Greggs concession in the Dordogne. Can you imagine the foot-stamping media outcry if a school in Kent were to introduce *boules* into the curriculum?

It will never happen, of course. Cricket will not be taught in French schools, there may be the odd after-school club run with the wide-eyed zeal of missionary-like expats in Brittany and there's nothing wrong with that so much, though I'd suggest local variations like using a three-day-old baguette as a cricket bat, but it will never catch on. When most English people these days don't 'get' cricket you can hardly expect the French to pick up the baton to make up the numbers, even if they did invent the sport. Yes, you read that correctly. The French invented cricket. I mean they didn't, obviously, but in so far as most French people really don't understand the English love–hate relationship with France, there are some mischievous souls here who occasionally like to prod the wasps' nest with a stick and they'll release entirely baseless statements like 'Hastings still belongs to France', 'Yorkshire puddings were an Escoffier creation' or indeed, 'France invented cricket,' and then just disappear back into the undergrowth and await the swivel-eyed 'How Dare They?!' over-reaction. Anyone who's ever seen the reaction to me affecting a perfect forward defence shot with a baguette outside the *boulangerie* of a morning, something that happens with increasing regularity as some kind of dementia takes hold, will realise that not only did the French not invent the game, if they did they'd deny it. Besides which, just imagine how long the lunch would be?

I don't go out of my way to be different here, that happens naturally, but I prefer solitude when I'm listening to the cricket. Imagine lazy, hazy summer's days lolling flamboyantly on the hammock under an apple tree in the orchard while in the background the radio crackles atmospherically as it brings word of another backs-to-the-wall effort from the English batsmen. Sounds idyllic, doesn't it? Sounds like the stuff dreams are made of. Well it is exactly that: a dream. With three kids, two horses, three dogs, two cats and two chickens, like I ever get the chance to lie down in the orchard listening to cricket! In previous drought months Natalie and her fellow gardening friends had all been praying for rain, but now after the brief and inevitable, 'Well, it's good for the garden,' they weren't happy. Too much rain, apparently – too heavy, wrong type; I think it's pretty nigh on impossible to please gardeners. They spend their time trying to harness nature and then give off when nature then throws a few obstacles in their path, and they stand there under a helpful tree, shaking their heads at the whole thing.

The horses love it, though. Junior sees inclement weather as a sign that the Norse gods haven't forgotten him and he stands there angrily facing the driving rain while Ultime, like the wife who's had enough of this nonsense, stands just behind him seemingly tutting. Logistically, the weather was posing problems for them, however. Being that it was ostensibly spring, they had more basic needs to attend to and while the horizontal rain no doubt added to their sexual excitement, the extra ingredient of mud and no little surface water meant that when Junior, as he sometimes does, took a little run up, they would end up sliding around the paddock like some particularly filthy equine Torvill and Dean, all legs, snorts and heated pouts.

They were the only ones keen to venture outside – the builders had, at some point, downed tools and hadn't been seen for a fortnight, and also it seemed that Samuel hadn't been out for months either. He had been on a school trip at the end of March where the whole class went to Île d'Oléron for a week, from which most of them returned with some kind of virus rendering them all bedridden and exhausted, or 'teenage' as it used to be called. Our doctor wasn't happy.

In the continuing efforts to improve my French it was decided that I would take Samuel to see the doctor, which inspired no-one with confidence and irritated the doctor even more than usual. A confirmed and openly honest misanthrope, it appears that one of his few pleasures in life is the occasional visit from Natalie, where they can just chat about horses and paddocks and the like. When I turn up, he looks me up and down, rolls his eyes at what I'm wearing, angrily remembers my 'unmanly' request for a vasectomy and can barely look me in the eye after that. He's an old-fashioned doctor and therefore it was something of a surprise when, while examining Samuel, he declared that school trips should be banned. That generation of adult normally mock the mollycoddled kids of today and their weak antibodies, stressing the importance of dust and muck in their diet in order to build up an effective immune system. Not this doctor, 'They should be kept indoors,' he said, clearly not wanting the business.

School trips, he declared, are basically a petri dish of germs and it's no wonder most children come back ill, especially with meningitis, he whispered menacingly while poking a massive cotton bud down poor Samuel's throat. Various blood tests, swab tests and a lot of poking about later and it was decided that Samuel had *Staphylococcus aureus* throat carriage, something so serious that not only does it not have a catchy shortened name but a lorry-load of antibiotics was needed, lots of rest and Samuel needed to be quarantined. In other words, stay in bed, don't talk to anyone and just pop some pills; this hardly constituted a massive change in behaviour for Samuel who had taken to spending almost all of his time in his room anyway, voraciously watching any film that came his way and eschewing daylight like an albino owl.

Not that there seemed to be much daylight to enjoy – it was just heavy dark clouds followed by wind and rain. The swimming pool, which we had prepared earlier than any previous year, lay there mocking us and in between storms Maurice would run out and check the temperature.

'It's twenty-one!' he'd declare. 'It's never going to be ready in time.'

Maurice's birthday was coming up and we desperately needed the weather to improve or we would have a dozen six-year-old boys running around the house, causing mayhem and noise, leaving some things lying around and breaking other things. It would be carnage. I had lost money by cancelling gigs, Pierrot's vet bills were mounting up, I had to bite the financial bullet and put the pool heater on and then hope for the rain to stop. If not, Pierrot wouldn't be the only one in crisis.

23

A FÊTE WORSE THAN DEATH

In the course of travelling the world as a stand-up comedian I have had guns pulled on me, faced down violent stag parties, coped with a room full of soldiers fresh off the front line, been chased to my car by angry Nirvana fans, threatened with beatings, stabbings and 'runnings over'. I have landed in Manila in a damaged plane in an electrical storm, overturned a camper van in a mad airport dash in France, had ashtrays thrown at me by angry hecklers, been sexually assaulted by a prostitute from Djibouti, collapsed on stage through intestine failure and been whacked in the nuts by an overzealous security guard in Mumbai. But nothing, nothing prepared me for Maurice's sixth birthday and the dozen French kids that he invited. I have never felt more out of my depth, never been less in control.

Like a grizzled 'Nam veteran, I'm still getting flashbacks.

It's one of those things that you agree to without really thinking about the consequences, but from the moment the invites go out to the end when you survey the wreckage of your home, it's chaos. Firstly, and I really don't understand this, you don't sign off an invite to French people with RSVP. Why the hell not, it's French isn't it? It means *Répondez s'il vous plaît*, everybody knows that. But no, it's not used in France. Which surely begs the question why it's bloody well used in Britain? Was it a pretentious middle-class whim that just caught on? I don't get it. So there I was in the ridiculous situation of being told to delete RSVP from my beautifully designed party invites because the French, presumably for the first time in history, didn't want to see some of their own language.

No, I said defiantly, I'm leaving it on. Natalie pursed her lips and raised her eyebrows, her default 'Don't say I didn't tell you so'. By the time the eve of the party came around, we had had three responses and one of those was from the mother of an invitee I had accosted in the supermarket, and who had looked shocked and not a little put out when I asked if her son was coming to the party.

'Of course,' she said and looked at me like I was mad.

To my mind it's not just that it's rude, though it most definitely is, but it means that the planning, be it for food quantities, games, goody bags, etc. is nigh on impossible; and I can't work without a plan. That's why they don't sign off with RSVP, because they bloody ignore it! It's like a zebra crossing on a French road, it's a trap for unwary foreigners and laughably redundant.

'I don't know how much food to buy!' I said, completely flummoxed by the clear breach of – double irony here – party invite etiquette.

'Daddy, just buy enough,' Maurice said, with a very Gallic shrug.

It would have helped enormously if the kids had arrived in dribs and drabs, giving us some time to acclimatise to the situation, allowing us to dip our toes gently into calm waters before they become choppy. Here, though, surely by fluke as I doubt seriously whether they could actually organise themselves to that extent, everyone arrived at the same time. Everyone. It was like a sudden invasion – one minute there was quiet and a bit of nervous anticipation and the next minute there were a dozen French six-year-old boys running and screaming about the place. To start with they were very demure and respectful, full of 'Bonjour Monsieur' and the obligatory kiss on the cheek greeting. But the second the formal niceties were over they threw their hats in the air and went absolutely crazy. I like French kids, I like their manners and respect, but there isn't in my opinion any nation in the world that has noisier children. They scream incessantly and it is impossible to determine whether they are enjoying themselves or in abject agony, the noise levels are the same, the intonation identical and it's a total assault on your ears.

Suddenly, we had fifteen kids charging about the place, including our three, who I'm happy to report weren't doing any of the screaming (Thérence was actually, but he'll learn). The four adults – me, Natalie and her parents, who we had roped in for crowd control – looked at each other nervously. We had planned some games, but this unruly mob didn't look like they'd stay still long enough for any kind of diversion, especially one involving rules. As we stood looking at each other, deciding what our first move should be they all raced by, all screaming 'Trampoline! Trampoline!' And we all looked at each other, all wondering the same thing, 'Can we make that last three hours?'

It's a big trampoline, but it really isn't big enough to accommodate fifteen kids. The netting around the side was all that was keeping them in as they crashed noisily off each other, the whole surreal image could best be described as a dwarf riot in a cage-fighting ring. You know when you shake a bottle of Coke and inside you can see the bubbles at the top bouncing violently off each other? It was like that and it's a small wonder there wasn't a serious injury as twenty minutes later, their appetite for physical assault and anarchy unsatisfied, the kids tumbled out looking for the next opportunity to hurt themselves.

'Football! Football!' they screamed and went charging off again.

Now, there are rules with football, but I wasn't going to be naive enough to try and enforce them and from my vantage point as reluctant goalkeeper I could see that it was a brutal affair. They all followed each other like a swarm of locusts, and like locusts they showed no mercy or respect to anything that stood in their path – flower beds, the orchard, the dogs – they all took something of a pounding. Even Junior, surely a fan of mindless violence if ever there was one, took one look at the proceedings and went back into his stable. It was like a cross between the football match in *Bedknobs and Broomsticks* and an old-firm derby. And even being in goal was dangerous, as they decided that any shots should be taken from as close as possible, firing the ball repeatedly into my genitalia and then trampling all over me as they failed to stop in time.

Over an hour this brutality lasted, and by the end I was the one battered and bruised with cut knees, broken sunglasses, a suspected broken finger and swollen testicles. Having worked themselves up into a red-faced, sweaty mess they then stripped off and all jumped into the pool, dive-bombing each other and splashing about so much that most of the water seemed to be thrown into the garden. As usual I couldn't get in with them; no sensible adult would have tried as it resembled a shoal of angry, feasting piranhas, but my job, like that of an attendant at a local public swimming baths was to spot trouble and dangerous high jinks and a couple of times I had to grab a flailing six-year-old as they struggled to stay afloat. They would then cough up a litre of pool water, look a bit sheepish for a few seconds and then dive straight back in.

But finally, and thankfully after half an hour or so, they seemed genuinely to have run themselves into the ground. They actually seemed tired, spent even, meaning that the last hour or so of the party would be a relative doddle, with them just lying around without the energy for further noise or exertion. A veritable breeze.

'*À table!*' Natalie shouted to indicate that food was served and off they trudged, hot and exhausted to the table. I surveyed the spread: Coke, lemonade, fizzy green stuff, chocolate, vile-coloured sweets, jelly, lollipops – basically a smorgasbord of E-numbers. We may as well have injected them with amphetamines. And all that was without the mountain of imported crisps that I'd brought back.

British cuisine is often unfairly marked down, more so for the way things are cooked rather than the ingredients themselves, but from the country that brought the world Fish and Chips, the Sunday Roast, Game Pie and Sausage and Mash, one should add the humble crisp. The French just don't get it! The most exotic flavour they have apart from *fromage* is peanut. Peanut! Who in their right mind would eat peanut-flavoured crisps? They taste like a jar of peanut butter with added sawdust; add an alcoholic aperitif to the mix and your mouth feels like it's been patioed. And you should see what they've done with Monster Munch. It's similar to what Steve Martin has done to the *Pink Panther* films, an ugly thing indeed. But because of this culinary blind-spot, every few months I drive back to the UK and stock up on crisps and other assorted snack food products that simply don't exist in a country that scoffs at the idea of convenience food in a bag. It's a kind of reverse booze cruise, we call it the 'Junk Food Junket' and I'd done my home nation proud with a selection of Wotsits, Skips, Twiglets and chilli-flavoured crinkle cut.

The next hour was one of the longest of our lives, though gradually the artificial energy burst died down and once again calm, or as near as possible, was restored, just in time for their parents to collect them.

'Thank you, Daddy,' said Maurice, when he found me later slumped drunkenly in the orchard, the sheer hell of the afternoon still etched in my face, 'that was the best party ever!'

I looked at him, tears welling in my eyes, 'I'm really glad you enjoyed it, son. I really am, because there is no way, no way on earth, we are ever doing that again!'

'Ha!' he laughed running off. 'You said that last year!'

I did too.

Late spring and early summer is fête season in France. It seems that there are more Bank Holidays *(jours fériés)* than actual work days, which is a good thing, and the *fête de l'école* is probably the family social event of the year around here; the annual end of school year production by the middle school is held in the cavernous *salle des fêtes* and is open to the general public as well if they're prepared to buy tickets. It is, to put it mildly, a world away from the school plays that I was ever involved in.

There's no crushing attempt at forcing nine- to ten-year-olds to interpret Molière or, as in my case, Goldoni's *A Servant of Two Masters* which is a subtle and nuanced piece in the hands of professionals but which was grudgingly 'stropped' through in our all-boys comprehensive and we had even volunteered for the roles. There were no volunteers here, however, as the whole school was roped in and Samuel, who had played the major role the previous year, was largely relegated to the chorus, much to his chagrin. He has, since last year's triumph, set his heart on becoming an actor and therefore being asked to fill in a succession of minor characters was difficult for him but possibly good practice for the potentially lean years to come.

Of course, the danger with insisting that every child play a role (sometimes quite obviously against their will) is that the quality may dip occasionally as some poor kid, feeling pressganged into public performance, may just offer up their lines in much the same way as a hostage might be forced to read a eulogy by their captors. The words are there, but the subtext and the body language just scream 'For the love of God, help me please!'

Last year's spectacle was a sprightly production about the people of the world; there were good songs, some nice set pieces and the 'message' about getting on with different people was clear and not too heavy. This year, however, was a more ambitious project. A new departure from the traditions of message and parable; this year they decided to dramatise their school trip. Like I say, it was ambitious. The trip to Île d'Oléron for five days in March had already left its mark with Samuel's virus but this was an opportunity to show those who hadn't gone, us parents in other words, what exactly had taken place. The fact that the vast majority of 'us parents' were relieved not to have been there at all and had in fact enjoyed a few days of relative peace and quiet wasn't considered, as here were the full five days in minute detail.

I remember my school trips and can only say that I would have been horrified if any of them had been dramatised for public consumption. Some of the more ambitious trips our boys' school organised were taken in conjunction with a local mixed school, which made the whole thing far more of a learning experience than most parents realised; but this was obviously a sanitised version of Samuel's break. Though, just exactly what details they left out was difficult to imagine as after two hours of bum-numbing performance the whole thing felt longer than the trip itself, and Thérence decided to add extra entertainment for those sitting around us by pretending to have his own burping competition. Almost two hours of detail about what they ate, the coach journey there and who had vomited on it and a list of every species living in the sea just off the West coast of France was enlivened massively by a strange vignette where the headmistress had apparently broken her nose by walking into a wall. It would be cruel to suggest that the damage may have been self-inflicted after a few days away in the company of a hundred or so schoolchildren, but it was news to us anyway and a brave acknowledgement that not everything had gone completely to plan.

The whole thing culminated in a harmonised version of Trenet's 'La Mer' which was very well received, though the encore that followed felt a bit forced as the audience by this point was decidedly fidgety and ready for a drink and refreshments. Of course, this being France, 'refreshments' meant a five-course meal with a full bar. The parents had prepared the *amuse-bouches* to go with the aperitifs and I personally had contributed mini *croques monsieurs* and some smoked salmon and watercress pinwheels, both of which I was very proud of and so while Samuel was asking me to deconstruct his performance I may, unforgivably, have been distracted trying to see how my food was going down with the locals instead.

Samuel was pleased with how it had gone and was obviously relieved that the whole thing, the months of rehearsals and the pressure, was now finally over and they could all get on with their lives. The evening had, in fact, barely begun and the first course of the meal wasn't served until half-nine as the band started late and as always with these things, there was a raffle to be endured and speeches and congratulations and so on. This was to be the headmistress's last year, possibly as a result of the nose incident, and there were many heartfelt congratulations on a job well done, all of which pushed the meal back further and further but that simply doesn't matter here.

There was no-one stomping their feet restlessly saying it was too late to be keeping kids up (I may have done once or twice actually) and as dessert arrived at a quarter to midnight, the whole thing resembled more a successful French wedding rather than a school play as children ran around everywhere and old women danced together to the jaunty strains of old-time *musette*. Loud, animated discussions were taking place at every table as the bar did a roaring trade and Samuel, playing one of his most important roles to date, was able to go to the bar for me and keep me well-stocked with French-language improving wine. I know! Sending a child to the bar for you! One can only imagine the drama some people would make out of that.

We were one of the first groups to leave, at around one in the morning, and we only did so then because we needed to check on the zoo at home, but it was a great evening. We had been in the area a few years by now and had been told by some that being accepted around here could be very difficult, it's a very close-knit, rural community. Large families all living in the same area inevitably means that 'outsiders', while not being ignored exactly, find it difficult to integrate and that, socially at least, people tend to stick with their own. We had found it quite the opposite. We have good friends who we can rely on and the community, largely via the schools and seeing other parents, has welcomed us warmly to the point where we are a fixture and that feels good. It means also that I feel less guilty about leaving Natalie and the boys when I go to work on long trips. I know that they're not alone.

Having said that, I would still much rather be at home obviously which is why when the summer holiday rolls around and Natalie and the boys want to go somewhere else, I'd rather stay put in my own house for once. There are people who would pay thousands to have what we have just for a couple of weeks' holiday so I don't see the point in us paying thousands to find something else that we already have. A holiday for me would be at home, a holiday for them is away from home.

I thought about this as I sat on the private beach of our campsite just outside of Biarritz. There's something about sitting on a deserted beach surrounded by dead jellyfish that makes you take stock. I once swore revenge on the entire jellyfish species for stinging me in Tunisia, but these flaccid, dehydrated beasts couldn't do any harm to anyone now and in a way I felt a kind of affinity with them; spineless creatures who had ended up in a place they didn't want to be.

I hate camping.

We'd been to this campsite before and it's a luxury, four-star affair with, like I said, a private beach, nice restaurant, good shop, friendly, welcoming atmosphere, etc. – but it's still a campsite. The first time we came we brought a large tent and it seemed like it took most of the holiday to get the bloody thing up, then our blow-up bed developed a slow puncture so that by the time the thing had completely deflated, about five in the morning, you'd wake up with a mouth full of grit. Samuel got bronchitis. I swore then never to sleep in another tent; so we had come back the following year in a caravan. Now, I can see the attraction of a caravan (sort of) but it's a stressful business. There's this stereotypical image of a driver towing a caravan and being completely oblivious to the traffic behind him, the beeping horns, headlights flashing and so on. Well I can tell you from experience that it's not ignorance, it's fear. Towing a caravan is incredibly hard work and an intense seven-hour drive while the kids argue relentlessly and your wife tells you constantly that 'you're going too fast' is no way to start a holiday.

Just positioning the thing on a campsite was difficult enough. The *emplacement* given to us was on a slight slope, but a slight slope in a caravan seems like a vertical incline and as I unhooked the thing from the car it began to roll down the 'hill' dragging me with it.

'Natalie! Put the chocks behind the wheels!' I shouted as I tried to stop the thing from crushing next door's tent.

'I think we should move nearer the hedge,' she suggested, completely unaware that I was losing control, in all senses.

'It'll be nearer the bloody sea in a minute, put the chocks in. NOW!'

'Well, there's no need…'

'NOW!' I screamed. It was an angry start to the holiday, and it somewhat set the tone.

The plan was that the two eldest, Samuel and Maurice, would sleep in a tent and Natalie, Thérence and me would be 'indoors'. I was utterly naive to think things actually might pan out that way though. It wasn't the boys' fault, there were violent storms almost every night so the tent wasn't really an option. We all slept in the tiny caravan which was resting precariously at an angle and which was not designed to sleep five. The evenings when we were trapped in by the weather developed their own theme, games like 'How Many Times Daddy Would Bang his Head', which the boys thought was great fun. Natalie was, as always, calmness and serenity personified. I hated it.

I tried to be positive, I really did, I tried to like it but I'm just not a camper. The filth, the lack of space, the damp, it all got to me. And there's this mantra that families on campsites keep repeating, 'It's good for the kids. It's good for the kids.' So is sensible footwear, so are cereal bars and non-alcoholic drinks, but I want nothing to do with them either. It won't wash with me that kind of delusion, I cannot for the life of me see how a family being holed up together in a damp tent or caravan is in any way enjoyable, and this 'sardine' approach to family living seems to me to be a tacit admission that, in most cases, there is no more sex to be had in the relationship. I mean, where are you going to go?

'Get the kids to bed, love, I'll meet you in the chemical toilet Waste Disposal Cubicle for a quick feel up... five minutes OK?'

It may be good for the kids, but it can put marriages under almost intolerable pressure. In the four years we've been going to campsites we've seen some huge marital rows, after some of which you just can't see how the marriage could ever continue.

And I don't care how luxurious it's supposed to be, the word 'luxury' shouldn't be used anywhere near a place that has communal toilet facilities. The men's toilets in the morning were a cross between the farting scene in *Blazing Saddles* and a refugee camp – though, to be fair, so is Stansted Airport on a Sunday morning and so is the Comedy Store dressing room before the late show on a Saturday night. But still, this is my holiday and I've paid for this?

'Clean Living Under Difficult Circumstances' is a very loose definition of what it is to be a mod, and campsites test that to its very limits. To maintain standards while everyone around you has clearly decided to stop fighting the elements and just give up on personal hygiene and sartorial basics takes some doing, but is thoroughly worth the effort because everyone on a campsite is smug about something. The retired couples are smug about their massive caravans and satellite dishes so they can watch *Countdown* from the South-West coast of France, the surfers are smug just carrying a board around the place with their wetsuits unbuttoned to their waist, the youth are smug about being young, and it goes on. Camping, caravanning, motor-homing is big business and the level of equipment and technology is staggering. On the night we arrived, while I struggled to prevent our caravan from falling off the precipice, a man opposite was manoeuvring his monster of a caravan with a remote control! He looked at me when he'd finished: I was covered in sweat, my trousers covered in grease, my Fred Perry shirt still stoically done up to the top and he with not a mark on him, just a patronising smirk on his very slappable face.

'It's still only a caravan, mate,' I muttered under my breath.

There's a limit to how many twenty-something skateboarders, white blokes with dreadlocks, youths pretending that baguettes are an amusing male-genital doppelganger, screaming kids, days with sand in your pants discomfort, hurricane winds and nights sleeping at an angle near a cliff top that I can put up with, and Natalie caught me snorting in derision as the tallest, blondest, fittest family I had ever seen erected the world's most complicated tent in just under two minutes.

'Isn't it tiring being you?' she asked.

And despite my obvious discomfort on the fraught journey back she was already planning the following year's camping trip. Already she had invited her parents and her sister, her brother-in-law and their children to spend time with 'us' at very same campsite.

'But who'll look after the animals if your parents are with us?' I asked. We had roped in Natalie's mum and dad to mind the menagerie whilst we were away and so I sensed an opportunity.

'Oh,' she replied, 'I hadn't thought of that.'

'I'll do it...' I ventured innocently.

'You mean you'd stay at home while we go camping, Daddy?' Samuel asked.

'Well, I don't see any option if we can't find someone to look after the house and animals,' I replied, pretending to be dejected at the thought.

'OK,' he said. Oh.

24

SHIPS IN THE NIGHT

After the obligatory nationwide shutdown in August, the builders returned to work at the end of the month. Whether they were mightily refreshed by whatever they had done for their *vacances* or just felt sufficiently guilty to finally get the job done they were on site for nearly four full days. The classroom for our courses was now almost finished, as was my upstairs office and meanwhile we were doing the background work on advertising, potential tutors, local hotels and so on. The whole project was beginning to feel more real and our excitement was growing accordingly.

We were still keen on doing writing holidays, but Natalie was also keen that we keep our options open, and also check out the opposition. She had booked herself onto a residential course in the Dordogne to do 'advanced sewing' or something which, while being a good idea, also presented a logistical headache. I was more than happy to cancel some gigs to accommodate her course (I never really need much of an excuse to stay at home when the sun is shining) but there was a limit to how much I could realistically forego. The plan was this: on my return from a weekend away Natalie would immediately leave for the Dordogne and on her return, five days later, we would just have time for a quick cup of tea and I would be off again. It wasn't an ideal situation – we would see each other for about an hour in total over three weeks.

That said, I was looking forward to a week or so at home alone with the three boys – a statement which, in itself, shows how foolhardy I seemed to have become and also just what a nasty piece of work optimism is; I've rarely relied on it in the past, I certainly won't do so again.

I am not a novice, either at childcare, domestic management or animal sitting; I do the majority of the cooking, a fair proportion of the cleaning and most of the ironing, therefore I considered myself to be a domestic goddess and didn't envisage any problems. I am an idiot.

Let's start with the animals. When I left for my weekend away at work the dogs were content, the cats came and went with ease, the horses tolerated me and the hens were laying. Everything worked. So either Natalie had told them deliberately to play up in her absence or they really do not cope well with her absence at all. Pierrot, while apparently almost back to normal, seemed to have stopped rubbing himself off on furniture and had instead started licking everything, and I mean everything. It was disgusting, not only for the constant 'lapping' sound but also because he insisted on watching you while he was doing it! (You try eating a meal at the table while the canine equivalent of the Marquis de Sade not only licks a sofa cushion but leers at you at the same time). Seriously, if Crufts ever decided to run a Best Pervert in Show he'd be a shoo-in. However, he was the least of my problems.

Toby appeared to be undergoing a total mental breakdown. After emptying my case, sorting through mail, reorganising the fridge and tutting at the state of the cutlery drawer, I was in bed by one o'clock. Toby was whimpering outside my door at three, then again at five and finally, for good measure, at seven. By the morning, however, far from feeling contrite, he was throwing himself at the patio doors like a bull ready for the off. He was due to have some jabs at the vets later in the week and I was tempted just to ask for a straitjacket, one coated with vitamins so that Pierrot would get his medicine when he started licking it.

The cats were a different story. I say cats, I meant cat. Flame had gone missing, he regularly stays out through the night but I hadn't seen him at all, which was a bit of a concern. Vespa, on the other hand, had left her mark.

'Daddy!' Thérence said. 'Daddy! Poo!'

'OK,' I said, 'I'll change your nappy.'

'No, Daddy. Cat.'

I went upstairs to find all three boys poking and prodding at some noxious substance, they were like policemen at a crime scene, unwilling to touch the evidence but advancing theories as to its perpetrator.

'I think it's just a furball,' I said, kneeling down and donning the Marigolds.

'Poo,' repeated Thérence, and he kept on doing so, despite the fact that his brothers and I were telling him it wasn't. Then we noticed what he had found in another corner of the room and it looked like a sandpit in a warzone. The contents of this massive pile of... of... I don't know what, either vomit or excrement, I don't know, it was like a beach after a violent storm. There were rocks, bits of wood, some plastic, piles and piles of sand and at least one dead bird. It was vile.

Something was up with the horses, as well; Junior I expect to be vicious, but Ultime seemed to be in a right strop with me too. Natalie insists that the horse manure be cleared and piled up every day, which is fair enough but what I didn't expect was the horses to follow me around and angrily crap on the space I'd just cleaned. It was an act of pure aggression and the fact that Ultime was at it too was very disappointing.

The hens had laid two beautiful eggs on the first morning and then, while I went off to get them some food, they not only trod on them but smeared them on the walls of their coop in some bizarre protest.

There was definitely something going on.

The boys, by contrast, were well behaved, if prone to disaster. Samuel had to have stitches in his forehead after falling off his bike, Maurice was missing his mum and when I finally got him to bed he insisted that he no longer needed a nappy; he hadn't actually needed one for at least six months to be fair, but the first night of Natalie's absence seemed a particularly fraught time to try and prove the point.

And then there was Thérence. Thérence, since I had got back, was having the kind of diarrhoea that makes a cat with the Normandy Beach landings in its stomach look healthy but also, on the first evening, he had to be carried back from the trampoline by a head-bandaged Samuel because he'd 'twisted his knee'.

'How do you know he's twisted his knee?' I asked sceptically.

'He fell and then couldn't walk properly on the trampoline,' Samuel replied, slightly hurt that I was suspicious of his diagnosis.

'Nobody walks properly on a trampoline!' I laughed. 'Put him down. Come to Daddy, Thérence, walk to Daddy.'

A beaming smile crossed his face, as he staggered two or three steps and then collapsed into a tearful heap. Have you ever had a two-year-old limp towards you? It's like watching a 3D TV charity appeal.

'He's twisted his knee!' I shouted.

'I know!' Samuel shouted back.

So, let's recap. The dogs were confirmed basket cases, the horses angrier than ever, the hens were on strike. I'd apparently lost one cat while another seemed to be able to turn itself inside out. Thérence could no longer walk, Samuel looked like he'd been hit with an axe and Maurice was quite possibly on the verge of a deep psychological setback.

Natalie had been away less than thirty-six hours.

In hindsight it was probably a good thing that the first few days of Natalie's absence were so chaotic, it meant that nothing, absolutely nothing, could faze me for the rest of the week. Every morning I awoke, tired yes, but in a state of heightened awareness; I was beyond domestic goddess now, I was a domestic ninja.

The animals, after a while, mostly stopped playing up. They had a couple of days treating me like a wet-behind-the-ears supply teacher, but then realised that actually I run a tight ship and won't put up with any nonsense. The hens stopped scuttling their own eggs, Toby stayed downstairs at night, Ultime got bored of pushing me around in her field and Pierrot even stopped peeing in his bed at night and spent the rest of the week relieving himself in Toby's bed during the day instead.

Only the ringleader, Junior, decided to carry on the fight, but was increasingly isolated as his support dwindled, which only made him angrier; he'd come marching up to me in his field, snorting away like a bluff old colonel, but then curiously run out of steam and actually avoid eye contact with me.

Of course, and Natalie made this very clear in the lists (and lists) of instructions that she had left for me, taking care of the animals is more than just keeping them fed and watered. There is the endless, and I really mean endless, cleaning up. Natalie's days were often spent in a permanent merry-go-round of poo clearance – frankly, I'd assumed that it had now reached fetish status and that really she secretly enjoyed the whole thing. There are the cat-litter trays, the chicken coop has to be scraped clean, Thérence's nappy has to be changed almost hourly as teething takes its toll on his bowel movements, the horse's field has to be stripped of manure every day and said manure piled up to form a steaming ziggurat in the corner of the field and then there's the fun, twenty-first-century parlour game – 'Hunt the Doggy-Doo'. It's all right and proper that dog mess be cleared up, especially when you have three kids running around, I have no argument with that; it's the logistics that we need to work on. We have two and a half acres and dogs, as far as 'evacuation' goes, aren't creatures of habit.

So, for a couple of hours every afternoon, I'd snap on the rubber gloves and just hunt and collect animal mess. I am not a man of compromise, and despite the filthiness of the job, the constant attention of following animals and millions and millions of flies, I decided that the only way I could maintain any kind of dignity was to don full mod regalia. White loafers may not have been the most practical footwear for the work, nor Sta-Prest trousers and a button-down collared paisley shirt, but there was simply no other way I could do it. There is little enough dignity involved as it is in excrement-gathering without dressing like a peasant. Inadvertently, this also provided entertainment for the local farmers who would stop their tractors and spend a few minutes staring at the mod in the field, like I was some kind of sartorial mirage.

I can't say it was all sweetness and light with the boys, either; it was full on and exhausting. I'd had this farcical notion that while Natalie was away I'd be able to get the boys to bed early enough to actually do some work in the evening. Fat chance! I got them to bed early, that was no problem, and although allowing them to watch a film in bed every night may not be everyone's idea of brilliant parenting, film can be educational – *Alvin and The Chipmunks 2: Le Squeequel*, for instance, is a metaphor for life. But by the time they were in bed I was knackered, my mind a mush of kids' needs, ironing, washing, shopping and animal droppings.

By the end of the week I was exhausted, far more tired than if I'd spent a week touring. But, and despite the bad portents at the start, all the animals were safe and well(ish), the boys were happy, clean and in one piece, the house spotless and the property, as far as I could see, entirely poo-free.

I languidly reflected on this on my last night as I sat on the terrace eating *noix de Saint-Jacques* cooked with chorizo and lemon juice, while sipping a chilled, crisp glass of Entre-Deux-Mers. The valley leading down to the river Cher was completely silent; it was a warm evening and even the crickets had turned the volume down, but just at that point as night fell and the bats began to swoop, it was incredibly still and peaceful. There wasn't a breath of wind and there was total silence as I lay back in my chair and closed my eyes, exhausted by the week but smugly satisfied, and then it began.

I'm no musician, so I couldn't pin it down, but it was wind definitely – a tuba maybe – or a trombone? Something heavy anyway, this was no delicate flute, and by God it was tuneless! It was coming from the woods about half a kilometre from the back of the house; there's a kind of summer house there on the edge of a lake and clearly – well, obviously I'm guessing – some child, probably in the early throes of musical exploration had been banished from the parental home and was even now balefully blowing their way through puberty and, judging by the instrument and evident lack of talent, impending teenage solitude. I'm a parent, I've encouraged music in my children, but here I had every sympathy with the parents, if indeed that's what the situation was. It sounded like an elephant with a grievance, wounded and slowly dying.

A full hour this wretched noise lasted. Occasionally there would be breaks, probably as someone tried to wrestle the instrument from this vandal, but it would always start up again. In the end I gave in and went to bed slightly miffed that my last evening wasn't completely as I would have liked but happy with a week's job well done.

When Natalie returned the next day I was ready for the inspection. She walked slowly around the place, spent too long talking to Junior for my comfort, checked her roses, looked under rugs and in time-honoured fashion dragged her finger along sideboards. She nodded in my direction and seemed about to offer some praise that everything was apparently up to scratch. Then, her eyes went past me to her prized orchid; her neglected, unwatered, and now ex-prized orchid and her expression changed.

'Got to go!' I said, and high-tailed it out of there before she realised that the orchid was only a small part of the house plant massacre. I got a text from Natalie a few hours later and I opened it with some trepidation, fearing more bad news, but by then I was quite stressed and short-tempered anyway; I was back on the road.

Terminal 2E of Charles de Gaulle Airport in Paris is relatively new but like most of the airport, it appears to have been modelled on one of the more convoluted M. C. Escher drawings and staffed by the kind of people even the less reputable budget airlines would reject on account of them being too 'surly'. It was opened in 2008; it had originally opened in 2004 but its roof collapsed killing four people (putting the British Airways Terminal 5 baggage fiasco into some perspective), and I don't think the confidence of the place ever really recovered from that early setback. When I first travelled through it just after its reopening it was quite clear that its baggage X-ray policy had been based purely on classic Buster Keaton.

Now the French love a bit of slapstick, but having the person at the security monitor sitting a good 25 metres from the actual X-ray equipment and with no means of communication to the other security staff other than turning the whole thing off and running down and telling them, was never going to last. Of course, this being France, tearing the whole plan up and starting again would be a public admission that there was something wrong in the first place, so the monitor has just crept closer over the last couple of years and now the security staff can communicate – OK, they can still only do this by shouting, but it's progress.

I don't begrudge airport security; I travel far too much to let it bother me. Generally if you obey the rules, there isn't a problem. Where I do get the hump – and I do get the hump – is when individual airports introduce their own arbitrary rules which differ from other airports. Surely airport security should be standardised? For instance, Stanstead Airport used to insist that your toiletries are stored in a clear, sealable plastic bag as does everywhere else, but at Stansted it had to match their dimensions exactly otherwise you had to pay for a packet of four new ones! That is simple racketeering and is illegal (or should be); Charles de Gaulle Terminal 3 briefly had a policy where only certain types of sandwich could be taken through security, one week ham and mayo was contraband but the following week salmon and cucumber was deemed acceptable, apparently fish-based snacks causing less of a threat to aviation security.

Every airport asks you to remove your laptop and phone; Terminal 2E in Paris asks you to remove everything electrical, cables included. And they watch while you do it. I had just come through security and felt like my electrical goods had been used in evidence against me as some kind of dilettante. I could tell the security guard wasn't impressed. She picked up the laptop and turned it over, for no good reason at all other than to show me who was boss; my phone she held like it had fallen in dog poo; she had clearly never seen a digital radio and just tutted at it; I thought she was going to vomit such was her reaction to my compact nasal hair-trimmer.

It's airport security, you just have to play their game. I once kicked up a fuss at Stansted, but the small point I was making at six o'clock on a Sunday morning really wasn't worth the alarm of having a machine gun pointed at me.

Terminal 2E also provides some of the world's most absurdly expensive food – it's like they thought, collapsing roofs and dignity-stripping isn't quite enough so we'll charge €12 for a chicken burger and €13 for a 'Jambon, Mimoulette et Poire' sandwich; that's just ham, cheese and pear right? Just because you name the cheese doesn't give it €10 extra worth of gravitas! But as you wander around the terminal you realise that they have to charge that much to pay for all the staff. In the space of 200 metres I had my passport and boarding card checked SEVEN times! On one occasion, I walked 5 metres from one check to the next, the second check watched the first check take place, eyed me suspiciously in the intervening 5 metres and then checked my passport with as much sourness as he could muster, clearly believing I could perpetrate some passport fraud in that small time.

So I was stressed and already tired when Natalie sent her text – my guard was down, something which I think Natalie has a sixth sense about. A dog, it seems, had 'turned up' at the gate; a small dog with either a hernia or haemorrhoid problem and the texts, a veritable flurry of them, were asking what they should do about it. As if my opinion in these matters counts for anything, as if I ever have a real say in the matter.

I have to say that it's not entirely unusual for stray dogs to turn up unannounced, France is one of the most dog-friendly countries in the world, they're welcome in restaurants and on planes – no-one bats an eyelid. But when the summer begins to kick in and the holiday season starts, some people would prefer not to have to pay kennel fees and dump their poor, generally elderly, beasts in the countryside. It becomes someone else's responsibility then, someone else's burden, in this instance, mine.

Ordinarily we are perfect for the job, an out of the way, single-track country lane; generally quiet yet easily accessible from two small local towns, ideal dog abandonment territory. But we had been less accessible than normal for the past couple of weeks as apparently those that run this part of the Loire Valley had won the tarmac lottery and almost every road and car park was in the process of being re-covered. No bad thing you might think, but in this case they had clearly forgotten to include the planning department and had left the placing of *'Diversion'* signs and *'Route Barrée'* warnings in the hands of either anarchists or rank incompetents. Usually the French will ignore a *'Route Barrée'* sign until actually faced with a non-traversable hole in the road, but these latest signage efforts were particularly spectacular. It was chaos and one thing the French road system doesn't need is added chaos. In the end the whole area seemed choked up and had just descended into a melee of incessant horn beeping and futile fist waving.

What I'm saying is that someone would have had to put in a special effort to dump their poor dog down our road while all these diversions were in place. Natalie went through the usual process and rang any neighbours and farmers nearby who may have lost a dog; she rang the vet who told her to ring the Mairie and they promised to send someone out, roads permitting. That's when she contacted me.

Getting the familiar sense that it would simply be a matter of course that we would be adopting the new stray, I decided to change tack and try a bit of reverse psychology.

'A new dog, you say? Why not? It's been a while since we took on an extra mouth to feed... how exciting!' Surely no one could mistake this heavy-handed sarcasm for what I really meant?

'Oh that's lovely. Speak to you soon. Bye then.' Not for the first time, I'd been completely out-thought.

I eventually arrived in Cyprus, where I would be performing for the next week, feeling like I'd been played, conned. And as I sat in the garden of the villa ruminating on how animals were effectively running my life, two chickens wandered into the garden, then a cat and then a chaffinch sat on the pergola above the patio and shat on me. I don't know if I give off some kind of chemical that attracts beasts, but they just seem to follow me wherever I go. I'm like some reluctant Pied Piper of Hamelin.

Natalie rang half an hour later, the dog apparently did actually belong to a local farmer who hadn't at the time realised that her dog was missing; a good thing, Natalie said, that the little thing was going home and though the boys were sad that it couldn't stay, they really appreciated that I'd said it could stay and that maybe we would look for a new dog when I got back. I was performing to the wrong troops I thought, what I need is to run away to the French Foreign Legion.

FOSSE AND BOTHER

La Rentrée is a major week in the French calendar. It's huge. It is much more than just the start of the new school year, it's like the whole country is drawing a line under the *grandes vacances* and everyone must knuckle down again. Not only do the kids go back to school, but everybody else comes back from holiday too and if not literally, then mentally. La Rentrée is a mindset: it's like New Year, a new beginning, a fresh start.

However, living in rural France means that, as far as business is concerned, there is very little difference between Les Vacances and La Rentrée anyway, and that's a good thing. It's quiet and sleepy and that's just the way I like it, it's why we moved here. You can tell it's La Rentrée, however, because the lunchtime news, in its continuing battle to ignore anything that happens outside of France, stops showing reports of booming French resorts and their markets that can barely cope with the demand for locally produced *moules* and now starts showing reports of French resorts unwinding in the late summer sun where locally produced *moules* are in plentiful supply. By far the biggest staple of French lunchtime news during La Rentrée, however, is the ever-growing size of a child's *cartable*, and I'm with them on this.

The *cartable* is the school bag, traditionally a satchel-shaped affair worn as a rucksack and which carries the child's books for the year. They are enormous and they cost a fortune. The first day back at school is different here; whereas children elsewhere may be comparing trainers or something, French kids are comparing their *cartables*; the size, the shape and whether it is an officially endorsed product of this week's fad, Beyblade, Ze Voice, etc. none of which will still be fashionable by the end of the school year. They are big business and at between €40 and €70 aren't cheap, and every year they get bigger; news bulletins regularly broadcast reports desperately concerned for the future of the French backbone as the pressure on small children's frail bodies as they return to school is very real. These reports are always accompanied by soft-focus images of small kids entering the school gates with these enormous, wide wingspan bags on their backs like they're wearing gaudy, slap-on wings, and having to turn sideways to get through the door.

They're right to be concerned too, these bags are utterly ridiculous, but after nearly nine weeks at home with their offspring you'll find very few parents moaning that vociferously about how it's affecting their kids. Nobody is keeping their child at home for fear of potential spine damage; the summer holiday is over, they're glad of a bit of peace.

It felt like new beginnings for us too. The building and renovation work on the classroom and the office was finally complete, we just had to decorate now, but it also meant that with the infrastructure finally in place we could get down to the nitty-gritty of what exactly we were going to be offering in our 'school'. Natalie's sewing course in the Dordogne had gone extremely well, luscious surroundings and sold-out craft courses proving very popular, but for now – and not knowing a great deal about craft – we wanted to stick with our idea of running writing courses, specifically genre-writing courses. We were determined not to over-stretch ourselves and therefore planned to run just four five-day courses over the following spring and summer, a relaxed beginning giving us a chance to get everything right.

Firstly, though, I had my office to complete. I finally had a room of my own and I wanted to get it up and running as soon as possible, as did Natalie who was looking forward to finally seeing the back of 'my' stuff which continued to ruin her shabby-chic house look. Having said that, and although we both wanted me to crack on with things, I wasn't thrilled about the prospect of more DIY.

One of the worst jobs I ever had was a temporary job in the summer of 1991, which I think may have been advertised as 'Highway Maintenance Assistant'. In reality, it was scraping up roadkill from the A24 in Sussex and it was one of those jobs which my dad, a no-nonsense Yorkshireman, would describe as 'character building'; a Yorkshire euphemism which apparently means 'potentially lethal'. These were the days before rampant Health & Safety and our equipment consisted of a paint scraper, a bin bag and our nerve. We didn't even have gloves or a luminous vest as we dodged the traffic, playing some kind of macabre version of the 1980s arcade game Frogger.

In my time I have been a bouncer, I've built kitchens in mobile mammography units, I've been sacked by Tesco three times, I worked as a housekeeper at the Gatwick Hilton for approximately twenty-five minutes (you really don't want any details, trust me) and I've been hired as a Minder for a Jewish rag trader until it came time for me to apply some pressure to a non-payer and my inadequacies for the role were cruelly exposed.

None of this is exactly diamond mining in South Africa, but I just wanted to show that, just because I'm in showbiz, I'm not afraid of work. I'll do what it takes to get by. I'm a trouper.

But I hate, hate with a passion, painting and decorating. I like the furniture planning stuff and I've never found IKEA shelving units or desks as troublesome as most people make them out to be; I'm handy with a screwdriver. The office, though, was four large walls and a floor, all of which needed painting, and as it stood empty it looked even bigger than I had planned (and I had planned big) ideal for a 'pacer'. When I write stand-up I do it standing up, and talk to myself as I pace around pretending I'm on stage, trying to get the rhythm right. Procrastination in the form of, 'No, I'm not sure what colours yet' gripped me. I also happened to mention online – a necessary evil these days – that I was painting and immediately started getting advice from 'decorating-bots' (usually companies who jump on a buzzword and try and sell you stuff). I hadn't even sought their self-satisfied painting advice in the first place, yet they were evangelical in their passion and 'support'. I felt less like I was painting walls and more like I'd wandered into the Church of Scientology and asked aloud if anyone had any advice for a newcomer.

According to this unsolicited advice, decorating, as with most things in life, is all about the preparation, four-fifths of it to be exact, said one zealous Twitterer, and I'm not big on preparation. Magazine and newspaper interviewers always ask that question of comedians: 'So, how do you prepare for a gig?' And then think I'm being flippant when I answer, 'Make sure there's nothing stuck in my teeth and that my flies are done up.' I'm not being flippant at all, that really is how I prepare to go on stage. The thing about painting is that because I detest it so much I haven't got time to waste 'preparing' anything, I need to get on with it, attack the job while I have a mind to do so. Preparation for painting the office was two coffees and trying to decide what in my wardrobe could possibly be sacrificed for the purpose. That alone took an hour.

The job did not start well. The roller extension pole, it probably has a proper name, snapped early on, which meant that the roller sprang back and hit me on the forehead leaving a perfect roller imprint. I thought this was ironic, as the paint was so thin it had barely left anything on the wall as yet. Seriously, the stuff was thinner than milk. We'd ummed and ahhed about not only what paint to buy, but where to buy it. Paint in France is very expensive, so I'd brought a load over from England, but it was already clear that this stuff would require about eight coats. The expat internet forums are alive with the whole English versus French paint debate for some reason and bits of it get quite tetchy as clearly some people, despite moving here, wouldn't buy a French product of any description while others regard it as nothing less than a betrayal to bring over English paint to put on French walls. I liked Reg from Burgundy's suggestion; just cover the walls in old Camembert boxes.

However, not wishing to lure the entire local mouse population to my new 'sanctum' I decided to change tack and buy local paint. Dark-coloured local paint; surely a darker colour would cover the wall more quickly? I bought an absurdly expensive *monocouche* (one-coat) paint and was immediately disappointed. It seems that 'one-coat paint' is one of those modern myths like 'economic trickledown effect' and cough medicine; they don't work, it's all a lie. After one coat the wall was supposed to be a deep red but it looked like I'd just got annoyed and thrown a glass of rosé at it instead. Further inspection of the instructions, or should I say my first look at the instructions, showed that in order for *monocouche* to work you first had to apply a *sous-couche*. Right. So let me get this straight, in order for one-coat paint to work you need to apply another coat?

This is exactly the kind of retail subterfuge that leads to uprisings and a storming of the barricades. If I need another coat, it's not bloody *monocouche*, is it? That's like buying a supermarket meal for two and the serving suggestion imploring that one of you stock up on bread first as the meal is a bit on the frugal side.

I spent all week in my new attic office, painting and repainting the same walls like a particularly dull *Groundhog Day*. The paint steadfastly refused to either cover evenly or, in some places, at all. I can see now how people come up with these modern decorating paint 'effects', after four coats they just give up and say, 'Sod it, that'll do. I'll call it dappled.' Mine looked more like a dirty protest. All week I was in there, the fumes and the exertion made me nauseous and aged me considerably so that every evening I emerged from the place looking like Dorian Gray's portrait, only a bit rougher.

I collapsed onto the sofa after one full day and though it was still early in the evening I didn't wake up again until about five in the morning. Natalie obviously felt it was better to leave my battered body where it was, which would have been OK if it wasn't for the fact that she'd also asked me to put the hens to bed in their coop before

I came in. It occurred to me now that I had forgotten to do so and I flew up off the sofa terrified that the weasels or foxes may have taken advantage of my neglect, but the hens were waiting at the back door for me, clucking away. Usually I find their clucking very relaxing, almost peaceful, but not on this occasion as they were clearly admonishing my absent-mindedness and had been waiting by the door for just such an opportunity.

Eventually, and after the mockery of *monocouche*, the painting was finally done and so, perhaps nearly four months behind schedule, my new office was open. There had been times over the course of the year I had thought it would never happen. Times when we hadn't seen the builders for weeks made the whole thing feel like some pie-in-the-sky notion, a fanciful half-baked ambition that, like wanting to represent your country at football, would be looked back on in later years with a kind of nostalgia and a shake of the head at the naivety of it all. Builders, French or otherwise, can do that to you, they make you doubt yourself.

I did point out to the builders at some point in July that the whole thing was supposed to have been finished at the end of June. 'Ah,' Monsieur Butard in one of his rare visits had replied, 'I didn't say which year.' He was only half-joking; it had taken him two months to decide that he couldn't install the stairs.

But finally I was in!

The walls were done, the skirting boards on, the floor painted and furniture erected. It is, even if I say so myself, a thing of beauty. I doubt it's to everyone's tastes, though; it is a 'boy's room' definitely. A boy with an excess of late 1960s furniture, a mountain of mod paraphernalia and, most importantly, a wife who refused to allow any of that stuff to be on display in the house. Actually, to be fair, she did at first and then gradually things would be sidelined, ceramic scooter models once prominently displayed would disappear and then turn up at the back of a cupboard somewhere; books whose spines didn't fit in with that season's new colour scheme wouldn't be completely removed but suddenly the shelving unit would have a curtain covering as if to hide offensive pornography rather than books with a prominent 1960s font.

I could see how the new office might have been a bit over the top, but I liked to see it as a Matt Helm, tongue-in-cheek homage to the golden age of James Bond films. It has the humour of *In Like Flint* but with the stubbornness of Miss Havisham; red and white walls with patterned rugs, bar stools, animal print cafe bistro chairs nabbed from the old Glee Club in Birmingham, one of my favourite gigs, and a magnificent dresser/radio/drinks cabinet from the late 1960s that still works and that took four of us to get up to this first-floor atelier. I have a record player for my vinyl, a CD multi-changer and no iPhone facility on the retro hi-fi. My office is old school.

I have a collection of guitars that I don't know how to play, a remnant from a time not too long ago when lacking in confidence, I started wearing a guitar on my back to give me added depth and kudos. I have a rowing machine and weights which I won't use but give the impression that I haven't completely let myself go, an Italia 90 edition of Subbuteo that only boys/men of a certain age could possibly appreciate and, inevitably, a cheese plant.

It is not only my room; it is an extension of me and contains everything Natalie hates in furniture styles, colour combinations, music, literature, films and footwear. Which is one of the reasons why it is 100 metres away from the house, presumably for fear of some kind of paisley contamination, and why she so happily agreed to it in the first place despite not seeing me most of the time anyway. All the things she'd wanted to get rid of now have a home, meaning that not only did she no longer have to tolerate their presence, but that she could fill her boots on eBay and plug the gaps.

She was like a woman possessed, an Erin Brockovich-like obsessive not in pursuit of truth and justice, but with the aim of hoovering up any stray Cath Kidston trinket and Toile de Jouy knick-knackery to replace my hastily dismissed collectibles. She now has the 'office' indoors (actually a landing) and what used to be a shared space has now been expunged of any presence I may have had there. I feel like Trotsky after he fell out with Stalin: the family photos look vaguely familiar but there's a grubby blur where the man of the house should be standing. It took me a whole six weeks to get my office exactly how I wanted it; but she had clearly been planning the move for some time and within an afternoon she was unwrapping eBay packages that had arrived without my knowledge, and I was history.

The office represented something else, though; in time, I thought, if everything goes to plan, most of my time away from 'home' will be spent here. I had started doing stand-up comedy in the first place as a way to make my name as a writer, but stand-up is all-consuming and it had swallowed me up. I was so surprised that I was actually able to make a living from it, I got terrified of being found out as a fraud, which is why I hid under the radar for so long. The office and the schoolroom, and not just because of the money invested in them, meant that this was the start of something else, time to start afresh. A new era for us, our very own La Rentrée.

Natalie made me four cushions to put in my new *pied à terre*, in the same way that some women used to hand their husbands a picnic lunch as they left for work, and it sounds like a nice gesture until you consider the fact that Natalie would make cushions for a stranger who fell off his bike, such is her need to produce the things. But they look good on my sofa bed and basket-weave high-back chair. And especially my fancy 1960s swivel desk chair, which is the most uncomfortable piece of seating I've ever come across, but which looks fantastic. Quite often, for instance, while gardening in bowling shoes or trying to navigate the rural Indian Railway network in a two-tone tonic suit, I am accused of choosing style over practicality. I hold my hands up – compromise on these issues really isn't for me, but Natalie is exactly the same in her own way.

Natalie's addiction to Cath Kidston, Cabbages and Roses and Kate Forman, farmhouse chic, insane inch-perfect frippery and the Goddess 'Cushion' meant that we had created a lovely house. Despite three young boys and the chaos of an informal animal adoption agency, she had put together a beautiful home. But not all of it is practical. A few years ago, during one of her occasional and cathartic scavenging hunts in the local rubbish dump she found a Victorian bath. A pretty little thing, no doubt, one of those baths that adorn old-fashioned adverts for soap in shops like Past Times, and she had to have it. I thought she meant to use it as one of those quirky planters you see in the more impractical, soft-focus interiors magazines, because as far as I could see the bath itself showed exactly why the Victorians were so uptight, why they refused to discuss anything below the waist. It was because they had no bottoms.

I have, despite putting on a few pounds in the last couple of years, retained my mod kitten-hips, something I'm quite proud of. I am of quite narrow build, but this bath was too narrow even for me. It is tapered to the extent that while I can easily get in the thing, the narrowness of the base together with the water means that I couldn't get out again. I'd get stuck and my fragile ego couldn't handle the ignominy.

So, while I do occasionally like a bath, I can't have one. The shower on the other hand had looked like the poor relation of the house for some time. It was badly fitted by the previous owners and with clearly no waterproof membrane behind the dingy, orangey-brown tiles, it had started rotting the wall in the room behind it and so finally we had bitten the bullet and decided to have the whole thing done up. Also, the authors that we intended to get in to run our courses would be using this bathroom and as it stood it wasn't up to scratch.

The shortage of plumbers, it turns out, is a worldwide issue, not just a UK one and without the convenience of an influx of hard-working Eastern Europeans it is even more difficult to get one in rural France than it is anywhere. Fortunately, one of our nearest neighbours is a plumber. Monsieur Cruchet is a small, mousey-looking individual who, like a millionaire who believes his entourage only like him for his money, is quite obviously paranoid that people only talk to him so that they have access to a plumber. He's a nice man, though, and despite flooding the house once because he forgot to reconnect a tap, or even because of incidents like that, he's generally available.

It was decided that the work should be done while I was away, that my presence while plumbers and assorted plasterers and tilers went about their messy business in the house was not going to be helpful. Apparently, having me fussing about and constantly asking them to clean up after themselves would not help with deadlines or costs; from experience, local artisans work better when I'm not there.

I was, oddly, quite excited when I arrived home after a fortnight away and was looking forward to seeing the new bathroom. It looked magnificent; a gleaming, white and chrome beauty with one of those large umbrella shower heads and with a wide, very un-Victorian, base. It had been finished earlier that day and was as yet unused and after a three-train, two-plane sixteen-hour journey looked like the mirage of an oasis in a desert. I soaked it up; washing the long journey out of my system, enjoying the temperature controlled forceful, yet relaxing, jet stream.

'Turn it off! Turn the thing off!' Natalie shouted, interrupting my shower reverie.

Apparently, while I was lost in my own world and lathering up like there was no tomorrow, the real world was falling apart. Water was bubbling up out of every other plug hole in the house, and even splashing out of the washing machine downpipe. The toilets had emptied and strange gurgling sounds, like a burping competition in a cave, echoed around the house. It was like a scene from one of those over-the-top disaster films, like *Earthquake*.

'Bloody Cruchet!' I shouted, 'What has he not connected now?' Worse, I thought, what had he misconnected?

Natalie rang him immediately and explained the problem. 'Hmm,' he said, 'sounds like a blockage.' Natalie had the phone on speaker as I stood there dripping onto one of her precious rugs; a heinous crime.

'No, really? A blockage?' I thundered sarcastically. 'Lucky you're around for such top-notch diagnosis.'

'I'll be back first thing,' he continued not hearing me in the background, 'in the meantime, don't use the shower. Or the washing machine. Or flush the toilet. *Bonne fin de soirée!*'

'He's not coming now?!' I shouted, the long trip and the subsequent disappointment inducing one of my 'Basil Fawlty' moments. 'He lives a hundred metres away. Get him back on the phone! What do you mean I can't use the toilet? Has he done this deliberately? I've seen *Jean de Florette*, you know. I know how these people operate.'

'Ian, calm down, he'll be here first thing, he—'

'Can I use his toilet? This is ridiculous!'

To be fair to Cruchet he did arrive first thing. I was yet to be convinced that he hadn't somehow screwed up the entire plumbing system but his explanation was definitely a plausible one. The previous shower unit had apparently been a rustic variation on one of those old 'hole in the ground' toilets for which the French were notorious. The shower base was plonked on sand and drained haphazardly into the ground below which was another reason why the walls were rotting and why the thing had smelled so badly. As Cruchet reasonably explained, the new shower had been linked properly into the drainage system which meant that if there was a blockage, as seemed likely, the system was now overloaded and backing up around the entire house. That is all waste, all human waste, that should have been going into the underground *fosse septique* (septic tank) was actually living in the wall pipes around us. We were living in a faecal compost heap.

He dug a trench outside exposing the pipe to the *fosse septique*. 'The blockage will be at the mouth,' he said, 'so if I make a hole around here the pipe will be full.' He pressed the button on his drill for added effect and began. Within seconds there was a fountain of waste water spouting up from the pipe as possibly years of back-up burst forth. Quickly Cruchet blocked the hole up again and called a *vidange curage* (a specialist septic tank emptier) that he knew to come and empty the whole thing, hopefully unblocking the system in the process.

A few hours later and a man with a tanker, big pipes, serious gloves and apparently no sense of smell whatsoever was emptying the *fosse*. 'There's your problem,' he said, fishing out a tonne of nappy wipes, a collection of household goods and a toy helicopter. About a year ago things had started to go missing around the house and we had also started to go through packets of nappy wipes like a busy maternity ward. We all knew Thérence was the culprit, but we had had no idea where he was hiding the things. Now we knew and we turned to look at him as he sucked nonchalantly on a massive strawberry ice lolly, the mess making him look like the Joker from the Batman films.

'Yum!' he said, a description completely at odds with the open sewer situation that surrounded us.

It's always good to meet people who are enthusiastic, knowledgeable and passionate about their work – to some extent it restores one's faith in humanity, and as I listened to the *vidangeur*, who had fitted us in at the end of his day when he had no obligation to do so, lecture me about my responsibilities towards my *fosse septique*, how I should be doing more regarding upkeep and general sewer maintenance, it struck me, quite genuinely, that the world needs people like him – and our neighbour, Cruchet, who had refused to take payment for the extra hours he had put in. Of course, *vidange* man was also standing on top of a pile of my family's bodily waste and wiping 'splashback' from his sweaty face, so the idea that someone whose life choices up until then had led to this moment was lecturing me, was all a bit much frankly.

'*Merci beaucoup!*' I said, handing over a cheque and narrowly avoiding a handshake. 'I'm off for a shower.'

After my shower, and also after a subsequent inspection of other plugs and sinks in the house to check that the problem was definitely fixed, I made my way out to my office. I had some notes to make on gigs I had coming up and I had to check the responses from candidate authors for the school. Whereas normally I'd wait until everybody was in bed for a bit of peace, I could now go to my office and get some work done while it was still fresh in my mind. I had a spring in my step as I made my way across the garden. I really felt that things were moving in the right direction; I could see a time when I would be home more, I had my own space for writing, everything felt good. Suddenly everything, like the *fosse*, felt unblocked.

I climbed the stairs to my office, two at a time such was my rush to get there, and as I arrived at the top I nearly fell over Samuel and Maurice who were in the middle of a noisy game of Subbuteo on the floor having also rummaged messily through my DVDs looking for something to watch; Vespa was asleep on my swivel chair and Pierrot was doing something unspeakable with my prized vintage dresser. Natalie was making some window seat coverings for the classroom below, happily humming to herself. Without looking up or even apparently breaking the beat in her tune she asked idly, 'What do you think of goats?'

I sat heavily on one of the barstools and untwisted the cap off a small bottle of beer. I took a long swig and surveyed the scene. *Plus ça change...* I thought, *plus ça change.*

Well, at least my French was improving.

MY QUINCE RECIPES

Turkish Delight

The recipe I use for quince Turkish delight is a variation of the traditional Portuguese recipe for *marmelada*. It is a tough recipe no doubt, but the rewards are great.

Firstly, peel, core and roughly chop up the quince – this will probably leave your hands looking like you've punched walls, but it gets easier from here.

Transfer the fruit to a pan, add enough water to barely cover the quince and boil until soft, around twenty-five minutes. Then mash the resulting pulp to make it smoother.

Once you have your mixture, weigh it and mix with an equal amount of sugar (my advice would be to weigh the empty pan beforehand rather than tip the mixture out and back in again), bring to the boil and stir until the paste that is forming no longer touches the side of the pan, which may take an arm-numbing hour and a half! If, like me, you'd prefer not to acquire burns to your hands and face from the spitting mixture, gloves and goggles are recommended.

Pour the paste onto greaseproof paper-lined trays and leave in a warm, dry place (I use the airing cupboard) for however long it takes for the paste to firm up and then chop it into sweets (I use a pizza cutter for this bit). Then, either cover in chocolate or dust with icing sugar.

Quince Chutney

A simpler and much less painful way to make something edible from quince is the chutney.

Peel and core your fruit and put it in a pan with sugar and vinegar – I use either cider vinegar or white wine vinegar but any will do – and then boil for a couple of hours, stirring regularly.

During this process, throw in whatever spices or extras you like – you can experiment with combinations though in the past I've added raisins, curry powder, cinnamon, walnuts whatever was to hand, and that's basically it.

Keep boiling and stirring until it thickens.

Sterilise some jars and pour the contents in, then store in a cool, dry place. It will last forever.

ACKNOWLEDGEMENTS

It's hard to believe that over ten years have gone by since this book was first published! There have been so many changes since then, and yet, as the French say, 'The more everything changes, the more everything stays the same.' So, a huge thanks still go to Natalie and the boys whose chaos in the face of my attempts at order remain and are the principal reason for the book's existence.

My thanks go to all at Summersdale Publishers then and now, Jennifer Barclay and Chris Turton, who believed in the book enough to push it and me hard, and to Debbie Chapman and Rebecca Haydon who have worked on this update. I'm very grateful to my agent Bill Goodall whose calm gets things done. Huge thanks also go to friends along the way, Charlotte Phillips, Alison Lyndon-Parker, Paul Thorne and Sonja Van Praag who all, at various times, told me to stop moaning and write it down. Lastly, my immense gratitude goes to the late, much loved Annabel Giles, for her vitality and encouragement.

ABOUT THE AUTHOR

PHOTO © STEVE BEST

Ian Moore is the best-selling author of the Follet Valley crime series which began with *Death and Croissants*. He is also the author of *The Man Who Didn't Burn*, the first in the Juge Lombard series. Ian is a well-known stand-up comedian on radio and TV in the UK and a husband, father of three boys, farmhand and chutney-maker in France where he owns a writers' retreat.

For more Moore, check out: **www.ianmoore.info**

Have you enjoyed this book?
If so, why not write a review on your favourite website?

If you're interested in finding out more about our
books, find us on Facebook at **Summersdale Publishers**,
on Twitter/X at **@Summersdale** and on Instagram and
TikTok at **@summersdalebooks** and get in touch.
We'd love to hear from you!

Thanks very much for buying this Summersdale book.
www.summersdale.com